Basic

HYDROPONICS

for the do-it-yourselfer

2nd Edition

A CULTURAL HANDBOOK

by

M. Edward Muckle

Growers Press Inc.
Princeton, British Columbia

First Published 1982
This revised edition published 1994

Printed in Canada
Cover; Ehmann Printing, Kelowna
Body; Webco West, Penticton
Binding; Canada Mounts & Library Service, Kelowna

Illustrations by; *Laurel McColman*

Photography by; *M. Edward Muckle*

Published by; Growers Press Inc.
P.O. Box 189
Princeton, British Columbia
Canada
V0X 1W0
Phone/Fax [604] 295-7755

A catalogue record for this book is available from the National Library of Canada

ISBN 0-921981-40-6

Table of Contents

Part I Introduction

Part II Hydroponic Systems & Methods

Part III - Media Based Systems

Part IV Water Culture

Dedicated to

All of the growers, researchers and others who have taken the time to share both their successes and their failures.

Their efforts have allowed me to advance my knowledge far beyond what I could have accomplished on my own.

Foreward

How time flies. It has been over a decade since I wrote the first edition of Basic Hydroponics. Since then much has happened and the first edition is very much out of date. Advances in equipment and technology have been made and as a result of working with thousands of growers, visiting research and growing facilities around the world I have certainly learned a great deal. Again with this edition I have worked to provide you with the essential information in Plain English so you can get on with enjoying the fun of hydroponic gardening.

Those who have the first edition will find many changes and a tremendous increase in the amount of information. Where there is a contradiction between the two editions, go with the information in this one. Many things that seemed impossible or simply unknown over a decade ago are now commonplace. My knowledge of these changes is the result of the co-operation of growers and researchers around the world who have freely and enthusiastically shared information. This book is my attempt to ensure the basic information is available to all who wish to use it.

The science and art of hydroponic gardening has spread around the world in common use both as a hobby and a profitable commercial method of plant production. It is still a field of discovery and adventure. While you need to observe the basics in any system there is the need for creativity in dealing your local climate and coping with the issue of what tools and equipment are locally available.

Remember that what appears today to be impossible may very likely be commonplace tomorrow as we learn more. You can contribute by taking the information in this book and using your efforts and imagination to do what has never been done before. Have fun and I wish you every success with your hydroponic garden.

Part I:
Introduction to Hydroponics

"Statistics show that of those who contract the habit of eating, very few survive."
Wallace Irwin 1875-1959

Chapter 1
Simplified Hydroponics

Hydroponics is the word that has become the popular name for the practice of growing plants without soil. It is commonly applied to all cultural systems which do not rely on soil to provide plant nutrition. In a 'Hydroponic' system, water is used to make the necessary mineral nutrients available to the plant. Root support can be provided by using an inert growing medium such as; sand, gravel, vermiculite, perlite, sawdust, rockwool, expanded clay, or even soil. The list is almost endless. Large plants such as tomatoes or cucumbers generally require stem support. The roots are not left to sit in the water at all times. If this were done, the plant would soon die from lack of oxygen.

The method of getting the nutrient water or 'solution' to the roots is not limited to any one system. As a result, many systems have evolved and been highly promoted. All successful systems have a number of basic principles in common.

1. Each system allows the roots to breath. This is necessary because respiration occurs in the plant roots and without oxygen the plant roots cannot take up water or nutrients. Additionally the roots give off gases and other materials which must be taken away for the plant to remain healthy.

2. Each hobby system uses the same basic balance of plant nutrients. Plants require some 18 elements to grow and thrive. To operate properly any system must provide these essential elements.

3. Each system provides for or, is designed to be used in an environment, where all other essential factors for plant growth are available; light, humidity, air and a good temperature.

This is the real realm of hydroponics. The roots of the plants. For those who don't recognize them, these are the roots of corn plants.

The 'Hydroponic' system is the one which serves the roots of the plants. Very often the complete environment is referred to as hydroponic which causes confusion for the novice. Lighting etc. is necessary but it is not a part of a hydroponic system, rather it is a part of a complete plant growing environment.

Nearly every container plant you buy at the local garden center, nursery or flower shop was grown using hydroponic technology. Why change a good thing when you get the plant home?

The simplest hydroponic garden to create is the one you may already have. Many people buy plants growing in what appears to be soil. In fact in almost 100% of the cases it is not. The 'soil' is a mix of materials with peat as the major component. Most commercial growers now use hydroponic technology to produce potted plants. While there is a limited nutrient residue in the pot when you buy the plant, it will require regular feeding with a balanced plant food.

The mistaken impression that the material in the pot is soil is the cause of many people feeling they have 'brown thumbs'. An incredible number of potted plants starve to death each year simply because the plant store didn't tell customers to feed the plants. Getting a 'green thumb' for your houseplants can be as simple as feeding your plants with a balanced hydroponic nutrient. Why waste time transplanting when all you need to do is carry on with hydroponics?

Hydroponics really is as simple as feeding plants instead of feeding soil. You can use an incredible variety of materials to hold the growing medium, if you are using one. Flower pots, dishpans, pottery, cans, in fact any container, just remember that if the container is metal or wood it should be lined with plastic. That way the wood will not rot as quickly and the metals will not be dissolved by the nutrient solution and upset the formula.

In the smaller simpler systems, if you are not sure whether it will work or not, try it anyway. Even if there is a problem you will have fun and learn from the experience.

Chapter 2
THE HISTORY OF HYDROPONICS

Contrary to the claims made over the past few decades, hydroponics is far from being the newest discovery in town. Dating back to Atlantis, and possibly even before, water culture has provided food and restful gardens to man for thousands of years. Canals, specialized lighting systems and very efficient recycling nutrient systems are developments of centuries long past which are only now being rediscovered.

In many areas of the world, Kashmir and the Andes mountains to mention just two, raft culture was an essential component of food production long before they were 'discovered' by Western civilization. Rafts of logs and branches were constructed and tethered to the shore of lakes. This framework was covered with vegetation which would rot quickly. Crops were then planted in this rotting vegetation. The roots of the plants quickly reached down into the water below the raft eliminating the need for watering. As the vegetation rotted, the minerals were released into the water providing a local zone of nutrient solution directly below the raft. The crops thrived and fed hundreds of people.

Two ancient, and readily recognized types of 'hydroponic' culture are seen here. A display of a rice paddy at Epcot in Florida and a bonsai tree. The rice fields were the basis of China's civilization and the bonsai trees have their roots in Indian medicine 1,000's of years ago.

In South America, especially Mexico, this system was carried even further as they developed more extensive production systems in areas with no lakes. Canals were dug with the soil being heaped up between the canals to provide the planting area. The canals were filled from local rivers and stocked with fish. Plants were watered using the canal water enriched by the fish effluent and rotting vegetation. This system provided a complete diet from one system for the local population and required a minimum of effort for a maximum yield.

Ancient Abundance

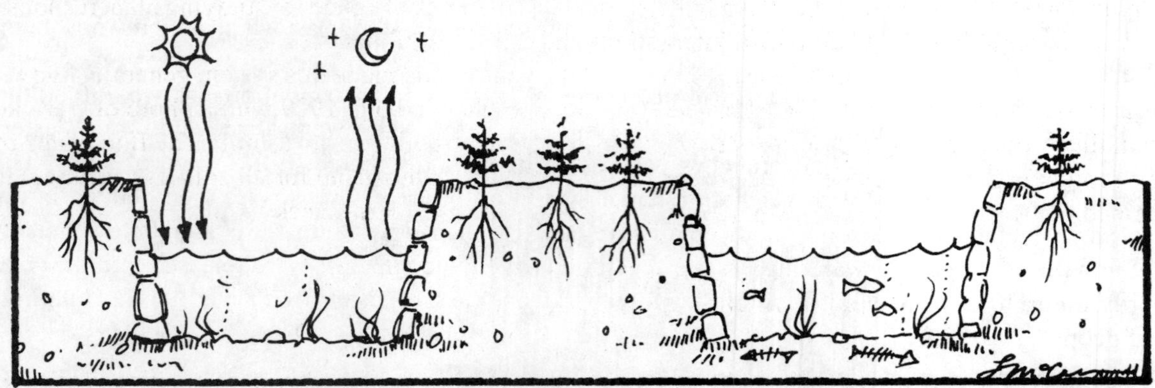

These Andean gardens show the ingenuity of the gardeners of antiquity. The raised-platform system produced yields which rival those achieved today, yet their only tool was the labour of construction. The effectiveness of the system is remarkable. Solar energy trapped by the canal water created a micro-climate protection against frost. Plant nutrition was provided by soil nutrients, plus a canal soup of nitrogen rich algae, plant and animal remains, and fish effluent. The canals were also fish farms where tilapia were grown as an additional source of protein. Irrigation was automatic with capillary action moving nutrient rich water from the canal to the plant roots. In times of drought hand watering required very little labour.

The modern history of hydroponics begins in the laboratories of scientists trying to discover everything but, how to grow food. Using water culture, they had proven by 1892 that plants required nine elements to grow. This was confirmation of observations made by field crop researchers as early as 1850. What spurred this field research was the beginning of shipments of grain from the New World (The US). Work on formulating commercial chemical nutrients began in 1860 and by 1920 standardized laboratory formulae had made their appearance. Yet the purpose of the scientists in the lab had nothing to do with discovering alternative methods of agriculture. The prevalent belief was that the water culture system would only work in the lab. This ignored the centuries old and well-known Chinese method of growing rice. To scientists, water culture was only good for studying plant response to various stimuli and the biological interactions and reactions of plants.

The big 'Discovery' which opened the laboratory doors and made this system generally known was made by Dr. William F. Gericke. The story broke in the media in 1929 with a photo of Gericke standing on a ladder picking tomatoes from a 25-foot plant growing in a washtub. The floodgates of promotion opened and Gericke's name for his system stuck as the name for all soil-less culture. He coined the word 'hydroponic' from a loose translation of two modern Greek words;

hydro + ponos
= water work

In his system water did the work of feeding the plants. If he had been more of a Greek scholar the word 'hydroponic' may never have come into common use.

Translated from the ancient Greek 'hydroponics' means,
'the sweat from the brow of a woman during child birth'.
So much for language lessons.

Fig. 18. The four basins covered 130 square feet. Six months after planting, the stage shown in the picture, 606 pounds of fruit had been harvested. The plants were allowed to grow one year and produced 1,224 pounds of fruit.

This plate is from the only book Gericke wrote "*The Complete Guide to Soilless Gardening*" published in 1941, and never reprinted.

This wheat, grown at Little Hanger L for the NASA programme is part of the research which will result in hydroponics going with man into space.

The original water culture jar is still in use in labs around the world today. This same jar, minus the air tube, would have been common in labs in the late 1700's as scientists attempted to determine what is essential to plant growth and productivity.

Researchers began exploring the possibilities for agriculture and the inevitable hype began. Fast talking salesmen had hydroponics doing everything but talking as they sold expensive equipment to gullible customers. The decades since are littered with the remains of these systems and these failures did a lot to hold back the general understanding and acceptance of hydroponics. In spite of the con artists, years of research the world over and the dedication of good growers has led to the very profitable application of hydroponics to commercial growing. It is also an essential part of the NASA program to move man into space, and feed him while he tours the planets.

Yet with all the research, the hoopla, and the promises; the principles of hydroponics haven't changed since Atlantis. The Hanging Gardens of Babylon were based on this simplicity yet they were known as one of the Seven Wonders of the World. Hydroponics today is just as simple. Changes exist only in the materials we use, the degree of control possible and our level of understanding about plant life.

Chapter 3
GETTING TO KNOW HYDROPONICS

How Hydroponics Works

Hydroponics is simplicity itself, feeding plants instead of feeding soil. Plants can only take up elements which have been dissolved in water. Some plants have evolved to trap insects in their flowers and dissolve them, but if you ever find a plant root with teeth it will be a startling discovery indeed.

For any system there are basic requirements.

First, Something to grow the plants in.
If you are using a grow medium it should contribute nothing toxic to the plants. Since gravel is one of the most commonly available materials we will use it as an example. If you take a container with drainage holes in it, say an old plastic bucket, and fill it with gravel, you have a place to grow a plant.

Second, You require a method of feeding and watering.

In hydroponics we combine the cycle of feeding and watering. You take another container, one without holes, fill it with water and dissolve nutrients in the water. Now you have a nutrient solution. It is a simple matter to pour the nutrient solution into the bucket full of gravel. Since it is full of holes most of the solution will drain out, but some will remain on the surface of the gravel and it is on this moisture that the plant roots will feed. The runoff solution can be collected and reused.

What I have outlined here is one of the crudest systems and it is labour intensive but I think it illustrates the basics of hydroponics. What you have done is provide a place for the plant to grow which neither contributes to, nor detracts from, plant growth. Into this place you have provided the basic food elements dissolved in water, in such a manner as to allow the plant roots to breathe. Simple! Well that is how hydroponics works.

Why Hydroponics Works

There are several very basic principles which have made the technology of hydroponics possible.

First: Plants can only eat (absorb, take up) elements in very limited combinations and only when these elements or combinations are dissolved in water.

Second: A plant makes no distinction between an element which is dissolved from a rock or broken down from organic matter by decay and decomposition. The elements are identical. No matter how many times it has been through a cow, calcium is still calcium. We humans have no ability to create elements so there is no such thing as an artificial element for plant nutrition.

Third: The formulation of nutrients has, as its basis, the plant itself. The process of determining the elemental makeup of a plant is very simple and accurate. The result of an incorrect formulation is a sick or dead plant so it is easy to tell when you are wrong.

Fourth: The plants are living organisms which, when supplied with fully balanced nutrition in the proper quantity, grow more quickly and produce more.

Fifth: The roots of the plants must breathe. They take in oxygen and give off carbon dioxide as well as other gases and compounds. The effluents must be removed from the roots and fresh oxygen provided.

Again it is clear that you must provide nutrients dissolved in water in a way which allows the roots to breathe to really get plants to grow. Of course a good environment is needed. The temperature must be right, the light levels need to be high enough and the humidity at the level the plant likes it. There is no limitation to where you can operate a hydroponic garden. Indoors or out, the garden will perform quite well as long as the climate is good for the plants.

This does bring up a common question. If hydroponics works outdoors why is it so much more productive than growing in the soil?

Despite all of the claims to the contrary, hydroponics is no more productive than what the 'perfect' soil garden would be. Plants are only capable of growing as fast and producing as much as their genetic blueprint allows. The reason we seem to get so much more production from hydroponics is that there are few if any 'perfect' soil gardens, while we have the ability using hydroponics to control all of the inputs to plant growth.

Additionally it is very easy to place a hydroponic system in a greenhouse and extend the growing season. This is a problem for the farmer with a 100-acre field. Climate control, a longer growing season and optimum plant nutrition all combine to provide yields per year per unit area, which are considerably higher than those generally obtained in the field.

Becoming a 'hydroponic gardener' is the first step to becoming a much better gardener than you would otherwise be. You have more control over your garden and it is much easier to provide everything your plant needs. Less work and better results. Now that is better gardening.

Chapter 4
UNDERSTANDING PLANTS

The Five Factors

There are five basic factors to plant growth; they are

WATER, LIGHT, AIR, MINERALS and ROOT SUPPORT.

Here is how they combine in Nature.

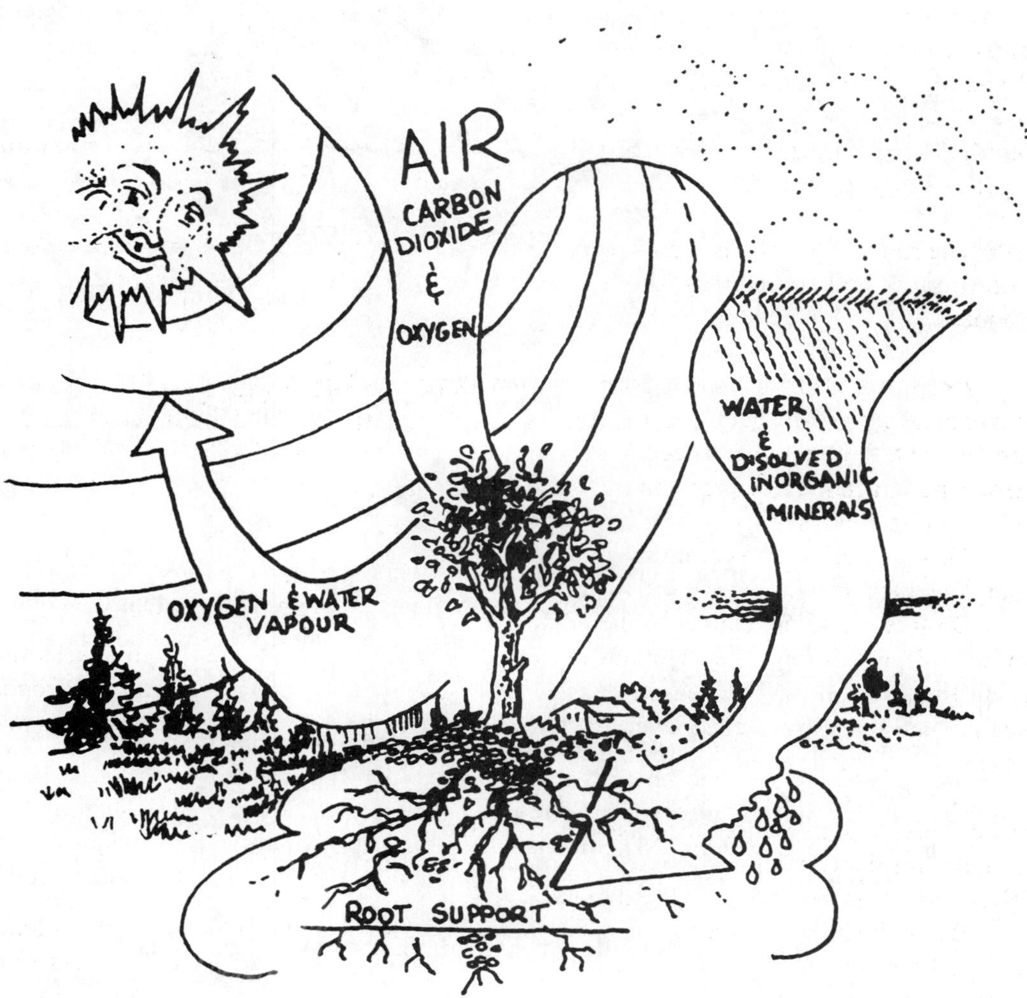

Since we are dealing in soil-less culture, let's have a quick look at each factor and how it affects the plants in our hydroponic garden.

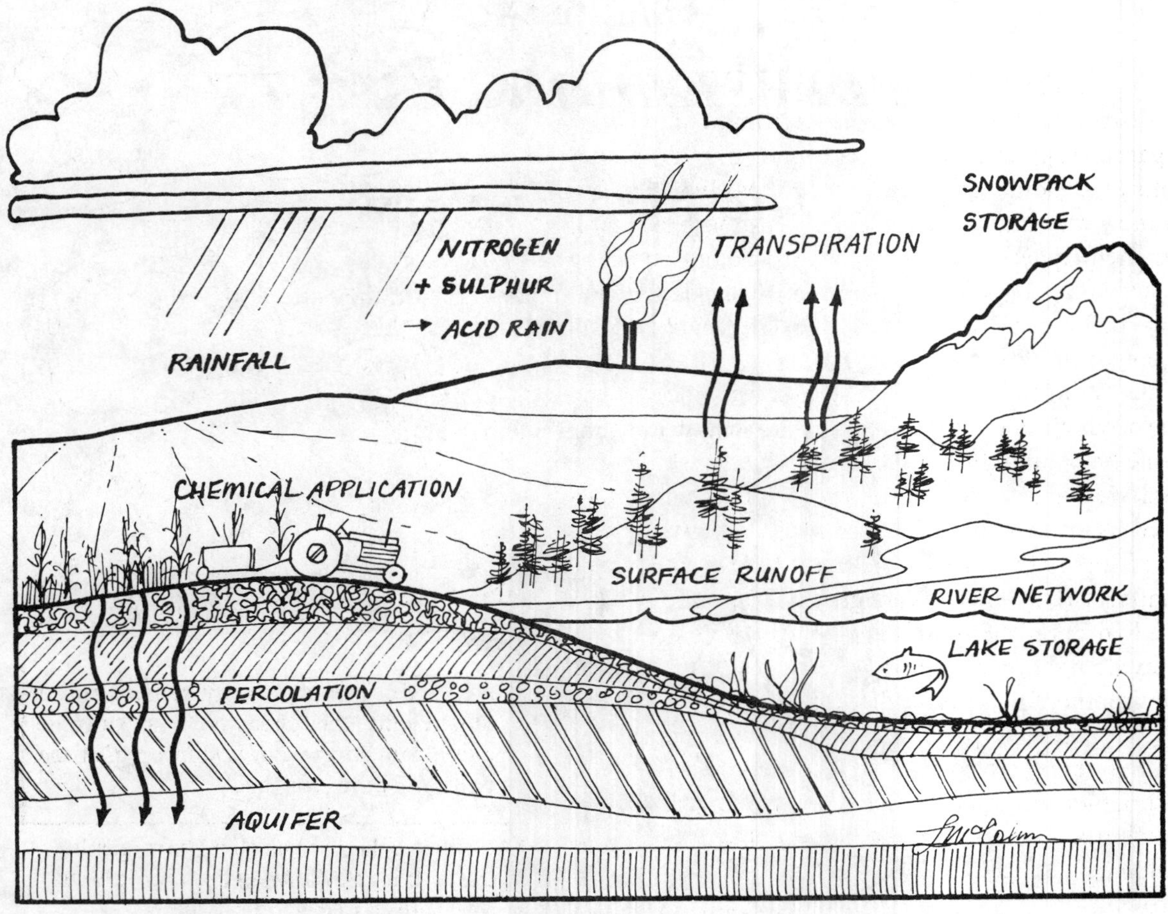

WATER

In Nature water comes from rainfall, lakes, rivers, and aquifers. With the pollution of the environment these water sources are too often contaminated. For outdoor gardens the volume of water used and wasted makes it uneconomical to treat or purify the water. Whatever cocktail of ingredients is in the water is what the plants have to deal with. This slows their growth and adversely affects their health.

Water is about 90% of the composition of plants and from its chemical formula H_2O we know that in its pure state it is composed of hydrogen and oxygen. The water we get for use in our gardens is far from pure but the volumes used in hydroponics are so much lower than field culture it is feasible to 'clean up' the water as required. The first step in setting up any garden is to get a water analysis, no matter where your water comes from. Even municipal water supplies can have some very nasty surprises these days.

We have the potential to provide water to our plants which is much more suitable than what would be used in an outside garden. A better quality of water means better plant health and growth. Later we will be discussing water in far more detail covering such topics as pH, osmosis, EC, ion exchange, temperature, transpiration, formulas, and aeration, plus many more. There is more water in your plants than any other single component so it does deserve a thorough understanding.

LIGHT

As mentioned earlier, light is not a part of hydroponics. It is a part of the environment in which a garden is placed. With the evolution of hydroponics into greenhouse and indoor locations, light has become a very important topic. Few Northern or Southern hemisphere climates provide enough sunshine year round for profitable plant growth in greenhouses. For indoor gardens we must provide all light requirements from artificial sources.

With the use of hydroponic technology from the ocean floor to space flight much research has been done on plant lighting. We know what sunshine does and we have some useful replacements when sunshine is inadequate or not available. The conversion of light energy by plants is the start of the food chain no matter where the plants are grown. The difference for the hydroponic garden is that we can often profitably provide lighting because we have created a protected environment which is limited in size.

The topics related to plant growth and lighting include photosynthesis, respiration, CO_2, humidity, temperature, and photoperiodism, to name a few. We have much to cover in the pages ahead on lighting. Light is the gasoline of plant growth, no gas, no growth.

HEY! I'm a high energy tomato not a mushroom. Just because you can see doesn't mean the sun is shining. Get me light or I quit growing.

The chart below shows that there is a lot more to the relationship between plants and light than just photosynthesis.

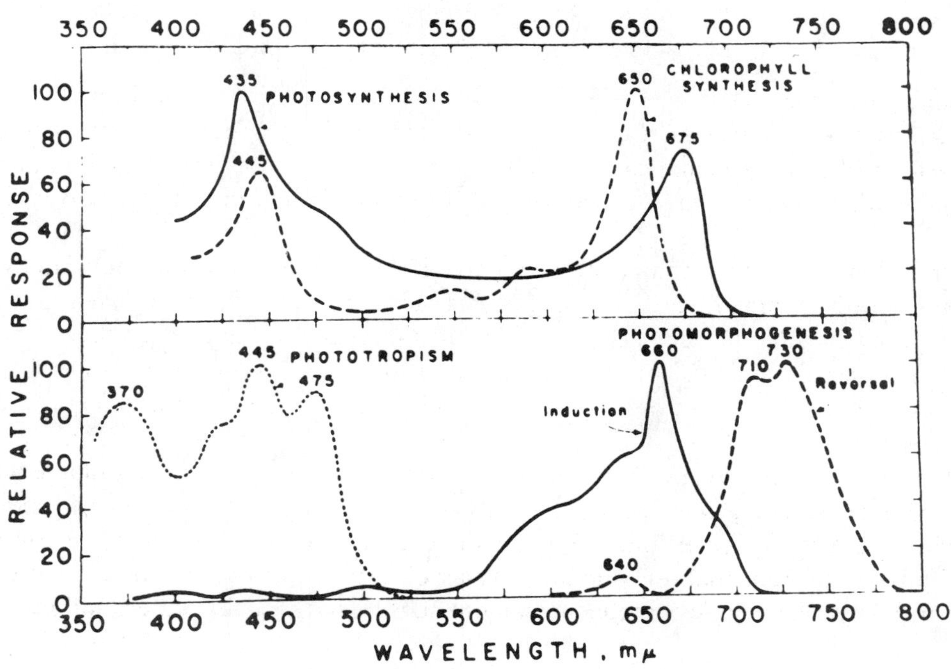

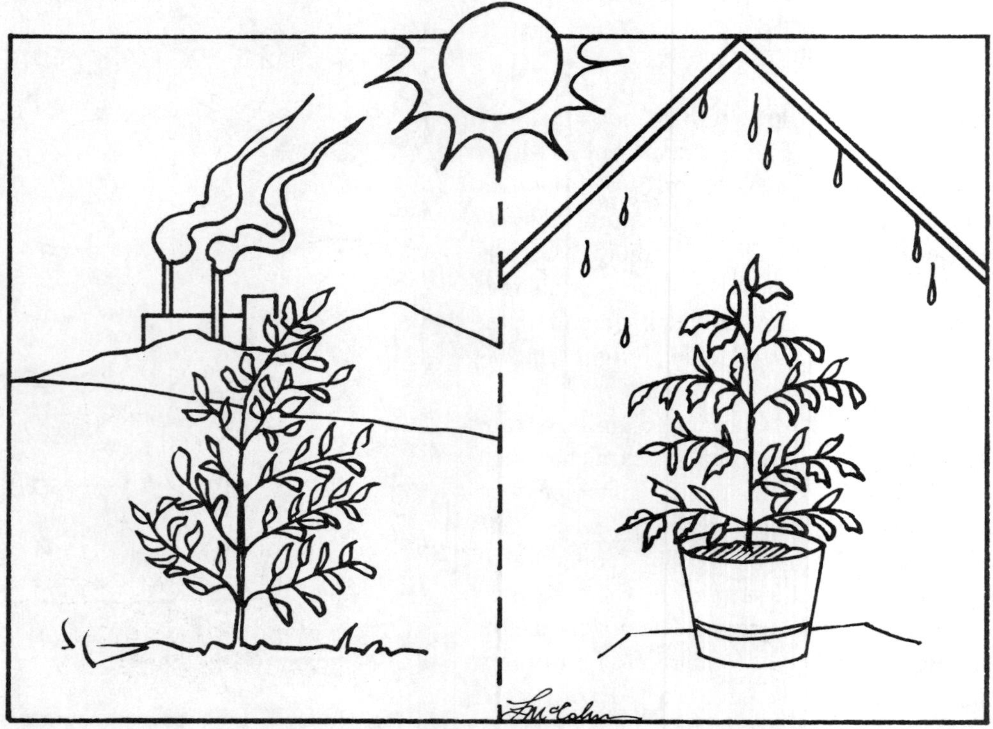

Air quality and behaviour changes dramatically when enclosed in a greenhouse. The air is still, humidity builds up rapidly, as does the heat, and plants can quickly deplete carbon dioxide levels.

AIR

According to scientists air on our planet is a mix of gases in these general proportions: Nitrogen 78%, Oxygen 21%, Carbon Dioxide 0.3%, Argon 0.93%, Neon 0.0018% with traces of Xenon, Helium, Krypton, and hydrogen vapour. With this description you might think there would be no difference between the air in a protected environment and the air blowing over an open field.

From the plant's eye view there can be some very considerable differences. The air plays important roles in plant growth. It provides the carbon dioxide which is about 40% of the dry weight of any plant. Air is what carries the moisture and oxygen away from the leaves of the plant and aids in transpiration. It is what takes the gases away from the roots. Air provides a tremendous buffer to temperature change around the plants.

When we move into a controlled environment we change how the air behaves. It is limited in volume and so the plants can remove all available CO_2 very quickly. Humidity can rise rapidly as plants grow more quickly and everyone has experienced the rapid increase in temperature in a greenhouse on a sunny morning. The other major change is the loss of the wind in an enclosed environment. This air movement has a very positive impact on the movement of water through the plant and if the water movement slows due to a lack of air movement so does plant growth.

We can't see, taste, feel or touch it unless it is moving or contaminated, but air is a major topic for discussion in any hydroponic garden environment. At least in a contained environment we have the potential of screening out airborne dust and other pollution which could clog up the stomata in plant leaves and stop growth.

There is often much discussion on the part of 'organic' growers as to the superiority of the food sources they use. The fact is that no matter how many times it goes through the cow, calcium is simply calcium, identical to that taken from a limestone cliff. Combining elements into fertilizer salts makes it easy for us to provide plants with the precise nutrition they require.

Try getting a custom formulation from a cow some time!

MINERALS

Much less than 5% of the live weight of plants is made up of the minerals taken up by plant roots. These minerals are the framing, the glue, the catalyst and the cornerstone of plant metabolisms. The plant metabolism is the primary link in the food chain which turns these elements into nutrition for all other species of life on the planet.

The fact that these elements are such a small component of the plant tissue makes it is easy to see why we use so little in a hydroponic garden. Field farmers who are used to spreading fertilizer at multiple tons per acre are amazed when we speak of parts per million as being enough for plants. We have the ability in our garden to ensure the plants get exactly what they need. Field farmers may have grown up on the idea that more is better but the hydroponic gardener knows this is a foolish notion. Better to give the plants what they need when they need it.

Few organic gardeners know what they are feeding their plants let alone what the optimum diet is. What they call chemical fertilizers are exactly the same elements contained in the chemicals they use to feed soil instead of plants. For those who don't realize it, a chemical is simply a combination of elements. Whether made by man or out of the back end of a cow these chemicals are made of identical elements. The difference is that we know exactly what we are feeding our plants in a hydroponic garden.

We will get to the specific elements and their roles in plant growth a little later in the book.

PLANT SUPPORT

This factor is really self explanatory. To stand up in soil plants need to hold on to something with their roots. The shallow growing media used and smaller root structures commonly developed by plants which do not have to search for food mean that plants often need support. For small plants the media is generally enough, but for larger vine crops plant support is used to keep plants upright. The purpose of both root and plant support is the same, to keep the plant oriented to the light source, keep spacing for good air flow, and keep the roots in contact with the nutrient solution.

This photo shows just one of the options for supporting plants. Clipping vines to strings or wires and plant stakes are also very common solutions to the need for plant support.

Summary

When using a hydroponic system, you are not directly affecting all of the factors to growth. Those controlled directly are water, minerals and plant support. The most important of these is the water.

The reason for this is simple. Water is the carrier for your mineral elements. It dissolves these elements so they are available to the plant. Your plants are about 90% water so it is readily obvious that it is a wise idea to know exactly what is in your water before you add any mineral elements. You use far less water in a hydroponic system, especially recycling systems, as the only water loss is through the plants. No spraying water over large areas and watching 95% of it evaporate.

The only change that occurs concerning the minerals is the elimination of a long, slow cycle which occurs in soil gardening. Plants cannot feed on organic matter, they can only take up elements in solution. In hydroponics the whole cycle of decomposition and decay is bypassed. The result is total control of your plant's nutrition. By using a proper nutrient formula you can guarantee your plants quicker, healthier growth with less effort.

Plant support can be a problem if you are using a water culture system and have no root support for a plant which grows quite tall. For this, and other reasons, the most popular form of hydroponics involves the use of grow medias which will be covered in detail. These medias provide a method of providing root support and often gardeners are more comfortable having something that looks like soil around the roots of the plants.

Hydroponics does not alter any of the other factors to growth but, the placement of the garden can have a dramatic influence on these factors as noted earlier. When you move your garden from the patio to a greenhouse or indoors you must carefully consider how you will deal with the other factors to growth to ensure the success of your garden.

Chapter 5
PLANT STRUCTURE & FUNCTION

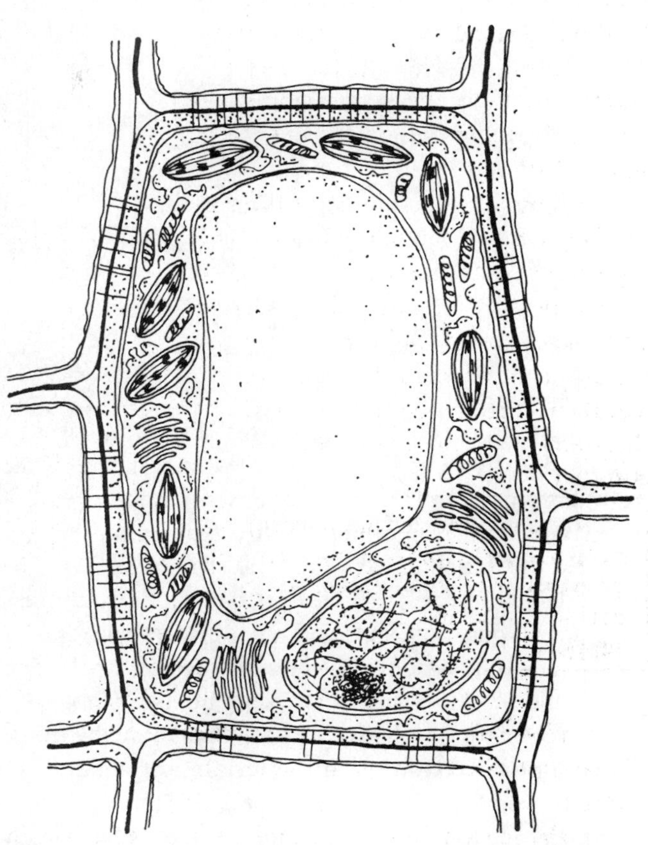

There are five portions of a plant which have functions of special interest to the hydroponic grower. They are;

1. **The Cell**
2. **The Root**
3. **The Stem**
4. **The Leaf**
5. **The Flower**

1. The Cell

First, What is a cell?

"A cell is a small, usually microscopic mass of protoplasm (living matter) bound externally by a semi-permeable membrane capable; either alone or interacting with other cells, of performing all the fundamental functions of life and forming the least structural unit of living matter capable of functioning independently."

What makes the plant cells in leaves so unique is the fact that they contain chloroplasts capable of manufacturing chlorophyll which is the essential compound for converting light energy to kinetic energy. This is the only living cell among higher organisms which can do this amazing conversion. Another interesting feature of plant cells is all external cells, especially those in the roots, are designed to absorb both water and nutrients. This process of osmosis is one we use to control the uptake of water and nutrient by the roots in a hydroponic system. By altering the concentration of nutrients in the solution we can affect the ratio of water/nutrient absorbed and in this way directly affect the growth of the plant.

All of the life processes of the plant appear to be initiated and controlled by the protoplasm in response to environmental stimuli such as temperature and the change in seasons, or the availability of water. The protoplasm itself is a complex, jelly-like, colloidal material composed of mineral substances, carbohydrates, fats, proteins and water. The exchange of elements and chemicals through the cell walls is in part motivated by the charge of the particle. This is a simple and glib explanation of plant cells. It is sufficient to show that we have the ability in hydroponics to affect plant metabolic activity on a cellular level via control of the nutrient solution and external stimuli in the environment.

All other components of the plant are merely specialized bundles of cells.

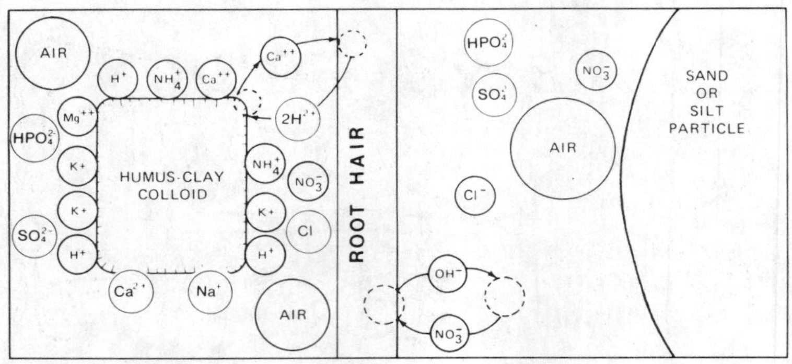

This diagram of all the things which can be in the root zone clearly shows that the root has an involved task in supplying the plant with minerals and water.

2. The Root

The root occupies its own environment separate from the rest of the plant. In most plants the dividing line is the root crown where the root joins the stem. Everything below the root crown is the root zone environment or the media environment. The dynamics of this environment are completely different from the aerial or atmospheric environment where the rest of the plant exists. From a strictly functional point of view, the job of plant support is secondary, especially in some hydroponic cultures. There is not detrimental effect to growth if plant support is supplied by other means as required by the design of the garden.

The physiological functions which are the prime work of the roots include absorbing water and minerals and other elements by osmosis through the root hairs. These two functions are dependent upon the rate of oxygen uptake by the roots, the respiration rate of the plant as well as the environmental conditions in the aerial environment. Few gardeners are aware of exactly how fast roots can grow, up to 6 inches in 24 hours. This growth is in response to a search for scarce water, a nutrient, or oxygen. It is the reason soil grown plants have such extensive root systems which often mirror in size and shape the upper portion of the plant. In a well run hydroponic system the root structure is considerably smaller as the roots do not have to search for any of the requirements and do not have to cope with root effluents. It is possible to grow a 30-foot tomato plant with a root structure which would fit in a coffee cup and still have a perfectly healthy plant.

Many critical processes take place in the roots, including nitrate assimilation and conversion. Another aspect of the roots is the function in some plants as a storage organ. Recent research has shown that we can control the development of tubers and storage roots through the manipulation of the pressure on the root zone. This has given rise to the development of a new class of hydroponic systems designed for this purpose.

The water and other nutrients from the roots are sent to the upper plant through the xylem vessels and receive carbohydrates and other foods in return through the phloem tubes in the stem. Possibly, the most important aspect of root zone control is the provision of adequate supplies of oxygen and air exchange. This oxygen is critical to the control of the over 1,700 microbes which exist in the root zone. The oxygen suppresses the growth of those which exist to break down organic material in an oxygen deprived environment and are the source of many diseases.

3. The Stem

Chiefly, a medium of support and conduction for the plant. It holds the leaves up to the sunlight and contains the phloem and xylem passages which connect the roots and leaves. The placement of these conducting tissues is used for typing or classifying seed bearing plants.

The stem is also an important structure for the grower. Constant visual monitoring of the stem size and placement of leaves, branches, flowers etc., can tell the grower vital information about plant response to the aerial environment and the need for manipulation of the root zone environment.

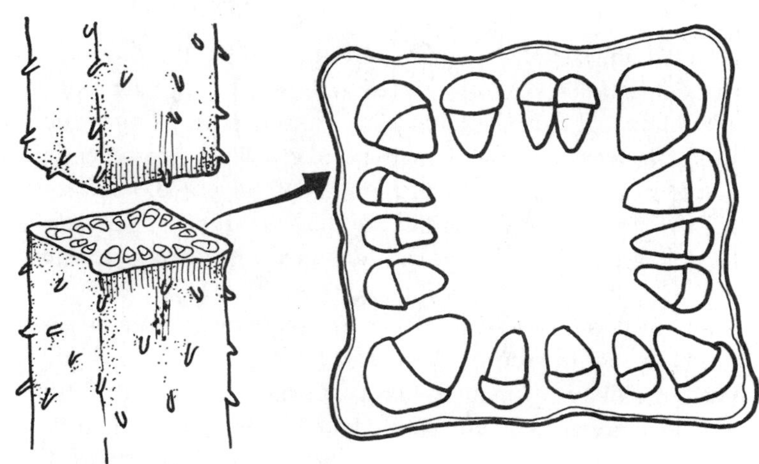

The stem is highway is the transport system which ensures that water and minerals reach the leaves, and the results of photosynthesis are available to all parts of the plant.

4. The Leaf

This is the primary manufacturing center in the plant. Both photosynthesis and respiration occur here. To permit the exchange of the high volume of gases involved in these processes, pores called stomata regulate the movement of carbon dioxide, hydrogen, oxygen and water vapour. The veins you see in the surface of leaves are veins through which the manufactured foods leave the leaf and water and minerals are brought in.

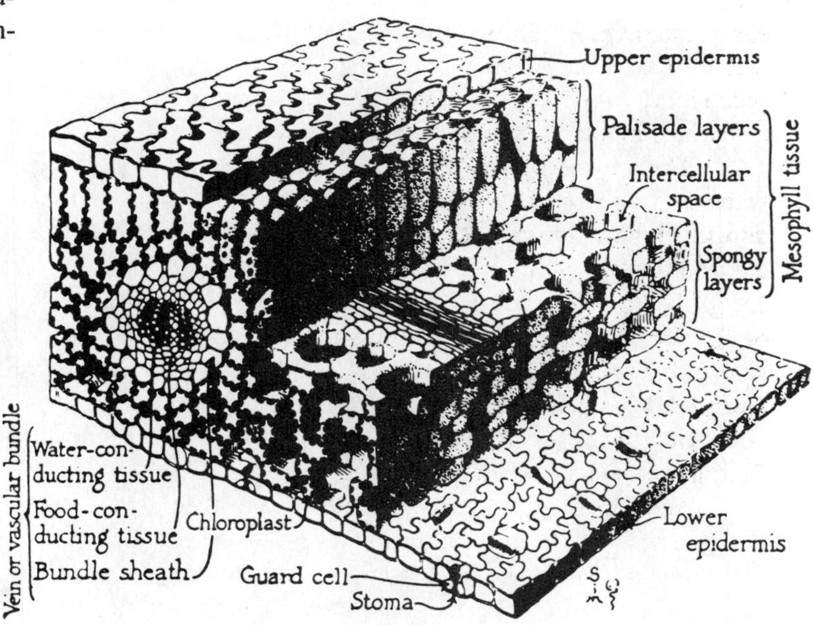

Fig. 9-4. Cross section in three dimensions of a vinca leaf, showing cells and tissues. (Transeau, Science of Plant Life, 1924)

The leaves are also the method plants use to talk to growers about the state of their nutrition and their response to the environment. Leaf shape, size, coloration, and curling, all speak volumes to the knowledgeable grower about what is happening in the plant. Whenever a problem arises the plant will always tell you through the leaves the cause of the problem and how serious it is. Learning the language of leaves for the plants you grow is well worth the time and effort required. You will become a superior grower because of this study.

5. The Flower

Being the reproductive part of the plant, the flower is of prime interest as both a product itself (for cut flowers like roses and orchids) and as an indication of what can be expected in size, quantity and quality of fruit. Not all plants are self-pollinating, which would make growers' lives easier, and some are harder to pollinate than others. This difference is due to the flowering habits of different plants. For pollination we are generally concerned with food crops and these crops can have flowers which are either perfect, male and female organs together in the flower, or imperfect where separate flowers are male and female. The imperfect flowers are either on monoecious plants (both sexes are produced by the plant) or dioecious where each sex of flower is found on separate plants.

Pollination of flowers is accomplished through several methods with more control being possible in the controlled environments where hydroponic gardens are mostly located. Perfect flowers (tomatoes etc.) can have enhanced pollination through the control of humidity and air movement, vibration, and tapping, as well as the use of bees. The monoecious and dioecious plants can require the use of insects and occasionally hand pollination. The resulting fruit size and quality are completely dependent on how well the flowers are pollinated so it is a process you need to observe closely.

Bees are tireless workers and very effective at pollination. They are usually present in outside hydroponic gardens. In the greenhouses, commercial growers have turned to the bumble bee in addition to the other options. Hobby growers must rely on such things as tapping the plant, and ensuring good air movement to enhance the sex life of their plants. For imperfect flowers a camel hair brush is often required.

Part II
Hydroponic Systems and Methods

The boat trip through 'The Land' exhibit at Epcot in Florida introduces thousands of people each year to the potentials and choices offered by hydroponic gardening.

Chapter 6
Choices

At this point we are going to have to get away from using the word hydroponics as the only system description. The number of different system designs is almost unlimited and to bring order to the chaos I put them into categories where systems have basic similarities. Following is a list of the categories and the subclassifications so you can see that you have many choices available.

Drip Irrigation - A basic component of most hydroponic systems.
Fertigation - Drip irrigation with plant nutrition for outdoor gardens.
Static Container - Where the garden is self contained without mechanization.
- Lluwasa
- Gericke
- Wick systems

Media Culture - The plant roots are located in a media of some type after transplant.
Soilless Culture - The media is organic in nature.
- Container gardening
- Drain to waste
- Recycling

Aggregate Culture - The media is mineral in nature.
- Recycling systems

Rockwool Systems
- Drain to waste & Recycling

Water Culture - No media is used other than to propagate the plants.
- **Nutrient Film Technique**
- **Deep Flow Technique**
- **Modified Flow Technique**
- **Aeroponics**
- **The Ein-Gedi system**
- **Ebb & Flow**
- **Porous Plate**
- **Grass production systems**

Even the foregoing is a general classification only. The range of modifications within each category and the combination of techniques by growers to cope with simplicity, climate, meteorology, available materials, energy supplies, skills, and financial considerations, is simply mind boggling. Contrary to advertisements for various commercially produced systems there is no such thing as the perfect garden which will answer every grower's problems and requirements. Anyone who makes such a claim is either a fool or deliberately attempting to mislead the public. As we learn more about plants and their relationship and response to the environment around them the less likely it appears that such a perfect system will ever be developed.

The basic principles governing both hydroponic systems and plant growth have not changed in 10,000 years. They must be followed for good results no matter what cultural system is used. Water replaces soil as the carrier of the nutrient elements to the roots of the plants. The delivery is accomplished in a way that allows the plant roots to breathe. These basics combined with our discussion on the five essentials for plant growth, and the fact that water flows downhill, will allow you to create your own hydroponic garden. It can be simple or sophisticated, manual or automated, indoors or out. All that matters is that you keep the basics in mind and your system will perform well. Forget one of the basics and you can expect trouble and/or dead plants.

Choosing The 'Right' System

Once you are comfortable with the fact that you will be responsible for the complete care and feeding of the plants, no matter what system you choose, you are ready to decide which type of system is best suited to your needs.

For any system you choose you will be propagating the plants in the same fashion as you would have used for your outside garden. The only difference is that you should choose the propagation media which is the same as the media to be used in the system you choose. You will have better transplant results by sticking to the same media throughout the growing life of the plant.

Step one is to recognize your individual personality.

Are you a stickler for detail who continuously monitors and adjusts or do you prefer to have a carefree hobby?

The stickler for detail who is willing to spend a lot of time in the garden will enjoy having things to fiddle with. This points to a recycling system with a minimum of media.

The carefree, throw it in and let it grow gardener, will want an organic media based system with the longest time between the times solutions must be changed or adjustments made to the system.

Are you adventurous or do you prefer the conservative approach with all the safe-guards you can find to guarantee success?

The adventurer will want to try the water systems which provide the maximum involvement with the plants and the most opportunity to learn from mistakes.

A conservative gardener will tend to the organic medias and a system which most closely resembles the type of gardening with which he or she is familiar.

Step Two is deciding what you want to grow in the garden

The choices are of course virtually unlimited so it is impossible to cover every plant and every combination possible in this one chapter. Even a book would be barely enough space. There are however, some basics to recognize about the plants no matter what they are.

1. Is it an annual or perennial?

How long will it be in the garden and will you want to move it around over its life, take it to shows or move it for display?

2. Green, flowering or fruiting?

What will you be harvesting, how often, and will the plant need to be removed at harvest?

3. How big will it get?

Plants do tend to get larger in a good hydroponic system and environment than they do in an outside garden. Be sure to allow enough space for the mature plant. Over planting results in overcrowding and disease.

4. How long will you grow it before harvest or otherwise using the plant up? Weeks, Months, Years?

The longer a plant's life the more you will tend to containerized growing for that plant to allow for other plants to be added and removed if you are growing multiple varieties.

5. Will you need to move the plant; seasonally, for display etc.?

Again containers will allow movement of plants. Removing plants from a garden such as NFT is impossible since root damage on the remaining and removed plants will result and your plants will suffer.

Every popular food crop has a different life cycle and growth habit. No matter what your favorite, it can be grown in a hydroponic garden. Lettuce and strawberries suit small spaces but kiwi needs a lot of space.

6. What is its growth habit?

Some plants will need support; tomatoes, grapes, cucumbers, peppers, others such as bananas need tremendous vertical height. Make sure that both the garden and the space you choose can support the plants you are going to grow.

7. How many different plants do you want to include in the garden?

Combination plantings demand you use containers due to spacing and irrigation requirements. Make sure you have the flexibility to use combinations of container sizes, as well as altering irrigation delivery within the garden. Tomatoes require more water than orchids. In addition you may need to split your garden into different irrigation systems to reduce the amount of compromise in feeding solutions.

This seems to be the dream of every hobby grower. A full crop of red ripe tomatoes. It is a high light, high energy, vining crop which needs room to grow and support for the heavy load.

Even NFT systems can be containerized to make crop variation and harvesting easier as this display at 'The Land' shows. In the background is a vertical aeroponic growing system for lettuce.

Step Three is to decide where the garden will be.

There are a lot of choices since hydroponic gardens free you from the necessity of having a plot of land. However, the space you choose may limit the type of garden which will operate well. It will also dictate what other type of equipment it will be necessary to purchase to create the proper climate for optimum plant growth. All your hydroponic system is going to do is feed and water your plants while giving the roots a place to call home.

Everything else is environment control equipment. What you need will be decided by where you want to grow. In addition the considerations in Step Two will decide what will have to be done to the space to make it useful for your garden.

The options are endless for your garden.

Top

A patio in Melbourne Australia turned into a flourishing garden of flowers and food using hydroponics.

Bottom

A parking lot in Tempe Arizona (Aquaculture Ltd.) becomes a productive hydroponic garden using recycling systems.

Imagine this as your maintenance free back yard in a town house or small city home. This completely hydroponic display was used by New Zealand Hydroponics to improve the appearance of their yard in an industrial area. Quite an improvement.

There are many self contained gardens which are ideal for indoor growing of all types. This 'Gardener's Delite' is a favorite with BC school children. An entire class can grow at the same time and see the results of their efforts. Even the teachers are fascinated.

A simple self watering, hydroponic planter can provide a home for a dwarf banana. Just keep in mind that some varieties can grow to 13 feet before bananas are produced.

Step Four is finding out the level of support you will have.

It is one thing if you can run down to the local store to buy a book, view a video, or talk to your favorite, locally knowledgeable, salesman. It is quite another if you have to deal by mail for everything and try to describe problems by telephone to someone who has never been in your particular area. Whether your supplier is local or mail order a big bonus is if you can locate other hobby growers who are growing the same crops you are.

Don't hesitate to ask stores for the names of local customers who fit with your interests. This will give you additional support as well as an excellent opportunity to see gardens in production and get opinions from growers like yourself. These same growers can make recommendations on the best books and publications for your library. Re-inventing the wheel is common among novices who have to go it on their own. If possible establish a relationship with a local commercial grower and plan to attend at least one conference every couple of years which includes a grower tour.

Step Five is to decide your budget.

The bottom line on any new system is how much you are willing to spend to start. Depending on where you are going to grow you will have to split your budget between the hydroponic garden and the environment control equipment required by your location. Don't get caught up in bells and whistles. Make sure you have the basics covered before you consider any toys, you can buy them anytime.

You don't have to spend a lot of money to get started so don't get fooled into buying high-tech controls for a simple garden. Balance your choices so your operational level is similar all the way through. If you have extra money then you can improve your hydroponic or environmental system on a selective, best result basis.

Step Six is to decide who to buy from.

There are now literally hundreds of stores throughout North America. Magazines, friends, the phone book, local gardening associations, are all sources of names of the stores. Get every catalogue you can lay your hands on; even if you have to spend a couple of bucks to obtain them. They will be not only a source of information, they will provide the opportunity to compare the range of equipment and services offered.

A beginner who makes decisions strictly based on price is in for some rude surprises and unexpected expenses. As a novice you may not be able to decide what the difference is between products which are described as achieving the same result. Quality never costs money, it saves you both money and aggravation over time.

In addition, the broader the range of products offered by the store, the more likely you will be able to get everything you need from one store. Many stores carry the same brands so you can do some price comparison and get an idea of what fair value is. Catalogues also tend to reflect the attitude of the company that provides them. A lot of colour and flash with a very limited product line is a bad sign. Look for extensive description, lots of information, and a wide range of product covering all areas of your requirements.

It is easy to gain insight on the way a store does business if you can pop in for several visits before you actually buy. Listening to existing customers is a really quick way to find out if the store caters to the type of gardening you want to do and if the staff is knowledgeable enough to give you the required support.

Chapter 7

THE SIMPLE SYSTEMS

Time now to look at how these systems are constructed and the special characteristics of each.

Drip Irrigation

While readers may immediately say, "This isn't a hydroponic system," I would suggest you consider the fact that you will install a drip irrigation system of some sophistication in virtually any hydroponic system you build. This system was originally designed to conserve water in desert areas by the Israelis but it was immediately seized by growers as a better way of delivering nutrient solutions.

I will only cover the barest details of drip irrigation to make sure you are familiar with it. For an in-depth study I strongly recommend the book ***"Drip Irrigation, for all Climates and Landscapes"*** by Robert Kourik.

Drip irrigation systems are composed of distinct parts;

the Source,
the Manifold,
the Header, and
the Delivery Device.

The design of the system starts with examining both ends of the system.

The Source to determine how much water you can deliver per hour and at what pressure.

Then the **Delivery Devices** to determine how much you need to deliver to all the plants in the system.

This irrigation device from 1900 shows that this technique was not recently invented. Rather it has been refined using the low cost plastic devices now common in garden centers and other stores.

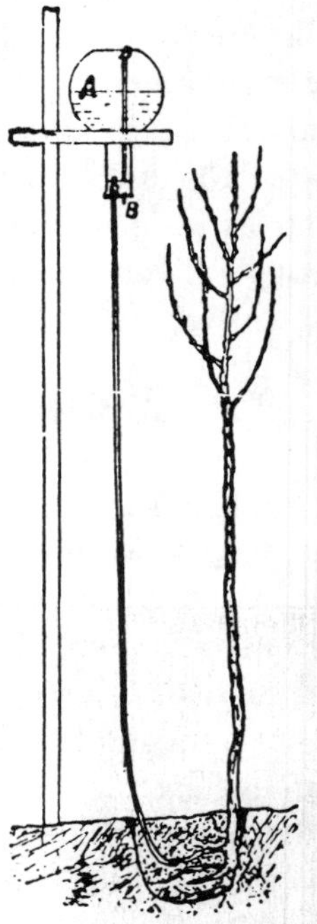

FIG. 152. — Device for starting growth in trees.

The Delivery Devices are available in a huge range of options from small diameter tubing, called spaghetti to overhead sprinklers and misters for propagation or climate control. Each plant will have a specific water requirement per irrigation period and the device you use will decide how long it will take to deliver this volume. By adding up the total delivery requirement you can figure out if your source can supply all of the volume at once or if you will need to split the system into zones which will operate at different times.

The rest of the design process is a simple matter of finding the easiest way to get water from the source to each of the delivery devices. The regular layout of most hydroponic systems makes this simple in most cases with flow calculations required only for commercial systems with thousands of plants. Hobby systems commonly require no tubing larger than 3/4" in diameter. For landscape applications the design is a bit more involved due to larger areas and lack of regularity.

The Source: This can be, and usually is for hobby systems, an outside tap. A wise precaution is to install a backflow prevention device at the tap. In some areas this is required by law.

Where the headers connect to the manifold it is a good idea to install flow control valves (any simple valve will do) to balance the flow to each header

When designing the system it is best to keep the headers of equal length and try to ensure that each is required to deliver the same amount of water through the delivery devices.

The delivery device can be as simple as a length of 'spaghetti' tubing, or it can be one of the devices shown below. The samples below are not by any means all that are available.

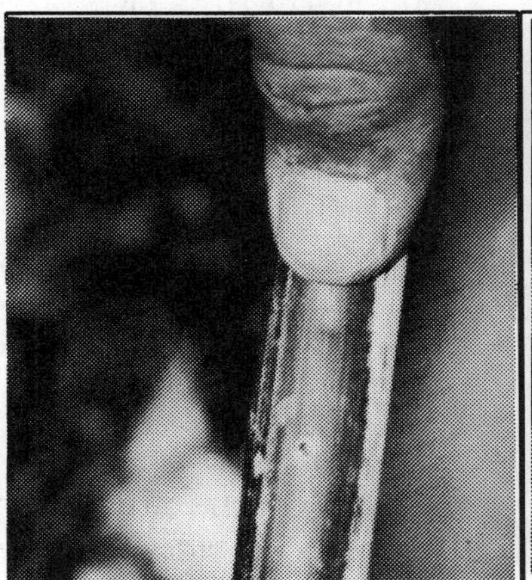

A dripline with emitter holes built in can be used as a combination header line and delivery device.

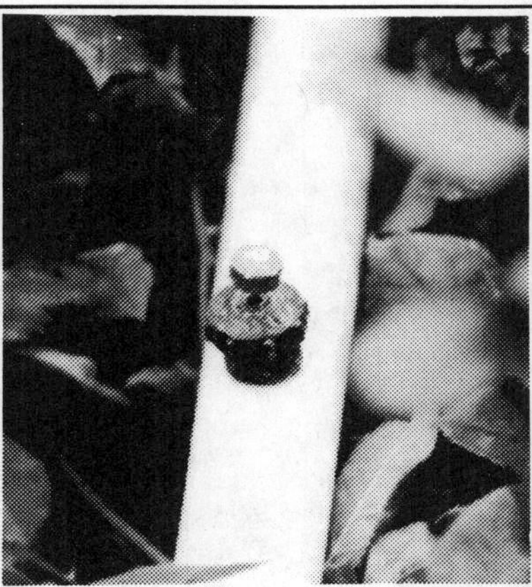

This spray device is used in a rose greenhouse as a delivery device. The disadvantage is the potential for salt build up on the stem and excess water on the lower leaves.

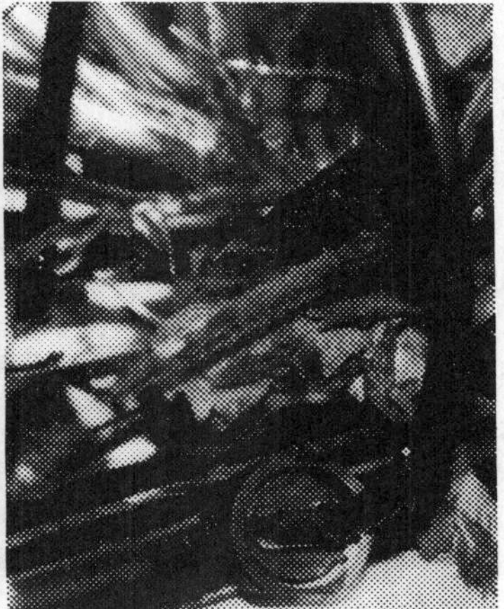

This delivery device is a dripper plugged into a header line with a tube to carry the water directly to the roots of the strawberry plant.

Fertigation

This is the simple system which allows you to turn any soil garden into an instant, automatic, hydroponic garden. It overcomes the problems of water shortages and poor soils at minimum expense. There is the additional benefit that all of your container plants and hanging baskets can be put on the same system, eliminating considerable work for you and ensuring better outside gardening results.

Installing a fertigation system involves nothing more than adding an injector to a drip irrigation system and using a full formulation hydroponic nutrient as an additive to your water. Hydroponic stores, nurseries, garden centers, irrigation suppliers, co-ops, farm suppliers and many other stores stock all of the components needed to install a drip irrigation system. There are two inexpensive injectors on the market which suit hobby needs very nicely; the Hozon, and the Mazzei injector. There are dozens of other options which are more sophisticated and it is wise to ensure you compare carefully before making an investment of more than $50.00.

The layout and design for a fertigation system is identical to that of a drip irrigation system. The only addition is a device to inject liquid plant nutrients into the irrigation water. There are many such devices. For the hobbyist the 'Hozon' or Mazzei injectors are generally adequate. For larger systems water powered injectors similar to the triple setup shown are the least expensive while still providing accurate dosing. They are popular with orchid growers, small commercial soil greenhouse fertigation and with apple growers using intensive plantings of dwarf varieties.

Static Container Gardens

These are gardens where the complete garden is in one container and the nutrient solution is located in a reservoir below the plant. The first of these gardens was the Gericke system which started hydroponics on the road to where it is today. He never did design a good nutrient solution for his garden, the first one was developed at the University of Southern California. No matter, there are good nutrient formulations today and his original system still works and can be improved upon quite simply.

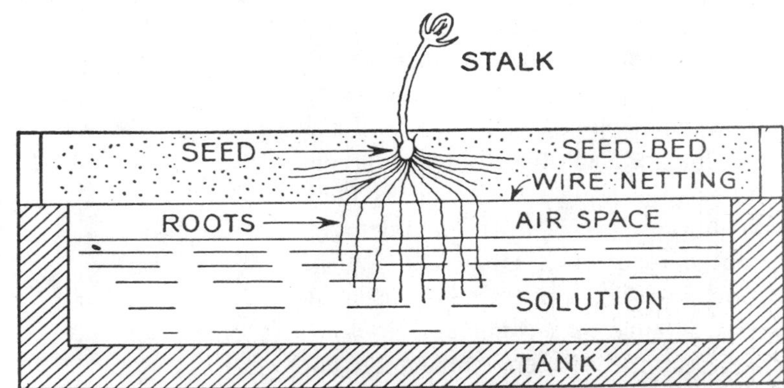

The 'Gericke System' shown here is the first improvement of the static container systems since the floating raft system of centuries ago.

The water proof basins or tanks contain the nutrient solution. Seedlings are planted into a litter tray or bed with a wire mesh bottom through which the plant roots descend into the nutrient solution below. Once the roots have reached the nutrient solution an air space is maintained between the level of the solution and the bottom of the litter tray.

This system is ideal for a quick and easy system on the balcony where the garden is out of the rain and the plants receive adequate sun. The bottom tank can be as large as you like, in any shape which is required, and the litter tray can be in components to allow easy handling. Today you have plastic screens available and peat or sphagnum based soilless mixes make an ideal litter at a low cost.

This type of system can be made very presentable for indoor applications. All you need do is spread decorative gravel over the media.

The large volume of solution makes control a bit more difficult and I would recommend you install a drain on the reservoir tank to make changing solution easy. The advantage is that the system does not require automation and can be left for days without attention. There is nothing to break down. A system to consider for the summer cottage where you want fresh veggies every weekend with a minimum of fuss. The productivity of the garden can be improved by using an aquarium air pump (or compressor for larger systems) to improve oxygen levels in the solution and to remove root effluents.

Lluwasa - Hydroculture

This system is over 30 years old and well established for houseplants in Europe. It makes more sense for houseplants than using the plastic pots and soilless media so common in North America today for killing houseplants and frustrating consumers. The system itself has 4 components and there is no limit to the size or shape of the garden. The components are The Outer Shell, The Inner Container, The Expanded Clay Pebbles, and the Water Meter. Many hydroponic and plant stores in North America sell ready to use systems in a range of sizes and colours, but you can make your own easily and inexpensively.

The requirement for the Outer Shell is that it look good for the location where you want the plant or plants to be and that i tnot leak nor leach any elements into the nutrient solution (no metal unless lined with plastic). Several Inner Containers can be put in one Outer Container. Where several Inner Containers are to be used the Outer Container can be topped with a cover with holes for the Inner Containers to ensure that the nutrient solution is not exposed to light.

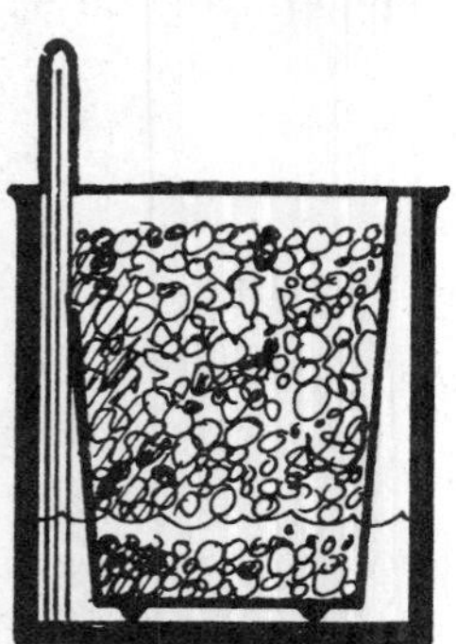

Hydroculture is as simple as the above diagram. A container that leaks (filled with clay pellets), inside a container that doesn't leak. What could be easier?

The Inner Container must be full of holes to ensure easy flow of the solution. There is a complete range of net containers used in NFT and other systems plus mesh bottom pots which suit this purpose admirably and range in size from 2" to 3 gal nursery. Failing availability of these use any plastic container of the right size and drill holes in the bottom and one third of the way up the side of the container. The holes should be about 0.25" (6mm) or less in diameter so the expanded clay pellets will not fall out. The Inner Container should sit on the bottom of the Outer Shell and extend upward to three times the maximum level of the nutrient solution.

Sizing the Inner Container determines the size of the Outer Shell and how large a plant can be grown. The diameter of the Inner Container should be at least 6 times larger than the diameter of the mature size of the stem of the plant to be grown and the height should be 1.5 times the diameter. You can transplant into larger containers over the years for large, slow growing plants.

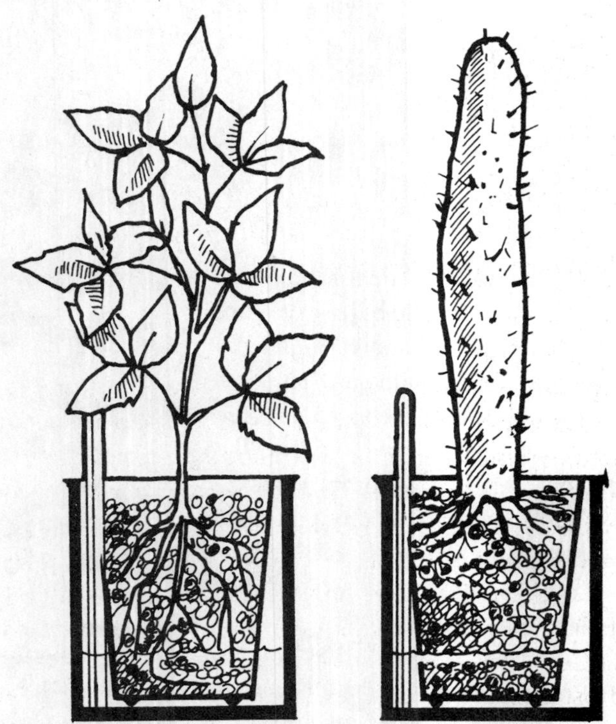

One advantage of hydroculture is it allows a plant to control its own feeding & watering. Each plant develops only the root structure necessary to reach its 'zone of moisture'. The result is a small root compared to soil grown plants.

The Expanded Clay Pellets are manufactured in Europe and North America and marketed under several brand names, Hydrostones, Leca, etc. Choose the size which is a mix of 0.25" to 0.375", larger, up to 0.5", if you will are making a planter for very large plants. It is possible to use expanded shale but it does not work as well and gravel has to be mixed with something like perlite to ensure proper movement of the nutrient solution to the roots.

The Water Meter is the key to the optimum operation of a hydroculture planter. You cannot see the level of solution in the planter so the Water Meter tells you what is happening. The nutrient solution should, at full, come one third of the way up the hydrostone in the Inner Container and at empty be completely gone. The solution should be replaced between 24 and 36 hours after the Water Meter shows empty. Commercial meters can be purchased but can be hard to find. You can make your own from locally available materials which will work very nicely.

Materials

A length of small diameter (0.25-0.5") PVC pipe equal to the height of the outer container,
a soda straw, and
a chunk of expanded polystyrene (from an old picnic cooler).

Procedure

1. Shape the polystyrene into a plug slightly smaller in diameter than the PVC pipe.
2. Set the PVC into a space between the Inner Container and the Outer Shell.
3. Drop the shaped plug into the PVC pipe and push the soda straw into the plug.
4. Cut the soda straw off at level with the top of the PVC pipe.
5. Fill the Outer Shell with water until it comes to 1/3 of the height of the Inner Container.
6. Mark the straw at that level.

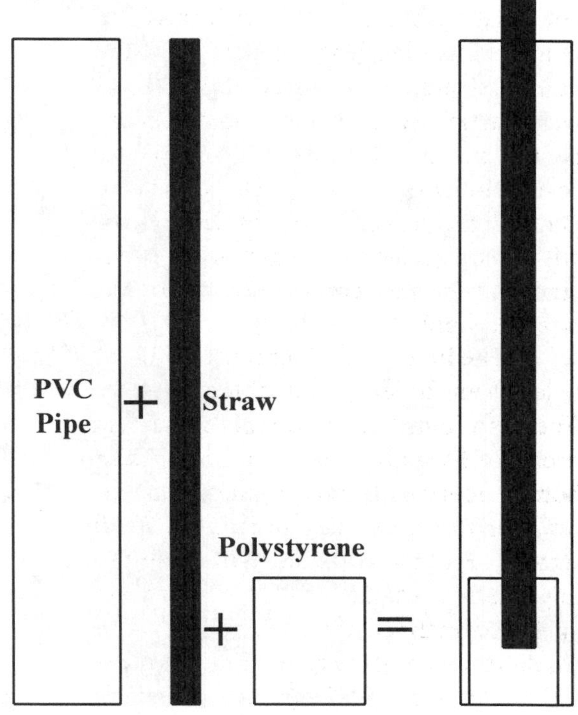

Cheap, simple and effective.

Operation of the hydroculture planter is a snap when you use the special time release fertilizers available from manufacturers in Europe. Using commercial hydroponic fertilizers or ones you make yourself are a bit more difficult as you really have to make sure you use a very mild solution as related to what would be used in recycling systems. The saving grace is that the Inner Containers can be lifted out and washed off when you notice a white powder on the top of the Hydrostones.

You can transplant any size of plant into a Hydroculture planter. Remove it from the existing container, wash all media off using cold water to reduce root shock and trim any dead roots. fill the Inner Container 1/3 full with Hydrostone and set the plant in the container, fill around the roots with Hydrostones. Fill the reservoir to the full mark on the Water Meter. Now all you have to do is wait until the reservoir has been empty for a day. Really tough plant care. The plant adjusts the schedule according to the season. You just do what the water meter tells you and enjoy the plant without worry in the meantime. No more over or under watering or forgetting to fertilize. Welcome to the 'Green Thumb' club.

Wick Gardens

These are simple gardens which can be made using containers similar to those used for the Gericke system. For the less than adventurous there are several single plant wick gardens on the market which operate quite well. The difference between a wick garden and the Gericke is that the roots in the wick garden do not go down into the nutrient solution. The solution is carried up to the growing media by a wicking material with good capillary action. For small gardens you can use cotton lamp wicks, the ones which would be used for coal oil lamps. Other options include sponges as shown in the converted Wardian case developed in 1840, or the capillary matting used by commercial growers.

A Small Portable Greenhouse.*—This is a sketch of a plan upon Ward's principle for trying experiments by the absorption of various medicated waters. D is the drawer under the soil; it is filled with small pieces of sponge, which may be saturated with any prepared water that you please. The drawer may be removed and the sponges washed for a fresh experiment. The glass may also be of different colours, to try the effect of different rays of light. Where there are children, this miniature greenhouse affords great delight. A small stage, removable at pleasure, may be fitted with the minutest pots, so as to take some of the smallest of the Roses and Myrtles, which will flower beautifully. The seeds also of the Yew-tree, Pinaster, &c., will add to the variety, as well as some of our indigenous Mosses, in rockwork. The bottom of the apparatus must be perforated with small holes to admit of the absorption ; and should this not be quite enough, some small skeins of worsted may be drawn up through the soil, which will have the effect of capillary attraction, and infuse the intended influence with great success.—*I. H.

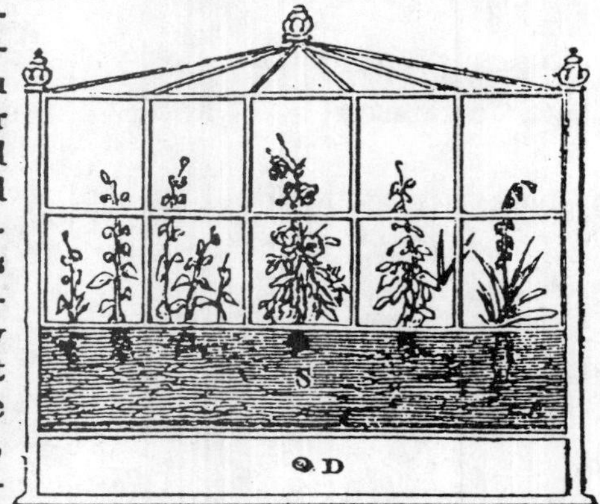

This description of the construction of a garden appeared in an 1841 issue of the 'Gardener's Chronicle. Who says hydroponics wasn't used until 1929 when Gericke made his announcement?

The critical component of the wick garden is the media used. It must have a strong capillary action to ensure the solution reaches all portions of the root zone. Consequently, aggregates and granular materials are useless. Soil is also a very poor choice ,as are most potting soil mixes sold for houseplants. Once wet these 'soils' compact and they do not allow plant roots to breathe well. The ideal media for these gardens is one which is at least 50% sphagnum peat which has not been sterilized. Sterilization collapses the cell structure and reduces the air space besides causing compaction.

The wicking power of the sphagnum mixes can be used to advantage in construction of the garden. A tube running from the media to the bottom of the reservoir, filled with sphagnum mix, is an ideal wick. The tube should be 3/4" in diameter and you will need one tube for every square foot of garden. You will get much better solution distribution if you use multiple tubes instead of trying to use one large tube. The top of the tube should bring the media it contains into good contact with the media in the root zone to ensure optimum solution movement.

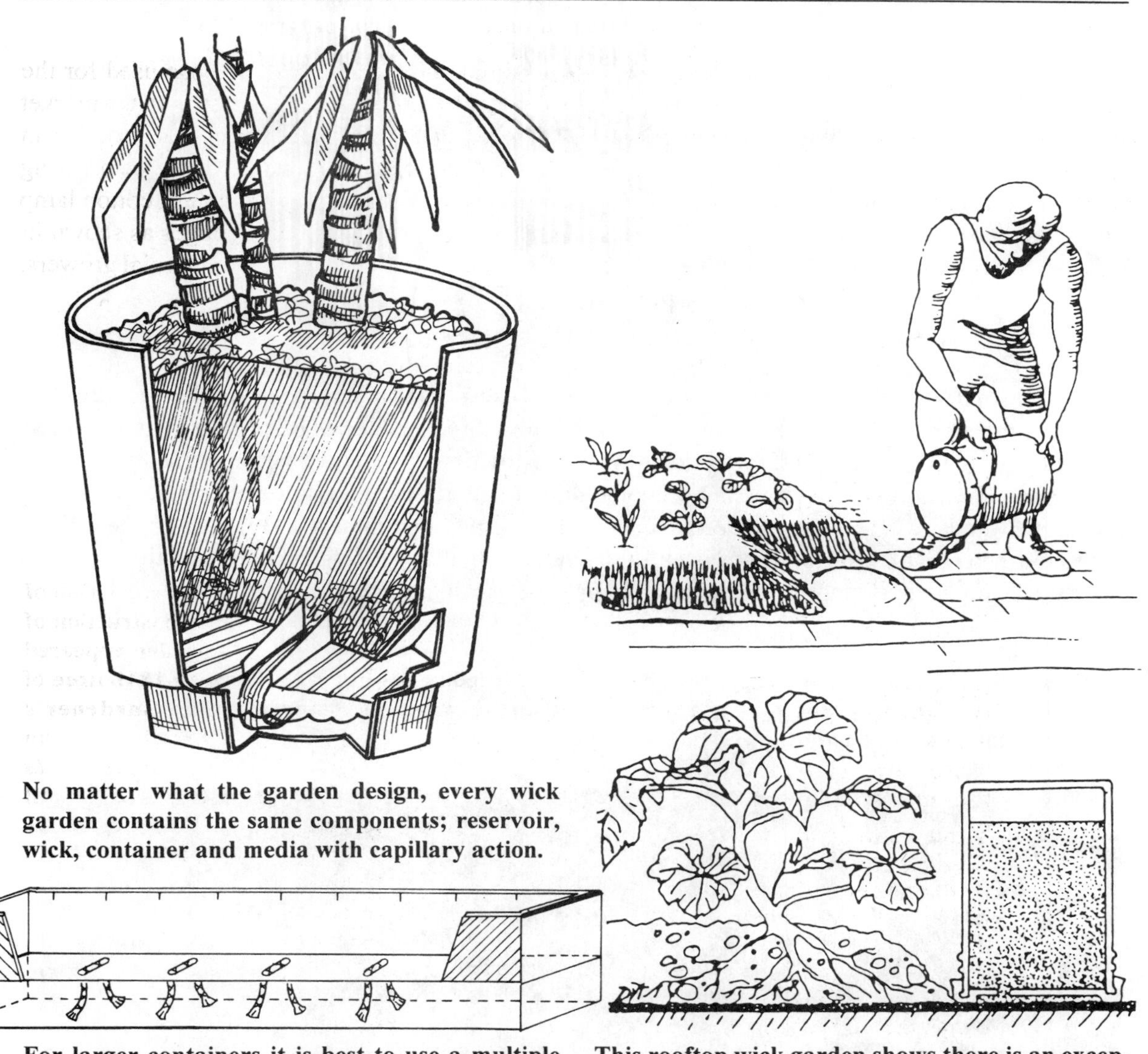

No matter what the garden design, every wick garden contains the same components; reservoir, wick, container and media with capillary action.

For larger containers it is best to use a multiple number of wicks distributed evenly over the bottom of the media container. The wick can be capillary matting, lamp wicking or sphagnum mix contained in a PVC pipe. The trick is to ensure even distribution of water and nutrients.

This rooftop wick garden shows there is an exception to every rule. The media is piled on top of capillary matting. The solution is provided by a 5 gallon pail with a hole in the lid. The matting carries the solution to all of the media which touches it. Ingenious and simple. Design by ECHO.

The best way of building these gardens is in two parts. This allows you to flush the media in the event you make a mistake with the solution and get salt buildup in the media. Remember that you do not want the roots down in the solution so any air movement slits in the bottom of the media container must be extremely fine. For larger gardens you can use multiple trays over one reservoir. Keep in mind that these gardens should not be placed where rain will fall on the media as it will drain into the reservoir, potentially flooding back up into the media also diluting your nutrient solution.

When operating your wick garden remember to keep nutrient concentrations low and let the reservoir go completely dry before refilling. If the media dries to any extent the wicking action will not readily restart from the reservoir. In this case pour a small portion of your new solution over the entire surface of the growing media.

Part III:
Media Based Systems

Chapter 8
MEDIA CULTURE

Most of the hydroponic gardens around the world use media of one type or another. To help you become familiar with the options we will look at them in three categories before we get into talking about how to build various cultural systems. The construction options are virtually identical for all media so there is no value in repeating the same thing many times. You will have plants, media, an irrigation system, a control system and in many cases a recycling drain. Not real complicated. What makes the difference are the characteristics of the various medias which can be put into three general groups, organic medias, aggregate medias, and processed mineral medias.

Media based systems grow more crops than any other hydroponic culture in the world. Environmental concerns have fueled a move to recycling media systems but the switch is occuring slowly. It is also the most popular system type with hobby growers.

This greenhouse drain to waste system in Israel is one of the most basic. The media is the desert sand. The nutrient solution is provided by a neighbour's drain to waste rose growing operation. Simple, low cost and effective. Proof a system doesn't have to be high tech and expensive to work well.

THE ORGANIC MEDIAS

The use of organic materials to replace soil is a habit well established around the world. Many people who purchase houseplants are fooled by the appearance of what they see in the container. It looks like soil, so it must be soil and can be treated accordingly. The result is of course the death of the plants. Soilless organic medias are the most popular with novice hobby growers around the world. This is quite possibly due in part to the fact most of the sphagnum mixes look like soil and the gardeners feel more comfortable when using them.

Commercial growers around the world use organic medias of many types because they are locally available and cheap. The media can be composted after use and there is no detrimental impact on the environment because of disposal. The low cost of these materials means the grower can replace them for each new crop cutting down the potential of disease carry over and eliminating the need for expensive and labour intensive sterilization.

There are an incredible number of organic materials available around the world which have been successfully employed in media culture systems. Virtually any stable organic material can be used so there are local options almost everywhere. The materials commonly used by commercial growers are discussed below but there are some considerations which need to be addressed with any of these media.

1. What is the air to water ratio of the media when wet?

If the media holds too much water due to non-rigid structure or too small a particle size, you will need to mix in another material such as perlite to 'open up' the media and provide more air to the roots. Most of the problems with organic soilless media are related to oxygen starvation because the air/water ratio is far too small. The plant roots literally drown.

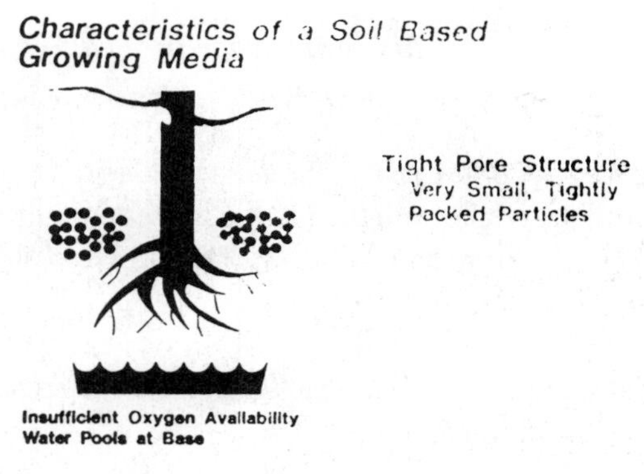

Finding out if the organic media you are using has the proper balance is quite simple and the process will also readily show the effect the container used has on this ratio. This process can be used for any media but is most often necessary with organic medias rather than aggregates.

Any media consists of 3 phases which are constantly in fluctuation as the plant grows.

The **solid phase** is the media itself and consists of all organic and inorganic material in the media. Many soilless mixes have a solid phase of 50% of the volume occupied by the media.

The **liquid phase** is the amount of liquid that is in the same volume of media when it is saturated. At 50% the media is waterlogged and useless for plant growth. A good liquid phase at saturation is 25%.

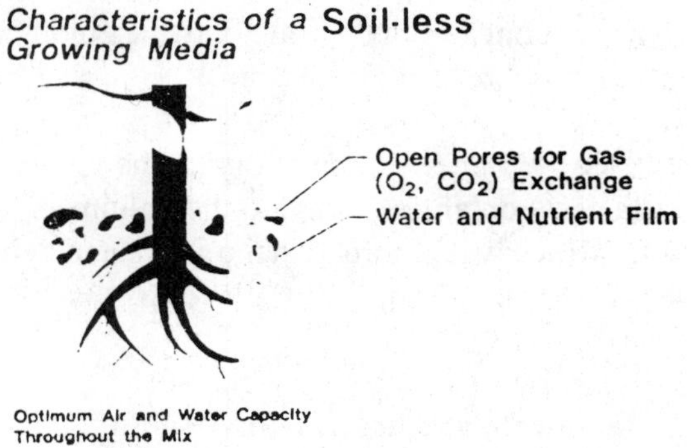

The **gas phase** is the amount of air that is in the same volume and is calculated based on the saturated state of the media. When the gas phase is too high the media is holding too little moisture and will require very frequent or constant irrigation. This means there is little reason for using the media as water culture requires the same level of irrigation and requires no media.

Testing for phase relationship of your media in different containers of the same volume

Materials required

The containers which you have the choice of using.
E.g., a plastic 10-liter bag, a 10-liter nursery pot and a mesh bottom 10 liter nursery pot. For the sake of accurate comparison in this case it will be easier to fill the plastic bag if it is placed in a second 10-liter nursery container.
The media you will be testing.
A graduated cylinder equal in volume to the volume of the growing containers.
Tape and plastic to seal the growing containers.
A marking pencil.
3 containers for water.
Paper and pencil for recording results.
Three pans capable of holding 10 liters of water (dishpans or aluminum roasting pans).

Procedure

This same procedure can be used to compare different medias. To compare medias, use identical containers for each.

1. Seal each container by using plastic and tape on the outside. Make sure the plastic is drawn tightly over the bottom and adhering smoothly to the side.

2. Place the plastic bag, no holes, into the spare nursery container.

3. Fill the spare nursery container with water to 1/2" of the top and mark the fill line on the outside of the container. Pour the water into the graduated cylinder and record the volume.

4. Place the same volume of dry media into each of the test containers, equal to the volume of the water which was recorded in the graduated cylinder. Tamp as you would for planting.

5. Measure a volume of water equal to that recorded for the graduated cylinder into the three water containers and mark each of them separately for the growing containers to be tested.

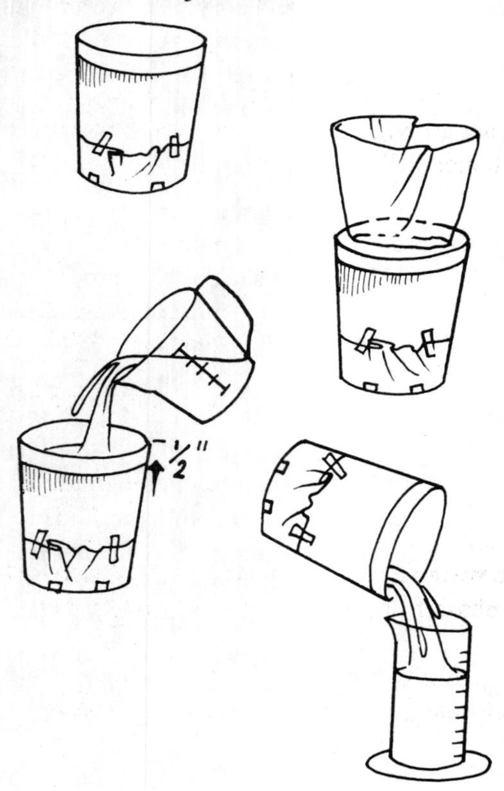

6. Remove the plastic bag filled with media from the nursery container.

7. Very slowly add the water from the assigned containers to each growing container. Add the water in small amounts to allow the media time to absorb it. Some medias are difficult to wet so this can take up to several hours. Once the media in each container has become saturated, a thin film of water will appear on top of the media, record the amount of water left in each assigned container.

8. Set each growing container in a collection pan and remove the tape and plastic from each in turn being sure all water released is collected in the pan. Hold each container in turn until all dripping stops. For the plastic bag make slits the same as you would for the bag in your growing system.

9. Once each growing container has drained thoroughly, use the graduated cylinder to measure the volume of water and record the results.

Calculations

You can now do the calculations which will help determine if your media is good for the crop you are growing (the air/water requirements do vary considerably from species to species), and which container will best suit your needs.

Total Pore Space - % Porosity

$$= \frac{\text{ml of water needed to wet the media thoroughly}}{\text{total volume of the pot in milliliters}}$$

Percentage of air phase at saturation

$$= \frac{\text{volume (ml of drained water)}}{\text{total volume of pot (ml)}}$$

The **water holding capacity** of the media can be calculated by simply subtracting the percentage of air phase from the total porosity percentage.

Using this procedure will allow you to custom mix medias to meet the requirements of your plants and provide key information for anticipating plant water use and irrigation requirements.

2. How well does the media 'wick water'?

A media such as a sphagnum mix with strong capillary action can remain very wet if there is a reservoir of water remaining in the bottom of the container. On the other hand, coarse woodchips will drain extremely well but will not draw water back up to the roots. This ability to move water will be a major consideration in learning irrigation scheduling in the garden. It will also be the deciding factor in the choice of container for the media. The stronger the capillary action of the media, the higher and narrower a single container should be. Medias with poor capillary action should be used in wide squat containers which also provide a small reservoir of solution in the bottom of the container.

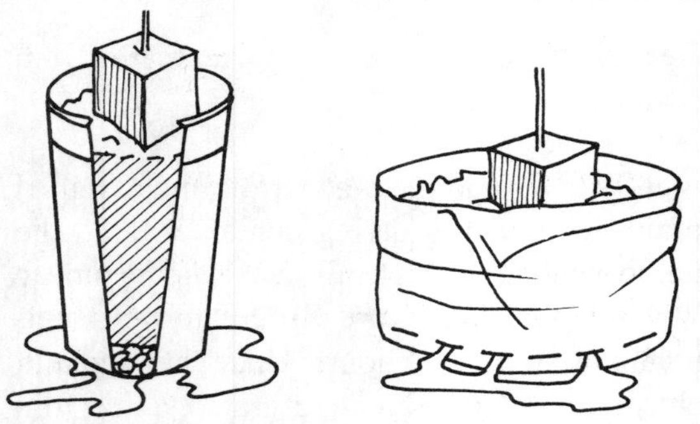

Ideally the growing container should suit the media. Tall & slim for high capillary action, short and wide for low capillary action

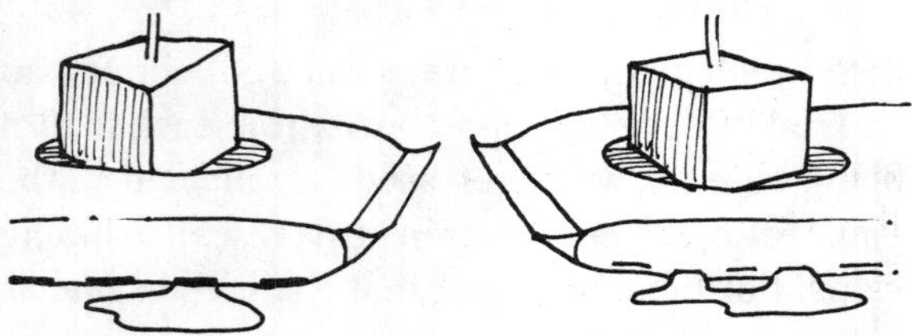

When bolster bags are used the drainage should be right on the bottom for high capillary action media and 1/2 to 1" up the side for low capillary action.

3. How much media should be used per plant?

Most growers use far too much media. They remember the need for large containers when soil is used in containers to grow plants. In media systems there is no problem with ensuring the plant will have a fresh supply of food and water on schedule. The more media you use, the less often you can irrigate and the less control you have over the root zone of the plant. This commonly results in slow growth in the early weeks after transplant as the plant attempts to fill the container with roots before getting serious about the upper growth you really want.

It is important to size the container to suit the plant. Too much media encourages additional root growth and reduces your ability to control what is happening in the root zone.

The less often you irrigate the less oxygen there will be for the plant roots, the more potential there is for salt buildup in the media, and there tends to be more disease problems with the plant. For a commercial grower with a proper irrigation and control system there is never any need for more than 10 liters of media per large plant (tomatoes, cucumbers, peppers) and a good grower will use as little as 5 liters. When growing smaller plants with a lower water/nutrient requirement the amount of media is correspondingly less. As a hobby grower the same applies.

4. Which containers are available for use with the media?

Among commercial growers, plastic bags are most often the choice for large crops. In some areas bolster bags are easily available and used. They are cheap and can be thrown away with the media, cutting down the time required to clean out a system between crops. For the hobby grower there are nursery containers with mesh bottoms which are ideal for the recycling systems most commonly used by the hobbyist. They ensure complete drainage and promote the best air exchange. The smaller crops are grown in a range of containers from 4" to 8" which serve quite well.

THE ORGANIC MEDIAS

An organic media, to be useful to a grower, must meet several requirements.

It seems the first requirement for most growers is that it must be cheap. I would suggest that cost be the last comparison you make, not the first. You will always make a better choice by leaving price till last.

The media should be able to be exposed to the nutrient solution for the full life of the crop without decomposing and it should not take anything from, or contribute anything to, the solution.

The media should have a good air/water ration when saturated and should not compact over time.

For the beginner another consideration is the CEC (cation exchange capacity) of the media. This is the ability of the media to hold the positively charged nutrients away from the roots of the plants when there are too many in the root zone and release them when concentrations reduce. This capacity has saved many a novice from disaster and a few commercial growers as well.

Peat Mixes

Peat is a dead organic matter harvested from bogs which are no longer growing. These bogs provide a habitat for a huge range of life. Many microorganisms involved in the decomposition process in the bog are not ones we want around the plant roots. Additionally these bogs provide a breeding ground for insects we don't want near our plants. For these reasons peat must be sterilized before it can be used. This destroys the structure and leaves a very small particle size. To be useful for growing the peat must be 'opened up' by amendments such as perlite and vermiculite. For our systems peat mixes are really only of value in propagation.

Sphagnum Mixes

Sphagnum moss or sphagnum peat as it is often called is harvested annually from living bogs. The bog environment is far too acid for the liking of most insect life and this combined with its high oxygen levels keeps detrimental microorganisms to a minimum. Sphagnum can be used directly from the bog with its larger fiber and structural integrity intact. It has a very powerful capillary action and a high CEC relative to other common medias. The pH of the moss is very low so it must be amended with a calcium salt such as dolomite lime. Most commercial sphagnum mixes are also 'filled in' with the use of perlite or vermiculite.

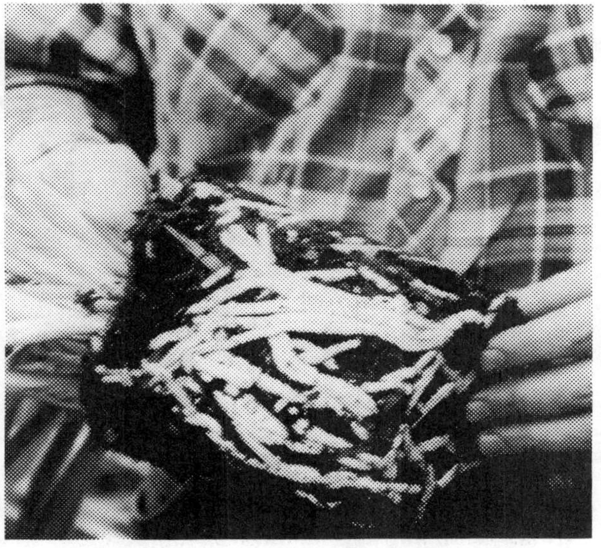

The white, healthy roots on this orchid, 9 months after division, show the results of a properly amended sphagnum mix. (Koch Greenhouses, B.C.)

Sawdust

This media is popular in many parts of the world. Anywhere you have a forestry industry and mills there is a cheap supply of sawdust. There are some special concerns which must be addressed when considering sawdust. First is the high requirement for nitrogen by some types of wood, especially cedar. These woods rob nitrogen from the solution and tend to decompose very quickly. Also, any wood with a high resin content should be avoided.

Never use fresh sawdust. Most mills supply growers with sawdust from the planner mill. The wood has been rough cut from freshly harvested timber which still has a high resin and moisture content, treated for short-term outside storage, then processed through the planner. Your first concern is the material used for treating the wood. Always try an un-aged sample of the sawdust with a couple of plants before using it in a system. The plants will very quickly show the toxic effects if the materials used to treat the roughcut lumber is toxic to plants. There are a variety of compounds used and several will decompose over the period of aging, a minimum of one year.

It is essential that commercial growers keep in touch with the mill supplying the sawdust to keep informed of any changes at the mill and to be sure the owner knows why you are using the sawdust. I know of several growers who lost crops because of a change in chemicals used at the mill and the ignorance on the part of the mill owner that any of the sawdust was being used to grow plants. The grade of sawdust to use is a medium/large particle size mix. Stay away from the fines and make sure there isn't a large percentage of chips in the mix.

The easy answer for hobby growers is to obtain the small quantity of sawdust required from a local commercial grower. Make sure you get it from the supply the grower used for his plants this year, not what he has stored for next year. He may also have some good growing advice for you.

Sawdust in bags is a popular system. You must be careful to keep the amount down to around 10 liters per plant for large plants such as tomato, pepper and cucumber. Some growers do this by placing two plants per bag.

Other organic medias

There is no shortage of other alternatives for local supply of organic media. Depending on where you live this could include rice hulls or coconut fibre to name just a couple. Explore the waste products provided by local agricultural operations and apply the same considerations as outlined above. If in doubt, try a plant or two.

THE AGGREGATE MEDIAS

Chunks, bits, and pieces of inorganic material.

Again we have a wide range of choices and some specific considerations which limit the choices. As long as the aggregate under consideration is clean and stable (will not contribute anything to the nutrient solution) the only thing left is the particle size. Too small a particle can clog up the drainage system or foul pumps and too large a particle doesn't provide enough total surface moisture for the plant roots. For propagation, smaller particles are best while for use in production growing a good mix of 4mm to 15mm (1/8" to 5/8") will do a good job. The only exception is sand where you have no size options.

Here is a quick list of the many aggregates which have been used successfully in the past and some notes on each.

Gravel

Often the media of choice for the beginner and used until the first time it needs cleaning. One round of backbreaking labour is generally enough to encourage investigation of other options. There is still one commercial tomato grower in the United States using a flood and drain gravel system. For those who want to use this media, try to get crushed granite gravel. The many sides will provide increased surface area for moisture to cling to. It is best to thoroughly wash the gravel before using and it should be tested in an acid solution before use for stability. (Low pH solution for 24 hours then check change in EC) River gravel which is much more rounded can also be used.

Sand

Coarse silica sand is really the only good option. It makes drainage possible. Sand beds tend to calcify over time due to evaporation (especially in tropical regions). Root aeration is poor unless a flood and drain system is used or the sand bed is very thin. While it is often used as a low maintenance medium in tourist attraction operations like Epcot Center in Florida or the Big Pineapple in Australia, actual production yields are disappointing.

The effort required to clean a sand bed system is shown here at the gardens of the 'Big Pineapple' in Australia. The irrigation tube is poly with built in emitters and a liner is used to direct drain water. Cleaning the roots from the system requires taking it completely apart. Time consuming and labour intensive.

Pumice

Everywhere there is a volcano there is pumice. There are two considerations which are important with pumice, structural integrity and mineral composition. The structural integrity is important because you don't want a material which will break down into dust at the slightest touch. The mineral composition of pumice varies wildly and if analysis is not available then do some extensive trials before committing your garden to this media. Pumice can also be used as an amendment for organic medias. When used alone it has a much better water holding capacity than most aggregates due to the very irregular shape and all of the holes. Cleaning is a real task due to the shape of the material.

Expanded Shale
also called oil fired shale.

This material is usually available in areas where oil is being extracted from shale. As long as all the oil has been completely extracted, it does have potential as a media and is being tested by commercial growers for crops like roses where they will be in the system for 5-7 years. Like pumice, it has excellent water holding capacity but is a real pain to clean. Size balance is the same as for the other larger aggregates.

Commercial growers are using the shales and clay pellets for recycling systems growing long life crops like these roses at Westbrook Greenhouse in Ontario. The durability provides a consistent root environment unlike the breakdown which occurs with sawdust or the compression in rockwool.

Expanded Clay

Take little balls of wet clay and pop them into a very hot oven (1,600°F). They expand up to 3 or 4 times and a hard, pottery-like, shell is formed. This is how expanded clay is made. The media is used in hydroculture planters. Expanded clay is made commercially in Europe and California so prices can vary widely depending on your location and shipping costs. A word of caution, all expanded clay is not equal, even from the same manufacturer. The clay is fired in kilns where other products are made and some plants use multiple fuels.

The best product is ordered specifically for horticultural applications. It has a consistent size, is fired in a well-cleaned kiln, and the fuel for firing should be clean natural gas. If you run across dirty colored material of inconsistent size and with many broken pellets, don't buy it. The pellets should be light in colour, clean, and consistent in size, with few broken pellets.

Beyond its use in hydroculture the pellets have become very popular with orchid growers as a replacement for bark. Pellets do have some capillary action but not enough for use as a wick. The pellets are light, easy to clean, and have a long life in gardens of all types.

Perlite

Perlite is a volcanic glass formed when lava cools very rapidly trapping small quantities (2-5% w/w) of water. When the glass is crushed and heated to about 1000 deg C, the trapped water vaporizes and puffs out the softened granules to form a white mineral foam.

Expanded perlite is physically stable and chemically inert. The porous nature of the cellular granules ensures a product that is light to handle, holds large quantities of readily available moisture and has a strong capillary attraction for water. Since it is free-draining, it is also well-aerated.

This has been a favorite amendment for soilless mixes for many years. Much work has been done to develop techniques for using it in gardens as a media by itself. The bulk of the research has been done in Scotland. Manufacturing techniques have improved and there are specific agricultural grades available. When used in containers, it is best in one which keeps a small reservoir of solution in the root zone. This reduces the wide swings in moisture level between irrigations when high demand plants are being grown. This is not necessary for lower demand plants.

Perlite does have a future potential as a media due to one factor not available with other inorganic medias. It can be reprocessed and reused. The only country in the world where this service is currently available is Scotland but the practice may spread as the environmental considerations of waste disposal continue to increase pressure on growers.

The irrigation scheduling is quite different from that used for rockwool. Irrigation timing is much less frequent, being based on reservoir replenishment instead of media moisture levels. This is a simpler regime to maintain but the same level of precision solution monitoring is required.

This tomato crop was propagated in perlite and is being grown in bolster bags filled with perlite in a greenhouse at Crop King in Ohio. The bags are slit for drainage so a small reservoir remains at the bottom of the bolster bag.

Vermiculite

Vermiculite has value only as an amendment to other media or for some propagation applications. By itself it floats until waterlogged and is then impossible to drain. It is available in a variety of grades depending on what effect you need in the soilless mix you are creating.

Other Options

Broken pottery or bricks

Smash it up small enough and screen out the fines. For locations where nothing else is available, this makes a satisfactory media which can be added back into a local field after use with no detrimental effect.

Plastic

This covers a range of everything from packing peanuts to ground up telephones. You really have to be sure of the plastic and what the 'outgas' characteristics are. The gases given off by some plastics are toxic to plants. Most ground plastic is in pieces too small to be of use but you may run across a source and be able to add another step into the recycling process. If it is stable and within the size range, it can be used.

Processed Medias

Rockwool

This is one of the most commonly used commercial medias due to the high level of promotion by the manufacturers. The other medias where a manufacturing process is required have been noted but none have received the kind of promotion and publicity put behind rockwool. I mention this to make sure you understand that though its use is widespread, the reason for this has nothing to do with it being so much superior to another media.

Mineral wool or rockwool as it is more commonly known, was first discovered in the United States by C.C. Hall in 1897. It was produced by using steel slag as a raw material. Since that beginning, European technology has developed mineral wool into its present form by substituting either basalt or diabase as the raw material. However, some plants still use steel or copper slag as their raw material. While these slags may be adequate for use as an industrial insulating material, they are not generally suitable for use as an agricultural material because of their high iron and copper content. In addition some companies are trying to produce horticultural rockwool in plants designed for mineral wool insulation and the resulting products show problems with quality control. Properly made rockwool is an ideal medium because it is totally inert, sterile, porous, non-toxic, non-degradable, with high oxygen permeability and high water retention capacities.

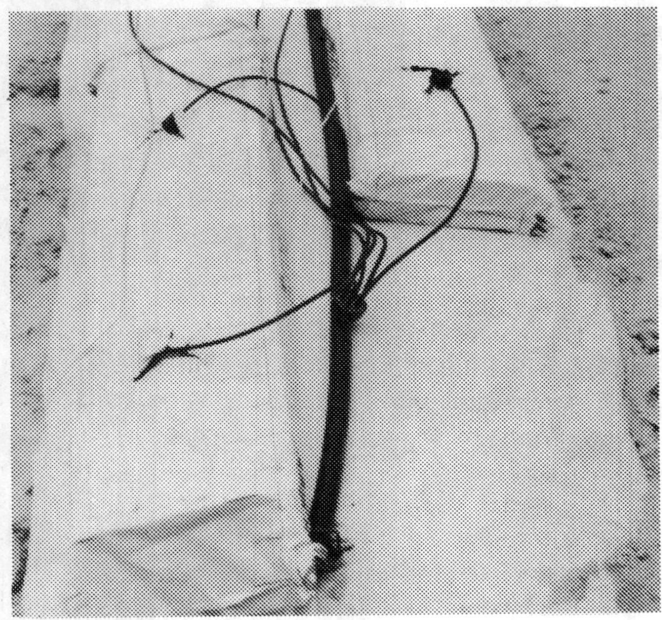

This is a typical setup for a drain to waste rockwool system. Note that the slabs are on a slope to encourage drainage. Emitters are placed where transplants in rockwool blocks will be set out.

The rockwool blocks (above left) are very popular with all growers. These blocks are in an ebb and flow propagation system at Bevo Farms in BC. The inset shows some of the sizes of slabs provided by a variety of companies. Many companies also provide culture recommendations for a variety of crops.

Rockwool is manufactured from basalt whose unique chemical properties produce an ideal growing medium. These characteristics include a stable pH level of less than 7. Also, it is well buffered to prevent wild fluctuations in pH levels. The manufacturing process entails heating the basalt to a temperature of 1500 degrees Celsius using coke as the fuel and a small quantity of lime to maintain fluidity of the molten mass.

This molten mass is discharged into a continuous stream over a series of four rotors spinning at a high velocity. When the molten mass strikes these rotors it is drawn into fibers through centrifugal force. After the fiberization process, a phenolic binder and wetting agents are added and it is then fed through a large curing oven to produce a blanket of 70-80 kg's/cubic meter density. This material is then cut into the various forms required for use as an agricultural substrate.

Horticultural rockwool has more than 95% porosity and retains more than 60% of water by volume to provide adequate oxygen and nutrients to the root system.

After reading the above you may be tempted to run out and buy some rockwool. There are however some other considerations, one of which is cost, especially when slabs are used. The other is the cost of disposal after use. For the commercial grower this will be a major problem in the future. It can be used as a soil amendment but there is a limit to how many tons per acre. For the hobby grower the considerations are different. Most hobby systems are recycling and it makes little if any sense to use rockwool slabs in a recycling system.

Rockwool is not limited in its availability to slabs. There are blocks, cubes, and 'flock', unbonded rockwool fibers. These other sizes and forms are well suited for propagation applications. Disposal problems are considerably reduced because there is very little used per plant in propagation which is the major application in the commercial industry. The flock or loose rockwool is available in a range of densities and has found favor with some orchid growers. Hobby growers have found cubes and blocks equally attractive for propagation.

Chapter 9
CREATING A MEDIA BASED 'HYDROPONIC GARDEN'

There are few differences in garden design for systems which use media. The dividing line for the organic/aggregate systems is the irrigation requirement. Aggregate systems have irrigation requirements that are so high it is not really feasible to use them in drain to waste systems. On the other hand the most common application for rockwool slabs is in drain to waste systems.

DRAIN TO WASTE SYSTEMS

Drain to waste systems are very popular with commercial vegetable growers and some cut flower growers find it useful. Few hobby growers have picked up on this system since most tend to do their hydroponic gardening indoors or in the greenhouse. For the hobby grower this system presents the opportunity to create instant outdoor gardens under an incredible variety of conditions.

There are environmental considerations for drain to waste systems, especially in commercial operations where the volumes of waste solution are quite high in the eyes of the public who do not understand the composition of the solution in the waste water although the volumes are mere fractions of the wastage which occurs in field production. These considerations should not be of concern to the hobby grower who can 'recycle' drain to waste solutions into the soil around trees, shrubs and other plants around the garden.

North Americans move on the average every 18 months according to one survey I read. This in spite of the dramatic increase in interest in gardening over the past decade. Who wants the backbreaking labour of preparing the quasi-concrete left in a new subdivision as an excuse for soil, just to leave the results to the next occupant? I have a feeling this may be a reason behind the high level of interest in simple hydroponic systems.

By using the drain to waste hydroponic technique you can have a garden flourishing in your backyard within days with almost no labour and usually at less cost than a prepared bed system. The drain to waste garden can make your most underutilized yard space very productive. Almost any vertical surface; fences, posts, trees, shed or garage walls, patios or the house itself, can become the framework for your instant garden. Unlike in ground plantings you won't have to worry about roots attacking your foundation walls or creeping into the pool.

The drain to waste technique of hydroponic culture is just as simple as it sounds; no fancy systems, no reservoirs, just provide the nutrient solution to the roots of the plants and allow the excess solution to drain into the ground. Really it is nothing more than a containerized drip irrigation system using a simple injector to put the nutrients into the water. The solution concentration is low enough that little will reach very far into the ground before it is used up by other plants. Trees make a point of sending roots into the area of drainage to claim the waste solution for their own.

Virtually every media has proven successful for this type of system; soilless mixes, perlite, rockwool, sawdust, even amended soil. The key to the media in the container is the amount of air in the mix combined with its water holding capacity. A good quality soilless mix sold to commercial growers for the purpose is ideal. I have seen one cubic foot container bags of soilless mixes available in garden centres, nurseries, hydroponic stores, etc. which are ideal for this type of system. They can provide a really 'instant' garden without the need to even look for containers.

Creating your own media for the containers can use up excess materials or use those ingredients which are locally and inexpensively available. The characteristics you want in the final mix are as follows;

1. Water holding capacity in the media itself.
2. A granular enough mix so that at least 30% of the volume is air space.
3. A pH of 6-7.
4. Excellent drainage of excess moisture.
5. No decomposition of the material during use.
6. No release of minerals into the nutrient solution over time.

Providing the above general characteristics are descriptive of your final mix there is no limit to what materials may be incorporated.

So what are the specifics of creating a drain to waste system? Well if it is to be a houseplant system, use the plants you already have, in the containers in which they currently grow. All you have to do is get a premixed hydroponic nutrient and follow the feeding instructions. You can't get much more instant than that. The same applies to any containerized plants you may currently enjoy. If your watering cycle is adequate for the plants, i.e., they don't wilt on hot summer days, then follow the instructions on your nutrients for the feeding requirements.

The system which will provide the most impressive results for the beginner is an automated, combination system for;

a backyard containerized vegetable garden ,
a landscape fertigation system,
plus your existing hanging baskets and container plants.

To get started you may want to simply try a new vegetable garden until you get used to the idea. There is a special consideration with outdoor gardens, the potential of rain. If you are in a relatively dry climate where it rains only once a week or so, and not too heavily, you can ignore it. In areas of higher rainfall it is advisable to place a cone shaped cover over the container with a hole in the centre for the plant stem to prevent the rain from washing all the nutrition out of the media.

First the equipment

An outside tap is essential for an automatic system. If you only have one, it is simple to place a Y-valve on it so the system can be left connected all summer. On the side of the valve you will be using for the system a back-flow prevention device is essential, and in many locations, is required by law.

You will want to check and learn what your water pressure is. High water pressure (over 40 psi) can damage the system and actually blow drippers out of the lines. If you are unsure a 12 psi pressure reduction valve is an inexpensive bit of insurance. For large gardens with many feet of tubing you will be better off with a 20 psi valve due to the higher pressure loss over distance. Each of these types of valves shows the maximum water flow in addition to the psi rating.

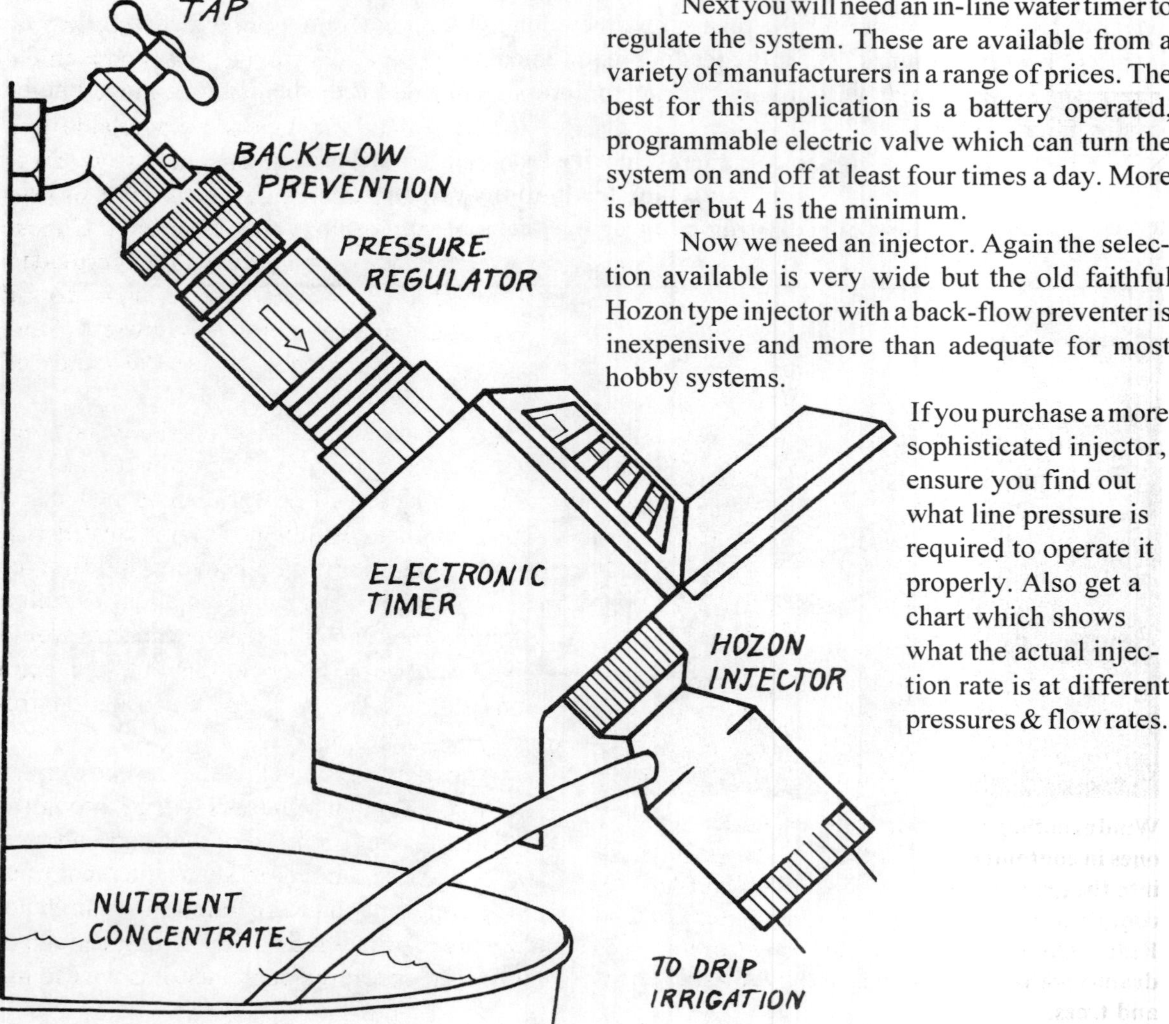

Next you will need an in-line water timer to regulate the system. These are available from a variety of manufacturers in a range of prices. The best for this application is a battery operated, programmable electric valve which can turn the system on and off at least four times a day. More is better but 4 is the minimum.

Now we need an injector. Again the selection available is very wide but the old faithful Hozon type injector with a back-flow preventer is inexpensive and more than adequate for most hobby systems.

If you purchase a more sophisticated injector, ensure you find out what line pressure is required to operate it properly. Also get a chart which shows what the actual injection rate is at different pressures & flow rates.

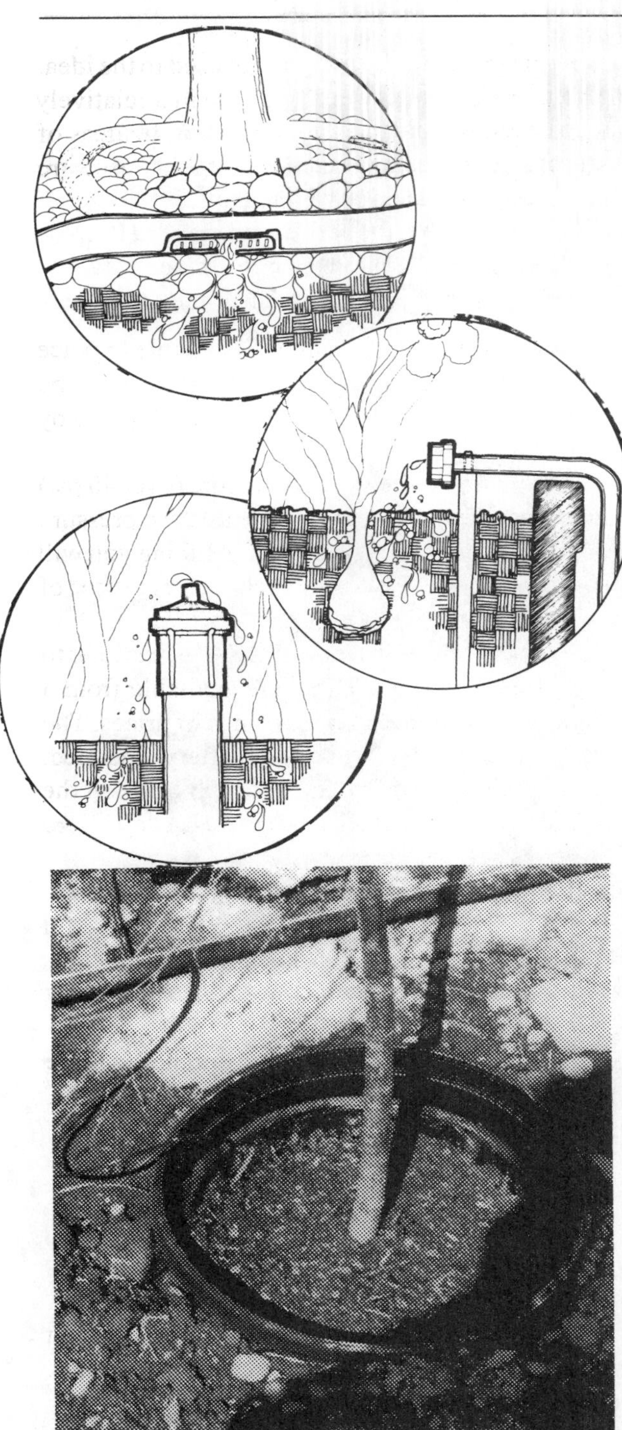

Windproofing outdoor plants, especially the taller ones in containers, is simple. Sink a large container into the ground, then set the smaller plant-holding container into it. Using the same system as Don Kato (see next page) you can create an inground drain-to-waste or recycling system for larger plants and trees.

The rest of the system is simple drip irrigation. The hose most often used is 1/2 inch black utility hose. It is inexpensive and the insert fittings are easy to install. There are also a variety of fittings available for every possible situation. This type of equipment is available from a wide range of retailers from hardware and plumbing stores to your favourite garden supply dealer. Since the hose is black it will pick up a lot of heat if left sitting in the sun. Whereever possible the hose should be protected from the sun's rays. or you will be giving your plants a drink of boiling water on a hot day.

There is one feature which I consider essential for the drippers used in this application, no matter what brand you decide to use; they should be pressure compensated. This means they will deliver the rated volume no matter how many ups and downs in your main hose, or how far the dripper is down the line. Other convenient features are shut-offs and easy cleaning.

All brands of drippers are available in a wide range of flow rates so choosing your size is simple. Drippers are rated by the volume of flow they will provide in one hour of "on time." Choose a dripper for each container which will provide a flow rate of 1 gph (4 liters/h) for every 4 litres of media in the container. You can use more than one dripper per container to provide the increased volumes if required.

The containers themselves should be sized for the plant you are going to grow in them. Most herbs and a variety of flowers can be grown in 1 gallon containers. Plants such as rose bushes will need the same size of container you would use for tomatoes, peppers, or cucumbers, about a 5 gallon container. These sizes are larger than we would use in a commercial operation but, the extra volume allows you to keep the irrigation frequency to 4 times per day.

Most growers don't realize just how much extra water the plants outdoors will go through as compared to plants indoors or in the greenhouse. This is because the breeze keeps the plant transpiring constantly and at maximum volume. For windy areas, where the wind is strong enough to overturn an unsecured container, it is wise to use a windbreak. This will prevent mechanical damage to the plants and keep transpiration rates within reasonable levels for plant growth, besides keeping your containers upright.

Really the only criterion for the containers is that they must hold the media and leak. If you were to decide to use for example, clay pots for aesthetic purposes, the drainage can be much improved by putting a layer of gravel or hydrostone in the bottom. In addition the drain hole itself should not be sitting directly on the ground. Raising the containers off the ground has the added advantage of keeping slugs out of the containers. A sprinkling of any sharp-edged material around the base of the containers will also solve your slug problem. Crushed shells are effective and present no hazard to children or animals.

Don Kato at Naramata BC has proven that field hydroponics is possible. He created growing gulleys in his field using sawdust to isolate the plant roots from soil borne diseases. The profile was covered with black plastic and a drainage tube laid in the channels. The field was then relevelled with sawdust. A drip system provides the solution to plants set directly in the sawdust or in containers set into the sawdust. When rainfall flushes the system the solution is adjusted accordingly.

GREENHOUSE DRAIN TO WASTE SYSTEMS

For greenhouse drain to waste gardens it is advisable to place weed barrier and white plastic on the floor to prevent weed growth. Alternatively you can collect the waste solution for use on the outside garden. Your plants will definitely thank you for the consideration. There are areas where the soil itself can be a prime source of disease for your plants. This is especially true in areas around water (rivers or lakes) and boggy land.

To keep this potential to a minimum in your greenhouse you should prepare your greenhouse floor properly. Cover the ground with a good thick layer of quicklime (about 1/4"). Cover the quick lime with a layer of plastic, black/ white plastic black side down preferably, white if that is all that is available. Now put down another layer of quicklime 1/8" thick, and cover with a final layer of plastic.

With plastic on the floor it is essential to collect the drain water and direct it to a collection point for disposal. This dramatically reduces the potential for disease, helps with humidity control and means you don't have to walk in a lake when you enter the greenhouse. The commercial grower is advised to properly 'profile' the floor of the greenhouse to provide the necessary drainage and keep the containers up out of the waste water for proper drainage. The hobby grower can accomplish the same by raising the containers on bricks and using a rudimentary plastic lined channel.

Greenhouse systems can use any of the medias; TOP sawdust in bags, MIDDLE rockwool slab, BOTTOM Carnations propagated in rice hulls and being grown in rockwool slabs.

OPERATING A DRAIN TO WASTE HYDROPONIC GARDEN

Operation of these gardens, for the hobby grower, is very simple. The same nutrients as you would use in any other hydroponic garden, Nutrilife Hydroponic Nutrients or similar, are mixed into a concentrate tank. This can be anything from a 5-gallon pail to a 45-gallon drum, preferably plastic. If you are using a Hozon type injector with a 16:1 injection ratio only one concentrate tank is needed. For higher ratio injectors two tanks will be required. Check with the manufacturer for specifications.)

For the Hozon type injector the nutrients are mixed at 4 times the maximum strength recommended for a recycling system. This is the highest concentration at which all of the elements can be combined in one solution. Initial mixing should be done, using hot water and the components should be thoroughly dissolved in the recommended order.

Irrigation Timing for Drain to Waste

Outdoor Container Systems

Setting the timer is a simple procedure. For outdoor systems, turn the system on and time how long it takes until solution starts to drain out the bottom of the containers. Turn the system off. Once you have completed transplanting your plants into the containers set the timer for 4 irrigation times, each equal to 1/2 the time it took to saturate the containers.

The first irrigation should occur just at sunrise and the last 3 hours before sunset. The irrigation times between should be equally spaced. For the first day leave the system as set. On the second day, time how long it is before the containers begin to drain from the start of the second irrigation cycle.

Reset your irrigation times to 25% longer than it took for the containers to start to drain. Repeat this reset procedure every 2 weeks when plants are young and every week during the heat of the summer.

Greenhouse Container Systems

For greenhouse systems you will be using smaller containers with a greater requirement for irrigation and lower plant transpiration due to the change in environmental conditions; higher humidity, lower air flows. You should invest in a timer which can provide at least 10 'on times' per day for optimum control. In the greenhouse it is important to put the plants in charge of the irrigation cycle. The greenhouse environment is more variable than outdoors due to more rapid changes in temperature and the plants do not have the advantage of outdoor breezes. For the hobby grower using a smaller greenhouse these swings are much more dramatic than in a larger commercial greenhouse.

Putting the plants in charge is not difficult. Raise a container up onto a tray, high enough that a collection container can be used for the drainage from the growing container. Drill a hole in the tray so the waste water will drain into the collection container. (***see diagram***) Now it is a matter of understanding the changing plant demands during the day. Early in the morning the plant will need more plant food. As the day goes on, and temperature and light levels increase, the demand for water increases so you want to be sure there is no build up of food in the container. Toward evening the plant has less demand for water and more for food. The cycle follows the light and temperature levels in the greenhouse.

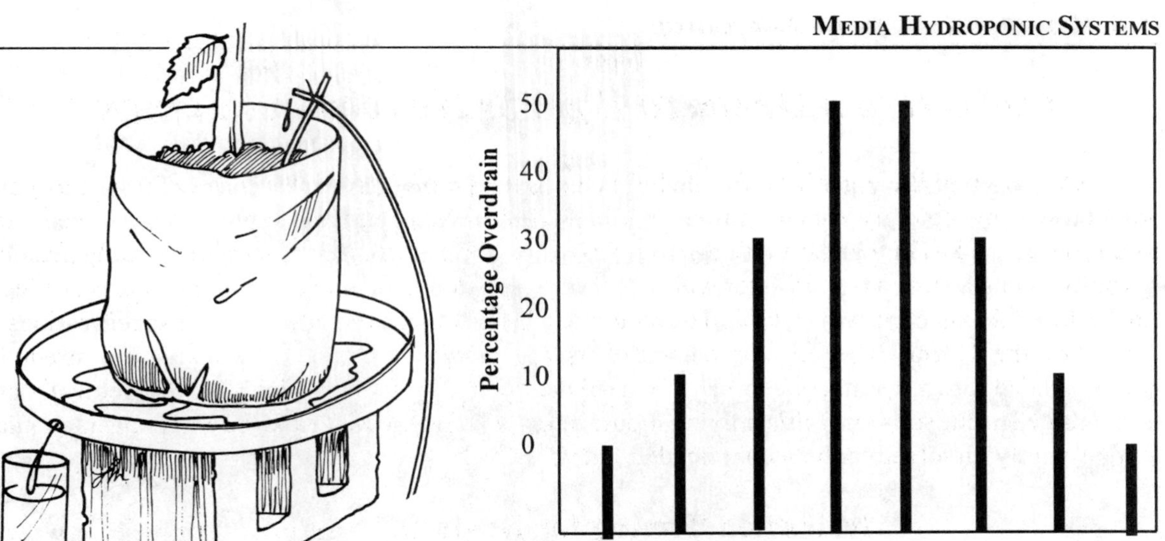

Overdrain collection is easy to do. It provides accurate measurement of the overdrain and makes EC &pH testing easy.

This overdrain schedule is for a long, sunny summer day. It should be adjusted for daylength, media testing, and light levels.

To follow the plant demand in irrigation requires a bit of time and regular monitoring of the drainage from your sample container. This container will also provide needed information on pH and EC, which we will cover in a later chapter, which will tell you how to manage the nutrient solution itself. Commercial growers should have one drain collection sample for every 1,000 plants in the greenhouse at a minimum, well distributed through the greenhouse. Your day length will of course vary over the season so begin by dividing the longest day of your season into ten equal intervals beginning at sunrise and ending one hour before sunset. This will give you the irrigation intervals. The number of irrigations required will be fewer in the spring and fall due to shorter day length and at maximum in the summer.

For the first irrigation in the morning you do not want any drainage from the growing containers. As the day progresses you want to increase the drainage from the growing containers in regular increments until the first irrigation after 12 noon which should have a drainage volume equal to 50% of the volume of solution delivered to the container. The overdrain should then be tapered off in equal increments to 10% overdrain for the last irrigation of the day. This will be modified according to solution manipulation which we will cover under EC and pH control.

Keep in mind this is a general pattern for days when there is sunshine. Commercial growers can, and should, use special light sensors to ensure the irrigation pattern matches available light. For the hobby grower the best simple tools available are the Farmer's Almanac and local long range weather forecasts. If extended periods of rain and overcast are due, the overdrain should be reduced along with the irrigation frequency to ensure there is enough food concentration in the container for the plant on lower light days.

There is one other situation often forgotten by both hobby and commercial growers. Solution temperature. How would you react if you were awakened in the morning by a bucket of ice water? Well, the response of plant roots is to go to sleep just at the time they should start working. This can put considerable stress on the plant and open the potential for disease. Ideally the nutrient solution should be delivered to the plants at 20C (68F) every time an irrigation occurs. Achieving this is not difficult for a hobby grower. Instead of using the outside garden tap as the source for water (straight off the cold water main) use a faucet in the laundry room and adjust the taps to provide the required temperature. All that is entailed is a few extra feet of hose and the result is much happier, more productive plants. Keeping the solution cool is a priority as well. If headers are exposed to sunlight the solution in them will get very warm and can burn tender roots. Shading all irrigation tubes & hoses will keep the solution cool.

CULTURAL CONSIDERATIONS

Every annual plant that will grow during your local growing season will do very well in this type of hydroponic garden. You can grow many annuals which would perhaps require a longer growing season than you have by starting seeds indoors and ensuring you have large, vigorous transplants, ready early in the season.

The range of potentials for hobby gardeners is extensive. Consider all the 'luxuries' you can grow with little effort in a greenhouse, outdoors, or in a well-lit grow room. Radishes are quick, easy, and provide a flavour crunch to any salad. These 'bird' peppers will provide the heat necessary for the hottest cuisine in the world. The I-melon is ready in a Northern greenhouse months before other Northern gardeners even consider transplants of tomatoes and can produce so late you can enjoy your last melon for New Year's Eve.

Perennials will also do very well in hydroponic, drain to waste systems, as cut flower growers, e.g., rose growers, have found to their profit. The key here is how cold your winters get. Many perennials cannot stand hard freezing, the majority prefer that the root temperature not go below -4C for any extended period. Here you have a major advantage with container gardening. The perennials can be cut back in the fall if required, and moved into the greenhouse into the back portion of a heated garage, or even rolled into an unheated basement, to wait for next year's growing season.

There is another option with the perennials as has been shown with dwarf apple trees. You can use an oversize container and place insulation inside before filling the container with media. This will eliminate the necessity for moving the plants in all but the most extreme climates. Remember however to cover the container when the plant loses its leaves to prevent excess water from getting into the container. When it freezes it will cause extensive root damage.

Both Canadian and Israeli researchers have found that the combination of dwarf root stocks, fertigation and plant support have the potential to provide production for a wide range of hard and soft fruit crops. Really, a portable orchard which can survive many climates.

Take advantage of the structures existing in the yard to provide plant support. No matter how expensive the fence, it won't look as good as grape clusters hanging down, tomatoes turning red for many feet along the fence or cucumbers shading your cool crops. You can also use the location in the yard to decide how much and what type of sun the plants will receive.

Vertical space is very flexible space for this type of garden. Vine plants can be trained along the top edge of fences and shade smaller greens grown in hanging baskets. The hanging baskets are also excellent for growing such things as strawberries.

In areas of high rainfall it will be necessary to cover the containers with plastic until the plants are large enough to provide their own protection. High volumes of rainwater would leach all of the nutrients from the containers.

ADDITIONAL APPLICATIONS FOR THE HOBBY GROWER

When you are looking for maximum flexibility in greenhouse production, the drain to waste system is an excellent tool. You have the added advantage of automatically feeding and watering your plants while you are on summer holidays. Just be prepared for a jungle when you return if your garden includes vine crops.

The other area where you will find this system useful is on balconies and anywhere else you have hanging baskets which seem to instantly dry out in the summer months.

Drain to waste systems are easy to operate and inexpensive to install. Really, just a more advanced form of drip irrigation which can even be applied to plants growing in the ground. So use your imagination, have fun and kiss goodbye forever to weeding, digging and all of the work parts of having a productive backyard garden.

Tips and Tricks for Drain to Waste Systems

1. Do not allow drain water to collect in the growing area. Ensure the waste water runs to a collection point for disposal.

2. In colder areas the plant growing containers should be set on an insulating material to prevent high heat loss to the ground and resulting low root temperatures.

3. In marshy or low lying areas with high water tables, cover the ground with lime before laying the ground cover. Put a layer of lime over the ground cover then lay the white plastic. This will really help prevent contamination from the ground.

4. For outdoor systems, set containers on something to raise them slightly and sprinkle crushed shells around the container to keep slugs away.

5. If there are ants in the area, coat the side of the container at the bottom with a sticky material. This will prevent the ants from carrying aphids up onto your plants.

6. Raw water tends to be colder than the plants like. Use a reservoir to warm the water and do pH adjustment. This works well in greenhouse systems. For the outdoor garden consider using a mixture of hot and cold water to ensure the right temperature.

7. When setting up the irrigation system use garden hose connectors or quick connect fittings to put the system together. They will make it much easier to drain the system before winter.

8. Calculate the dripper size for the smallest container and then use multiples of that size for the larger containers. That way you will never use the wrong dripper by mistake. Plus you will only need to keep a few extras of one size.

9. Check the pH and EC of your raw water every month and do a water analysis at least once a year.

10. Once a week over the growing season, check the pH and EC of the drain water from a good sample of your containers.

11. Whenever possible use an organic media which can be composted after use. This will reduce the urge to use the media for more than one season and cut down on potential disease problems.

12. At least once a week blow all header lines to remove any debris in the lines which may clog your small tubes or emitters.

13. Establish a regular weekly schedule for carefully examining each plant in the garden for mechanical damage, disease or evidence of insects.

14. During summer months an irrigation in the middle of the night will be of benefit to the plants. No over drain on this irrigation.

15. Soaking clogged emitters in vinegar overnight often is all it takes to clean them.

Chapter 10
RECYCLING MEDIA SYSTEMS

Turning a drain to waste system into a recycling system is a matter of a bit of plumbing and the addition of a solution reservoir. This is the most popular type of system with hobby growers and is rapidly becoming the legislated system for commercial growers in various parts of the world. Recycling systems are the most water efficient and environmentally friendly. They have the additional benefit of being ideal for indoor operation for the hobby grower. The wet carpets which result from drain to waste can test the temper of a non-gardening spouse with no sense of humour.

Defining the difference between a media based recycling system and a water culture recycling system is really a matter of arbitrary opinion. The systems look very similar in design and operation including controls so I use three factors to draw the dividing line.

1. The number of plants per container.
2. The amount of media used per plant.
3. The number of plants serviced by a solution delivery device.

If you are confused at this point don't worry about it. These divisions are simply arbitrary. There are an ingenious variety of recycling hydroponic systems in use around the world today. Some use massive amounts of media while others use almost none. These systems are almost identical in basic design. Each has four basic design components;

the reservoir,
the solution delivery system,
the root containment system,
the solution recovery system.

No matter what the name or label attached to the system you want to build, it will have the four basic components. The size and specific installation of each component is affected by what you are trying to achieve with the system and the amount of control needed.

This system in Israel is a stacked system of polystyrene foam boxes. The solution is introduced at the top of the column and the black bucket at the bottom collects the waste solution which is carried back to the reservoir. As in any vertical system the bottom plants grow more slowly until the top plants have been harvested and there is more light available to the plants.

THE RESERVOIR

Hobby growers tend to use much larger reservoirs than commercial growers. The reason is they want a system which can hopefully be left without attention for days at a time. No matter what the other components of the system may be there are some guidelines you can follow when finding the reservoir best for your purposes.

Since hobby gardens tend to be mixed crop gardens there is a wide variation between the daily solution requirements for each plant. By considering the average requirements for the mature plants on a daily basis it is quite simple to estimate the volume of reservoir which will be required to service the plants over a 24 hour period. For estimating purposes, I use the amount of 1/2 gal (2 litres) of solution per plant for each day the reservoir is expected to service the garden.

The use of the solution is of course going to vary dramatically over the life of the plants. A seedling uses far less solution than a mature tomato plant with 6 or 8 trusses of developing fruit. A reservoir which has been designed to last for 3 days when the plants are mature may last for 2 or three weeks just after the garden has been planted. Keep in mind the longer the reservoir is going to service the garden the more potential there is for drift of the pH and the development of nutrient solution imbalance.

A procedure which has worked well in hobby gardens for years to help prevent these problems is the addition of fresh pH balanced water on a daily basis. When you use this procedure, cut the volume of the reservoir to 1 litre per plant per day. Each day the reservoir is topped up, until 50% of the original amount of volume has been added. Once this amount of water has been supplied, the reservoir is allowed to empty until 25% of the original volume remains and then it is time to start with a fresh solution. If you are using a submersible pump never let the solution level fall to the point where the pump is exposed. These pumps are water cooled and if exposed will overheat and burn out. They also add heat to the solution which is not needed on a hot summer day. External in-line pumps are a simple solution to these problems.

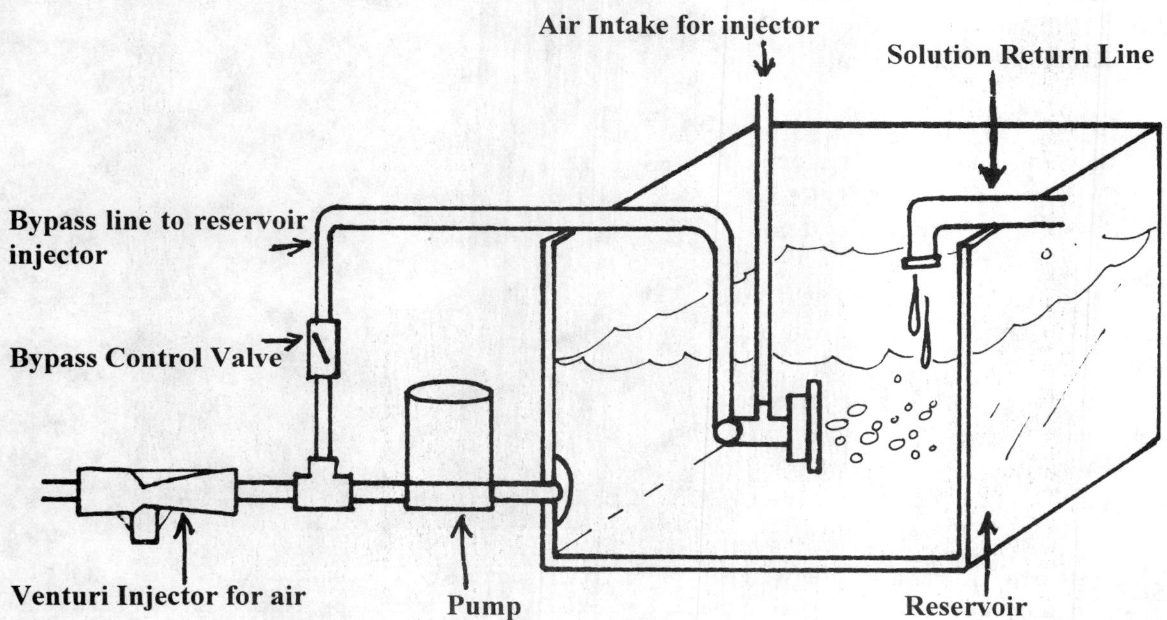

This procedure works only if you are using a well-balanced nutrient formula with the necessary amount of chelating agents as long term buffers. The concentration of the solution at the start without considering the influence of the raw water or the pH adjustment agent is under 2,000 ppm. This technique works more consistently when a sphagnum media with a high buffering capacity is used.

For recycling systems the reservoir is usually easiest to install at a lower elevation than the root containment and solution recovery system. Gravity is the most reliable method of recovering solution. Trying to do it in another manner requires the use of additional equipment which really presents the opportunity for more things to break down. This in no way means there is no application for an installation where the reservoir is at the highest elevation. If you are in a situation where there are frequent power failures, or a shortage of power it may be the only installation which can guarantee consistent delivery. For these circumstances you will have to size your delivery and collection reservoirs to match the frequency of cycling from collection to delivery.

Another thing to keep in mind is that the strength of the elevated reservoir must be far superior to that which will be placed on or in the ground. I once worked with a commercial grower who had installed this type of system. In designing his delivery reservoir he forgot that water weighs 100 pounds per cubic foot. His plywood and 2x4 construction of two 1500 litre reservoirs proved inadequate. The result was a properly impressive wave of water crashing the length of the greenhouse and a crop that suffered from too much and then no water at all.

FRESH SOLUTION

Make up a full reservoir of fresh solution.

As the plants use the solution, add fresh, pH adjusted water until 50% of the original solution volume has been added.

WASTE SOLUTION

Let the plants continue to use the solution until the reservoir level drops to just above the top of a submersible pump or the outlet connection for an external pump, then dump the remaining solution and start again.

Students at the Abbotsford Christian Academy use the 'top up' system for one of their greenhouses. A pump is used to get the drain solution back into the reservoir. The reverse of the most common positioning of the reservoir. Normally solutions are pumped out and gravity drained.

Reservoir Installation Considerations

There is only one specific requirement for a reservoir, it must hold water without leaking or leaching anything into the solution. For hobby systems there are a wide range of moulded plastic containers which are ideal. For commercial growers there are some large plastic containers available but it is more common to install inground concrete reservoirs. Lining is often used to keep the solution away from fresh concrete which will leach into the solution. Make sure you know what you are using as a coating or liner. Many petroleum based products will diffuse extremely toxic materials into the reservoir and contaminate your entire system so badly it must be replaced.

With the limited height in greenhouses both hobby and commercial, it is quite common to locate reservoirs below grade to provide maximum growing height for the plants. In the event that you have a leak in your reservoir you can find a range of diseases migrating into the reservoir from the ground. Make sure the reservoir does not leak. The inground location can provide a tempering effect on the temperature of the solution during the summer months but it can add to heating requirements in winter months. If you are in a location where winter ground freeze extends below a few inches you should insulate the tank and isolate it from direct contact with the earth.

No matter where you locate the reservoir, a light proof cover is essential. It must also keep out the potential of any debris falling into the reservoir, or any water from other sources in the growing area draining into the reservoir. If the reservoir is located where it is above ground all surfaces must be coated to make them impervious to light penetration. If you sit the reservoir on the ground a sheet of styrofoam insulation is a wise bit of insurance against winter temperature loss.

In the hobby greenhouse it is oftem best to use an inground installation. This keeps the benches as low as possible providing more room for plant growth. The top of the reservoir should be carefully covered and the area over the reservoir is often the ideal place for a transplant and workbench. Insulation (the shaded area) around the tank will help alleviate temperature problems.

THE SOLUTION DELIVERY SYSTEM

This system has many components and it should have built into it the ability to specifically regulate the quantity of solution which is delivered to each plant. Lets begin with getting the solution out of the reservoir. For this you need a pump.

As mentioned in our discussion on plant growth, the roots do produce effluents both gaseous and soluble solids. Your nutrient reservoir is the collection point for these materials in a recycling system. If they are allowed to accumulate unchecked, they will literally choke your plants and cause disease. Additionally there are over 1700 different microorganisms which can potentially live and develop in your reservoir and throughout your system. In combination quite a potential for problems which can be easily prevented. The microorganisms which present the highest potential for problems are the anaerobic, the ones that reproduce and thrive without oxygen, and don't fare well when high oxygen concentrations are present.

Your solution delivery system should provide two things to handle these problems both in the media and in the reservoir. A small injector on the output from the pump to the manifold will raise oxygen levels in the delivered nutrient solution to maximum and ensure there is full oxygenation of the solution. Air for this injector should be drawn from outside the growing area. The other essential is a venturi (a spa valve is ideal) built into a bypass taken off the output of the pump. The combination of nutrient solution and air being drawn through the venturi being pumped back into the reservoir should be a sufficiently powerful jet to give your reservoir the appearance of being vigorously boiled. This action will get rid of the maximum amount of root effluent gas and keep oxygen at levels that inhibit anaerobic organism growth.

Pumps

There are two types of pumps commonly used for hobby systems; submersible pumps and in-line pumps. Submersible pumps are water cooled; that is, the heat generated by their operation is absorbed by the fluid they are sitting in. This can tend to raise the temperature of the solution above acceptable levels if the reservoir is small.

These pumps can be a benefit to the greenhouse grower who has no tank heating for the spring and fall months. Reservoirs sitting in or on the ground can tend to get too cold during these months if they have not been properly insulated. The in-line pumps should be used for any indoor garden where the environment is very stable.

The best pump for smaller reservoirs is an in-line pump which is air-cooled and will not create heat problems in the reservoir. This type of pump is most easily installed in plastic tanks using thru-hull fittings commonly found in the marine industry.

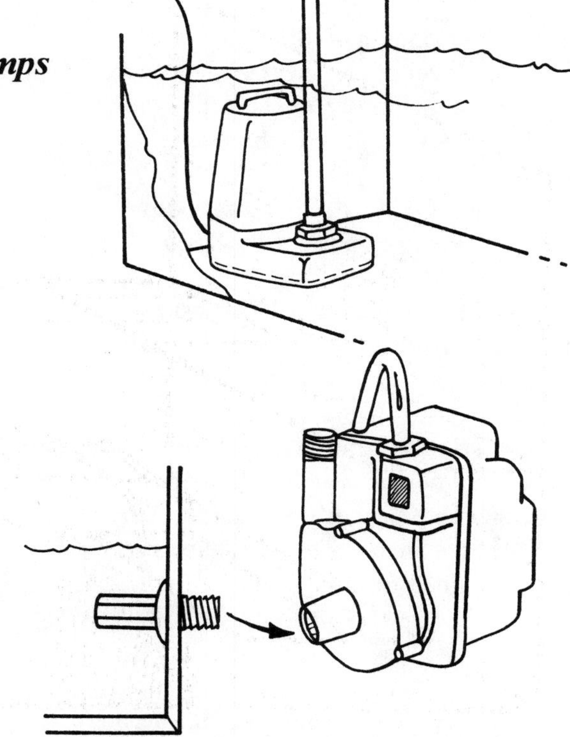

Above are the two most common types of hobby pumps used. For more power you can use the same sump pump found in wet basements. It has the added advantage of being external to the tank.

Delivery Tubing

The tubing used to get the solution from the pump to the plant root container is generally referred to in three parts;

the manifold,
the header and
the delivery tubes, with or without emitters.

For hobby systems it is seldom necessary to use anything other than 1/2" black poly hose for the manifold and header tubing. The delivery tubes (often called spaghetti tubes) will vary in size according to several things; whether emitters are being used, and if they are the size of tubing required to service them.

Emitters are convenient tools for the recycling hydroponic system. They allow you to vary the amount of solution being delivered according to plant requirements by using devices of different delivery rates on the same header line. (E.g., 8 litres per hour for tomatoes and 1 litre per hour for cactus.)

One common problem of the nutrient delivery tubing is clogging. This can be minimized or avoided completely in several ways.

Put a flushing valve on the end of header lines so they will automatically flush on every irrigation.

Instead of stopping off the header lines, fold them over or cap them so they can be flushed manually every time you make up a new solution in the reservoir.

Cover the drains with nylon stockings where they empty into the reservoir.

Use emitters which can be disassembled for easy cleaning in the event they do clog.

You will find it useful to have some sort of holding device which will keep the delivery tubes properly located at each plant. There are a variety of stakes and clips designed for this purpose.

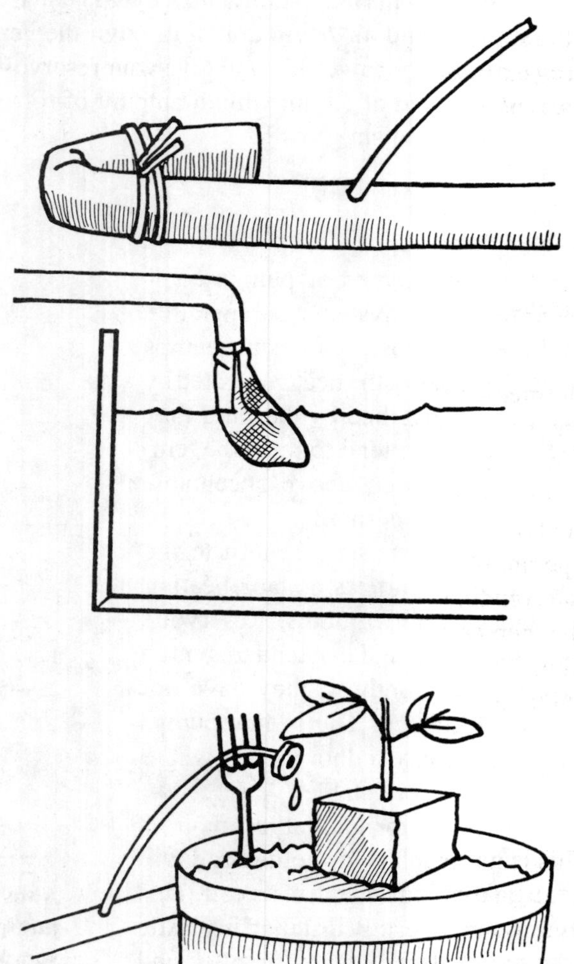

You can do your bit for recycling in your hydroponic garden. Old plastic picnic forks are free and they make great tube holders for the drip lines.

THE ROOT CONTAINMENT SYSTEM

Here your imagination is the limit. Every system which has ever been used has been successful to one degree or another. There are a variety of examples from the huge containers full of media used in the flood and drain systems which hold many plants in one container all the way to the small pots used to grow some flowers.

The common considerations of the root containment system are as follows;

1. Provide sufficient space for root development,

2. Allow complete drainage of the solution to the extent allowed by the media,

3. Keep the solution from being exposed to the available light and,

4. Channel the return solution to the collection system for return to the reservoir.

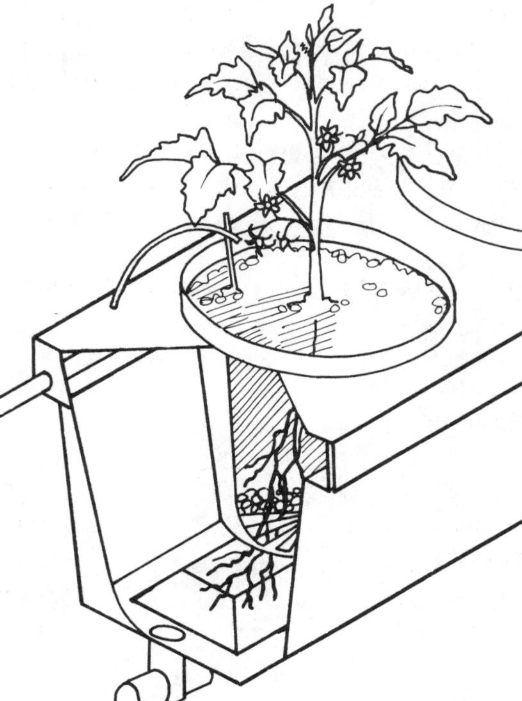

This cut-away view of the trays developed by the author shows all of the requirements being provided in a modular system which allows flexible installation. The cover allows the system to be used outside and keeps light away from the solution. The irrigation line fits on a lip under the cover to keep solution cool. The containers have a full mesh bottom and sit on the raised ridge in the bottom of the tray. Drainage is from the lower part of the tray and ensures there is no solution left near the container between irrigations.

The media which is to be used for root support will have an impact on the operation of the system. Soilless mix medias are very popular with hobby growers as they provide a buffer between the plant roots and the nutrient solution. This allows the hobbyist to make minor mistakes without paying major penalties such as would be exacted in an NFT system.

Media based systems require that a certain amount of flushing occur at each irrigation but, they do not operate well under constant irrigation regimes. Drainage is best enhanced through the use of individual containers for each plant which have a mesh bottom and a layer of gravel or hydrostone over the mesh when non-aggregate media is used. The characteristics of each of the medias which can be used in these systems, and how they affect system operation, has already been discussed. Remember to keep your containers small.

SOLUTION RECOVERY SYSTEM

This is generally built right in to the root containment system but, can be external. All we are really talking about is getting the excess solution out of the root zone and back to the reservoir. If piping is required, you will find PVC pipe is very easy to work with and meets your needs. Just remember to filter the return drain with a nylon stocking to get rid of bits of media and root which can be drawn by the return solution back to the reservoir.

Chapter 11
TIPS AND TRICKS IN DESIGNING YOUR HOBBY RECYCLING SYSTEMS

Containers

Choose your container to suit the crop you are growing. Using a container for each plant eliminates the potential of root damage on other plants when you remove a plant from your garden. It also allows you to change the position of plants in the garden as your requirements change with the seasons. Those who use an aggregate media will find that single plant containers make cleaning the media much less of a back breaking chore and will allow you to keep your system in continuous production instead of having to shut down a large portion for cleaning in the middle of the season.

Large multi-plant containers are good for crops such as radishes and carrots. They may also be used for growing crops where you expect to harvest all the plants at once or if you will be harvesting or transplanting to other containers before root entanglement occurs.

Modular Construction

The one thing you can be guaranteed is that your garden will change over time. You will want to try other systems or like most of us you will find yourself moving. Nothing is more frustrating than getting to a new location and finding out your garden is just slightly too big for the space. Modular components will ensure this will never happen. They will also allow you to rearrange your garden to make maximum use of available space as your needs change.

The modular design of the 21st Century Gardens allows the students at Fraser Valley College to take advantage of available space and change the garden configuration to suit the plants being trialled.

Plastic vs. Wood w/Liners

You can build a quick and easy garden using wood channels and lining them with plastic. This type of construction is good for experimentation and gardens where few watertight connections are required. Over time however you will find that the plastic liner will shrink and moving containers around causes holes. It can be very frustrating to go away for the weekend and come back to find the reservoir dry and the plants dead or dying because you missed a small leak in a plastic liner.

There is now quite a selection of commercially moulded trays, troughs and channels you can choose from to construct your garden. It is important to know the differences between them and find one which will stand up to the rigours of your application. Three processes are generally used to manufacture hydroponic containers; extrusion, injection moulding, and rotational moulding. It is not the process involved, but the material used to make the product which is important. It must not be brittle and it must stand up to exposure to high levels of ultraviolet radiation. UV is the prime destroyer of plastic products as greenhouse growers know. If the seller of a product does not know what the product is made of, and how it is protected from UV, find another supplier.

Many hobby growers take great pride in building their first system to fit their growing area. Unfortunately problems are associated with this type of installation. The havy plastic liners shrink over time as a result of contact with the nutrient solution. When you move the garden never fits and you have to start over. Take a tip and build your system in modules and make sure it is easy to replace your liners.

Mixing Different Medias

This is not a good idea in hobby or commercial systems operating on the same reservoir as each media has its own specific characteristics. It is okay to start plants in one media and then transplant to another growing media but, it is best to keep the growing container media the same throughout all containers serviced by the same reservoir.

Using Waste Solutions Elsewhere

You will periodically be cleaning out your reservoir and the solution does not need to be thrown away. It can be used on any outside garden or diluted and used in container gardens and hanging baskets.

Automatic H_2O Replacement Using Float Valves

This can be easily done but, it is wise to ensure that only a limited amount can be added. You don't want to leave for a month and have your garden operating on water only long before you return. You should not add more than 50% of the original solution volume without cleaning out the reservoir and starting fresh.

Using auto-refill from a solution backup reservoir can be dangerous if the reservoir is too large. The result is usually the development of nutrient imbalances if it is carried on too long. The auto-refill should only be used when the volume of solution in the reservoir is used by the plants within one photo-period and there is a constant monitoring program.

Setting the Fill Level

If you are going to use an auto-refill system you must set your float carefully. Keep in mind that if you are using a media based system the media will hold a considerable volume of water. Run your system to ensure all media in the system has been thoroughly wetted. Turn the system off and wait for drainage to stop, then top up the reservoir. Now turn the system back on and mark the solution level when drainage back into the tank starts. The difference between the mark you have made and the full mark is the amount of solution in your system which can be expected to drain back to the reservoir when the pump shuts off. Set the float on your auto refill valve so it will not open until the solution level falls below the mark you made when the drainage started.

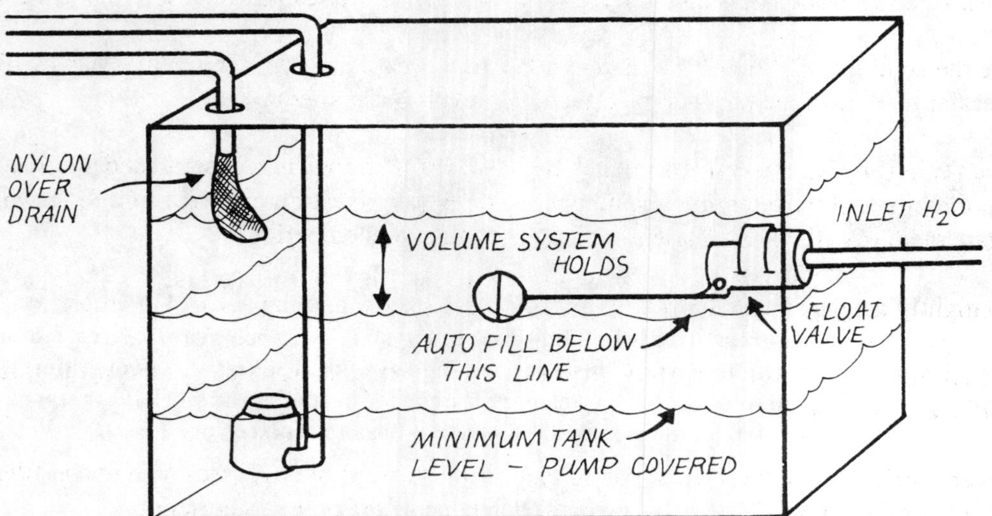

Recycling systems are simple to construct. No matter what the physical shape, every successful system will follow the same basic rule. Get a properly formulated nutrient solution from a reservoir to the roots of the plants in such a fashion as to allow the roots to breathe and collect any excess solution for return to the reservoir.

Tips and Tricks for Recycling Media Systems

1. Use an 'in-line' pump so there is no heat build up caused by pump cooling.

2. Connect the pump about 2 inches above the bottom of the reservoir to keep the intake above the sediment level.

3. Wherever possible install a bottom drain to make tank cleaning easier.

4. A few drops of hydrogen peroxide in the reservoir on a weekly basis will help keep algae and bacteria growth down.

5. When using an organic media always put a layer of gravel or hydrostone in the bottom of the container to act as a filter.

6. To grow root crops such as carrots and radishes use a soilless mix in a separate container and irrigate by hand on a periodic basis. The media needs to dry out a bit more to encourage storage root formation. Watch out with the radishes though, if the EC of the media gets too high those radishes will get very hot indeed.

7. Do not grow hot peppers and sweet peppers in the same system. The sweet peppers tend to ripen a lot hotter than you expected.

8. Keep all irrigation lines protected from the sun. The solution they contain can get very hot between irrigations.

9. Flush all manifold and header lines every time you start with a fresh nutrient solution in the reservoir.

10. Use the smallest amount of media possible and increase irrigation frequency. This will make it much easier to control the moisture and fertilizer levels in the media.

11. When using an aggregate media make sure the pieces are a good mix of small and intermediate size for maximum moisture retention. Remember to continue irrigation cycling through the night. Few aggregate medias will hold sufficient moisture for an extended period.

12. Do nightly irrigation as required by the volume of media and the age of the crop.

13. Use emitters which can be shut-off so you can remove plants from the system without leaving an open stream of solution.

14. Never restrict the intake side of an irrigation pump. Always put bypasses, valves and filters on the output side of the pump. Restricting the intake will cause the pump to burn out.

15. If you leave on vacation it is better to let the garden run itself for a week than have an inexperienced neighbour come in to experiment. Without pruning your vine crops will be a jungle when you return. If you will be gone for extended periods you may want to consider harvesting all large fast growing plants before you leave and starting again on your return.

16. Do your first irrigation just at sunrise and make sure the solution is at 20C (68F). In many areas this is slightly warmer than the air temperature at that time of the day and it helps get the plant working for the day.

Part IV
Water Culture

Chapter 12
INTRODUCTION TO WATER CULTURE

This is the oldest system of hydroponics and the one which holds the most promise for commercial growers of the future. As with any cultural system there are advantages and disadvantages. The original misfortunes of North American growers attempting to duplicate the results obtained by English researchers with the Nutrient Film Technique in the early '70's gave this cultural system a bad reputation. What they didn't realize at the time was that they were operating with incomplete information. Like building an internal combustion engine from blueprints which leave out the spark plugs.

In the past few years the advantages of water culture have become more obvious to growers and many different systems are enjoying a resurgence of use. Enjoying the benefits and advantages of water culture requires approaching the system with full recognition of what it is and how it operates. Water culture changes absolutely nothing about plant growth, nor the factors which make its growth possible. The major difference between this and other cultural techniques is the fact that little or no media is used.

The lack of media has several impacts upon the operation. Media acts as a buffer around plant roots in many areas dependent on the type of media.

It holds water available after irrigation has stopped.

It can play a role in stabilizing the nutrient solution and reduce swings in pH.

It provides plant support.

It can provide food for any of the several thousand micro-organisms which flourish in the root zone.

In short, the media goes a long way to protecting the grower from his or her own mistakes in operation of the hydroponic system. Also, the opposite is true. Media makes it much more difficult for the grower to maintain absolute control over the root zone and respond to changes in plant demand. For many decades growers have seen the protection as being more important than the control as they tried to operate wit a lack of information and thus needed all the protection they could get. Now growers have become much better educated and yields in media based systems have increased up to 20 times on some crops because of improved knowledge.

This same knowledge can be applied more effectively to water culture systems. What is this incredible advance which has made growers so much better? Simply a recognition of the fact that the root zone is a live ecosystem and as such requires a specific environment. The areas involved are so basic it is surprising it took so long for recognition to become common. After all, they were taught in biology courses in the 1800's.

Roots Require Oxygen

The oxygen requirement of plants varies with the species but exists even in those plants which grow underwater. Roots cannot grow, take up water or food, or even stay alive in an oxygen deficient environment. Water holds oxygen and is a major source for roots in hydroponic culture. Plants are capable of growing 'air roots' but, this is a survival technique to deal with an adverse environment not an option of first choice for the plants. It is much easier to maintain optimum oxygen levels in water than to try and do it in media as well.

Roots Require a Specific Temperature Range

Why something so basic should have come as a surprise is beyond me. When plant roots freeze, plants either don't grow or they die. When they are too hot, again they either shut down or die. The same thing that happens to all other life on this planet under the same circumstances. The temperature range for many of the plants we grow, in which roots remain active, is rather narrow. Some plant roots shut down if the temperature falls below 10C (tomatoes) others will survive to as low as 1 or 2 C (lettuce). Transpiration will stop due to root shut down in some plants if temperatures go above 30C, others are a bit more tolerant. The point is that it is easier to maintain the temperature of the nutrient solution within optimum ranges than to do the same for acres or even square feet of media.

A Host of Micro-organisms Exist in the Root Zone

A common reason for growers to switch to some form of hydroponic culture is soil borne disease. Nature is a very effective recycler. As environments change there are always organisms instantly available to recycle the remnants from the previous one. To these organisms, sick plants are food. All it takes to trigger hosts of these organisms is a change in moisture levels, oxygen availability, temperature, or any of a host of others. What damages plant roots causes these organisms to reproduce and thrive. Another group of organisms feed on the effluents from the roots.

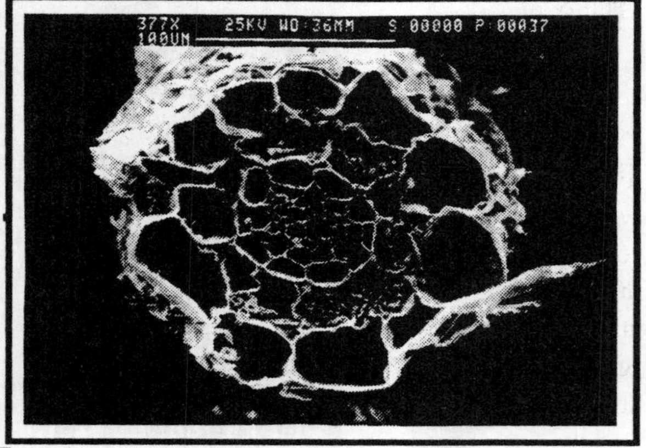

Mycorrhiza fungi help many plants increase their nutrient uptake. This electron microscope photo shows the fungus penetrating a root cell.

It is possible to influence the balance of these organisms through cultural practices and again this is much simpler in water culture. Many growers using media (especially rockwool) attempt to reduce costs by extending the use of the media through several seasons. They fail to realize that when they sterilize the media after a crop all of the microorganisms which have colonized the media are killed, both the detrimental and beneficial. This provides the opportunity for a complete new balance in the recolonization.

The microorganisms can be divided by their requirement for oxygen, the ones that need it (***aerobic***) and the ones that don't (***anaerobic***). On balance the aerobic ones tend to be much friendlier. Maintaining the oxygen in a water culture is, as earlier noted much easier, and there is no expense of either buying new media or sterilizing the old with all the potential problems involved.

Having fun is what hobby hydroponics is all about. Water culture systems allow you to stretch your imagination to create growing systems which are very unusual. This water wheel NFT system at NewZealand Hydroponics is a classic example of a fun hobby system.

Water is Not Pure H_2O

Water has been called the 'universal solvent'. Under the right circumstances it seems to be able to break down and carry away just about anything. Recycling systems use far less water than drain to waste systems so there is a smaller volume of raw water which requires treatment. On the other hand recycling systems require a purer raw water as it will remain in the systems. The changes in pH and mineral composition in a recycling system can result in unexpected interactions with even the most stable media. In a water culture system, only the water and its interaction with the nutrient solution and root effluents are of concern. Also the concern of quality control and consistency of media is removed so you can eliminate a factor beyond your control.

Summary

This clearly shows that water culture allows the grower to take control of the root zone. This is being done by many growers around the world but the key word is 'control'. Water culture systems have no buffer so the commercial grower must constantly monitor the system manually or have sensors in place and automatic control for optimum production. The systems will operate with less than optimum control, quite effectively, which makes it possible for hobby growers to have a lot of fun with water culture. Additionally, there is the factor that the shorter the period of time plants are in the system, the easier it is to operate the system. There is less time for the accumulation of problems. Many different water culture systems as well as adaptations and combinations are used. There is no shortage of imagination among growers and researchers so there are many examples of water culture for your choosing. The following are listed in the order in which they came into use.

Chapter 13
SOME WATER CULTURE SYSTEMS

RESEARCH WATER CULTURE

I am sure that at some point in your life you have seen or used the 'plant in a jar' technique of growing. Whether it was a beansprout experiment in school, grandma rooting a cutting she quietly snipped from someone else's plant, or the traditional science lab jar with a rubber stopper. This is the technique which has been used to explore plant response to nutrition in the lab and teach botany to students.

However even this simple culture has kept pace with the times. While the original is still used in the lab there are the modern day versions. Most notable of these is the Minitron II developed at the University of Illinois, Champaign Urbana. It places the original jar inside a completely sealed environment where computers can measure and analyze everything that goes into and out of the plant. Far beyond anything hobby or commercial growers will use but a current tool for furthering our knowledge of plant metabolisms.

This very high tech device is a Minitron II. The complete environment surrounding all parts of the plants is controlled and all inputs can be measured to very precise levels. It is much more sophisticated than the old water jars but is used for exactly the same purpose.

EBB & FLOW

This was one of the first automated irrigation systems developed for greenhouse applications. Originally it was an irrigation system only but there is no question that for a variety of smaller plants and propagation requirements there is a no more efficient system.

The principle of ebb and flow benches is very simple. Very little irrigation tubing is required to flood a waterproof tray thereby bottom watering many plants. Operation is easy. A pump is used to flood the tray to a specific depth, and hold the level for long enough for the media in the plant containers to be thoroughly moistened.

The water used to flood the tray contains properly formulated nutrients the same as required by any hydroponic system. This is an area where advances have been made to improve the operation of ebb and flow systems. We know a lot more today about plant nutrition than we did 100 years ago.

The plastics revolution has made it simpler to construct ebb and flow systems. Properly designed trays are available in a variety of sizes which can easily be used by the hobby grower. For those of you concerned about the increasing use of plastics in agriculture, the original methods of construction still work well. They simply require you have some basic skills and are willing to do additional ongoing maintenance.

Commercial growers have found Ebb & Flow to be a very valuable tool for a variety of crops. This range at Burnaby Lake Greenhouses in BC uses the system to facilitate complete automation of tray movement and the use of rolling tables to maximize area coverage. The system is used for many crops including cactus, propagation, orchids and potted plants to name a few.

No matter what components you decide to use, the construction is quite simple and your system will be composed of the following parts.

1. The tray (or trays) 4'x4' or 4'x8' are good sizes for hobby use.
2. The bench for the tray.
3. The irrigation system including pump & timer.
4. A reservoir for the nutrient solution.
5. Containers & Media.

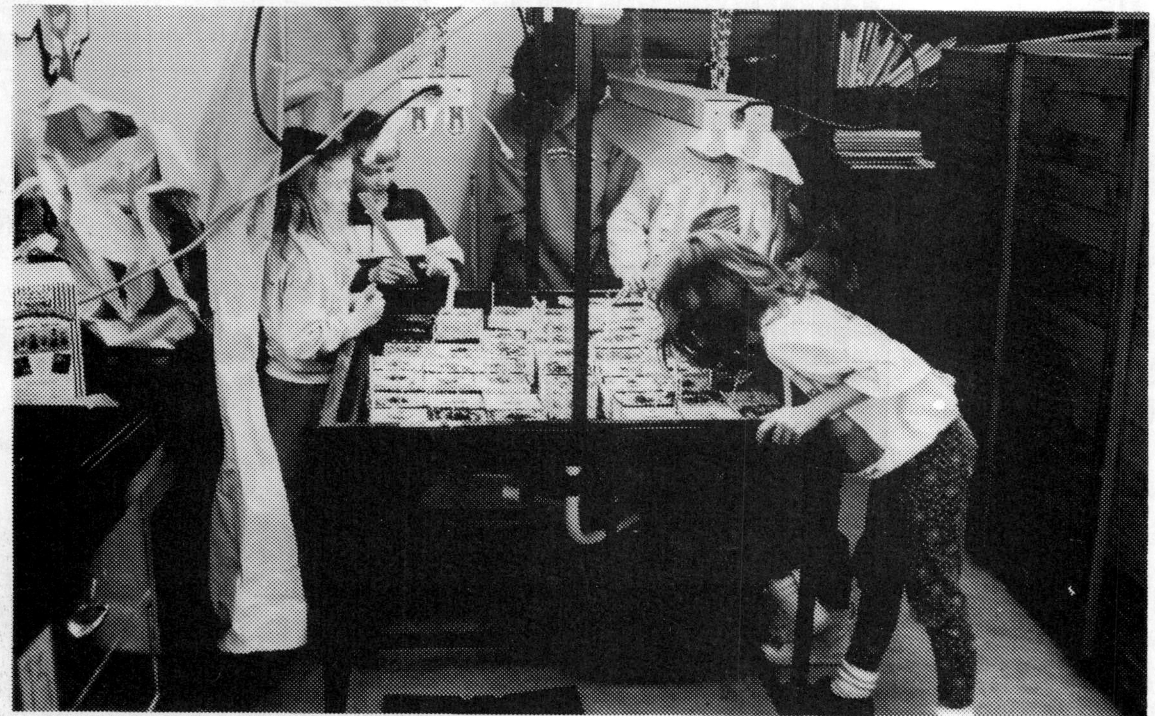

Ebb and flow systems are very popular with hobby gardeners of all types. This self-contained 'Gardeners Delite®' has proven to be a valuable teaching aid in BC schools. For an 'in-home' system this is one of the most useful styles you will find for a wide range of applications.

Really the same list of parts you would have for any hydroponic system. The difference with ebb and flow is that it is ideally suited for many growing applications. For the hobby grower these include;

Orchid growing - all types
Propagation - seeds and cuttings
Cut Flower Growing
Salad production
Herb production
Potted Plants

What these applications have in common is that the plants involved are short and do not require the support vine crops such as tomatoes or cucumbers do. For the hobby grower the ebb and flow system presents the opportunity to grow a variety of short and medium height crops in the same system with very little installation cost.

System Specifics.

The Tray

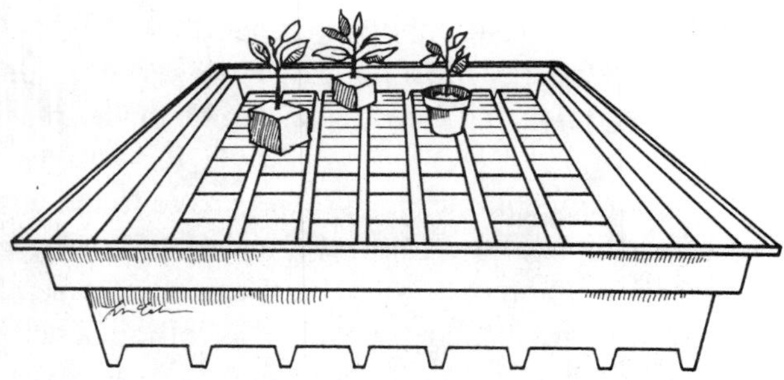

The key to a good ebb and flow system is proper tray design. Premade trays can be purchased or you can make your own but proper design is critical. Looking at the ribbing design in a commercial tray, you note the plant containers sit above the level of the lowest point of the tray. The ribbing also provides good tray strength so it will remain perfectly level on the bench. This ensures all containers are watered evenly.

If you are building your own tray the same effect can be achieved by building a flat bottomed waterproof tray and placing in the tray a grid for the plants to sit on. Effective for this purpose is the open grid light diffuser normally installed in fluorescent light fixtures.

By raising the containers (or media) you ensure perfect drainage, provide air pruning on roots and keep plants from sitting in solution. When building your own trays it is essential the material you use to waterproof the tray be non-toxic to plants and that it not interact with the nutrient solution.

The tray can be as large as the greenhouse itself as this specialty propagation greenhouse at Bevo Farms in BC demonstrates. The concrete floors have heating in them and are simply oversized ebb& flow trays.

Benching for the Trays

For proper fluid distribution it is important the bench be perfectly level. In home built systems the bench and tray may be one unit but, the requirement for accurate leveling still applies. The bench must also be strong enough to support the weight of the tray when it is full and contains a full crop weight as well. The tray must not sag under these conditions.

A quick and easy bench can be made from a piece of 3/4" plywood and a pair of folding table legs.

Many commercial growers have found ebb and flow trays to be the ideal tool for automation. Larger trays roll on conveyor, trolley or other types of systems, from the potting area down into the greenhouse and on through to the packing area after growth. A considerable labour saving. Ebb and flow trays are also ideally suited to rolling benches which can increase the use of growing floor space by as much as 25%.

The most common options for benching are; fixed with the bench providing the support strength (above inset) or, mobile with the tray being contained in a metal frame which provides the support strength (bottom). The stronger tray systems are easy to roll and thus transport large numbers of plants through various portions of the greenhouse.

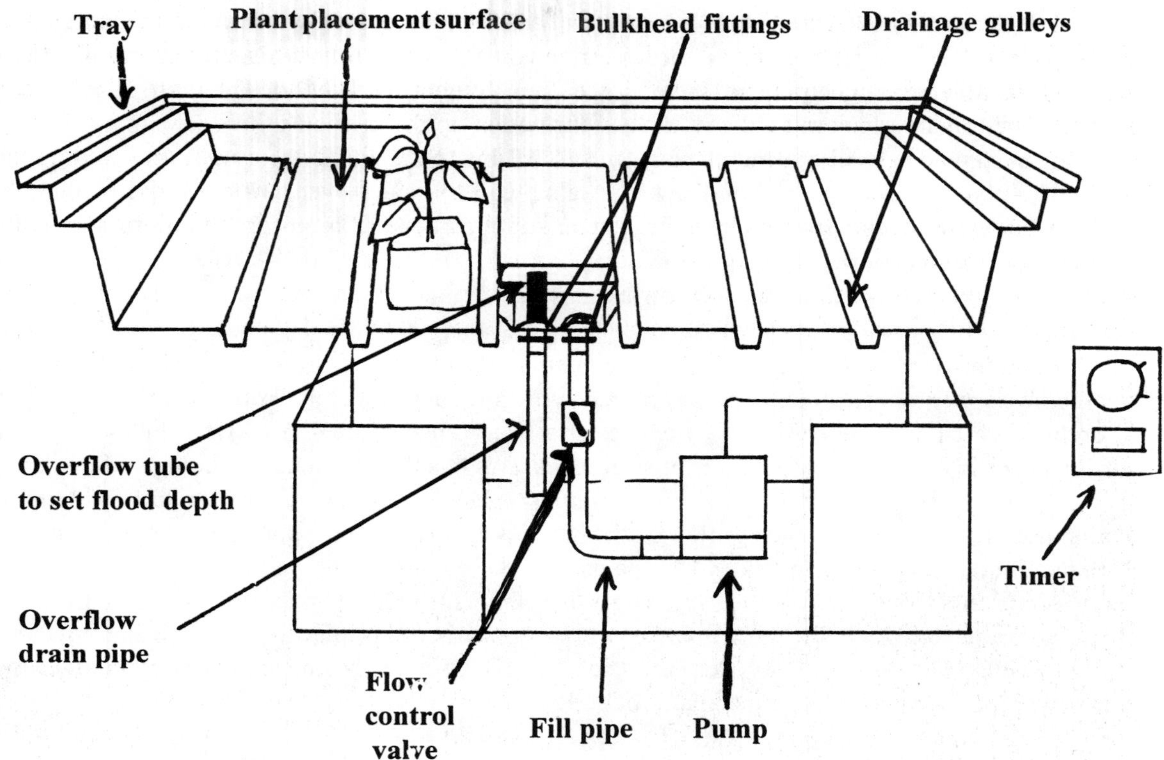

The Irrigation System

Irrigating to a specific level can be easily accomplished. The fittings normally used for this in hobby gardens are the thru-hull fittings made for the marine industry. The 3/4 inch size is adequate for the smaller trays (up to 4'x8'). For large trays it may be necessary to go up to 3 inch fittings.

The trick is to size the fitting so during the fill cycle the drain hole will remove solution from the tray as fast as the pump puts the solution in once the proper level has been reached. The fluid should rise 1/2" above the level of the tray the containers and media rest on.

To accomplish this there are several factors involved; the size of the fill pipe, the size of the drain hole and the output of the pump being used. The output of the pump can be controlled through the use of an in-line valve. A pipe equal to the desired fluid height in the tray is installed in the drain hole. This ensures the fluid reaches the desired level before the drainage occurs. The pump remains on for the time necessary to raise the solution to this level and then the solution begins to drain back through the same pump hose in simple systems.

Figuring out the required irrigation cycle is not difficult. You simply want to ensure the media stays moist enough that the roots never dry out. The timing between irrigations is determined by the media being used. The two most popular and easiest to control are rockwool and sphagnum based soilless mixes such as Pro Mix C or BX.

The timer required to control the irrigation cycle must be capable of the number of cycles required and the duration. Remember the only reservoir for the plant roots is the media they are planted in and this volume of media is quite small. The irrigation cycle will be more frequent than would be used for a recycling system where there is a larger volume of media used per plant.

The Reservoir

The reservoir will need to have a capacity of at least 50% more fluid than the amount required to fill the tray. The larger the reservoir, the less often you will have to change the solution. I would note here that the solution concentration will be lower than you may be used to. The reason is that this is a bottom watering system and there is no flushing action on the media as there is with a drip or top watering system. The media is therefore more susceptible to salt build up.

The plants grown in ebb and flow trays also tend to have lower nutrient requirements than tomatoes, cucumbers or peppers so the EC can be kept below 2 millmohs or 1300 ppm.

Containers & Media

As mentioned earlier the most popular medias for ebb and flow systems are rockwool and sphagnum based soilless mixes. Orchid growers will have success using hydrostone for the varieties of orchids which are true epiphytes. The easiest media to use is the 4" rockwool block which has sufficient mass for most small plant root systems. It also has the advantage of being self contained.

Soilless mixes should be used in the smallest mesh bottom container available. Commonly available containers include, the 1 gallon mesh bottom pot and the tomato and cucumber pots also used for bag culture. Rockwool flock may also be used in these containers.

If possible you should have all of your plants in the same media to make irrigation control easier. If you are propagating, the tray inserts filled with soilless mix can be placed in the ebb and flow bench with individual clear domes over each insert set. The 1020 flats with holes in the bottom make ideal containers for cut and come again salad production.

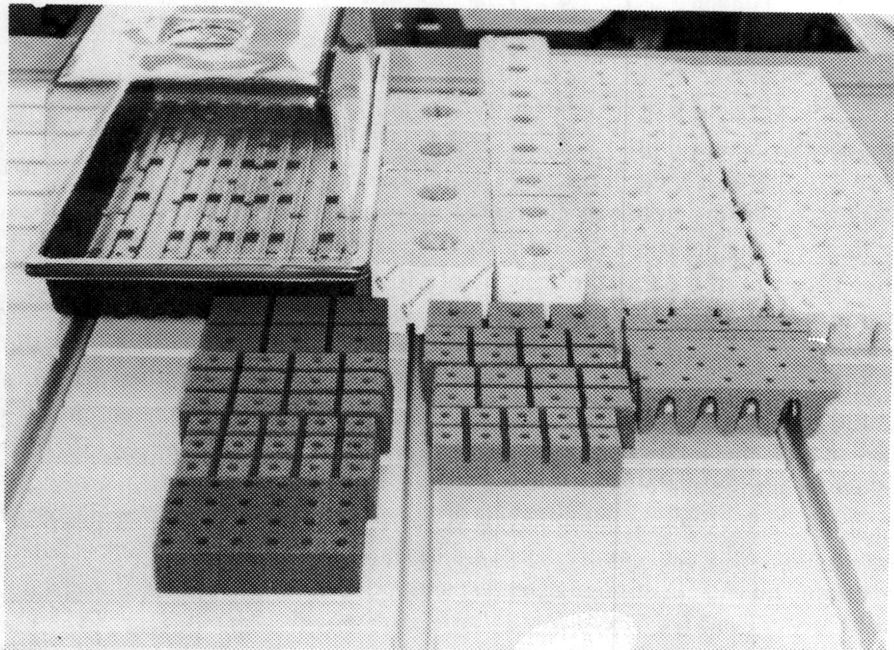

Hobby growers have an unlimited range of choices for both propagation and plant growth medias. Virtually any type or style of container with holes in it will suit an ebb & flow system. Many medias do not require containers. Shown here are oasis cubes and rockwool cubes and blocks.

Operating the system.

There is an aspect of ebb and flow culture which it is important to understand. The method of sub-irrigation results in nutrients accumulating in the media. Top irrigation of media or the usual flow of solution around small propagation cubes provides the necessary flushing action to remove excess nutrients. This action is not present in any bottom irrigated system. Therefore, it is wise to moderate the strength of the nutrient solution to the minimum required. Hobby growers can flush the plant roots each time it is necessary to change the solution in the reservoir.

No matter what the frequency of irrigation the solution does not have to remain in the tray for an extended time. Even with 8" azalea pots it takes only 7 seconds for all of the media in the container to be completely wet to maximum adsorption and absorption. Ebb and flow is becoming more popular for all sorts of container plants and growers should keep in mind that the salt buildup becomes more severe over time and should be closely monitored.

Ebb and Flow systems present a very flexible set of options for the hobby grower. The limitation is to the smaller self-supporting plants but on average most of the plants we grow meet this definition.

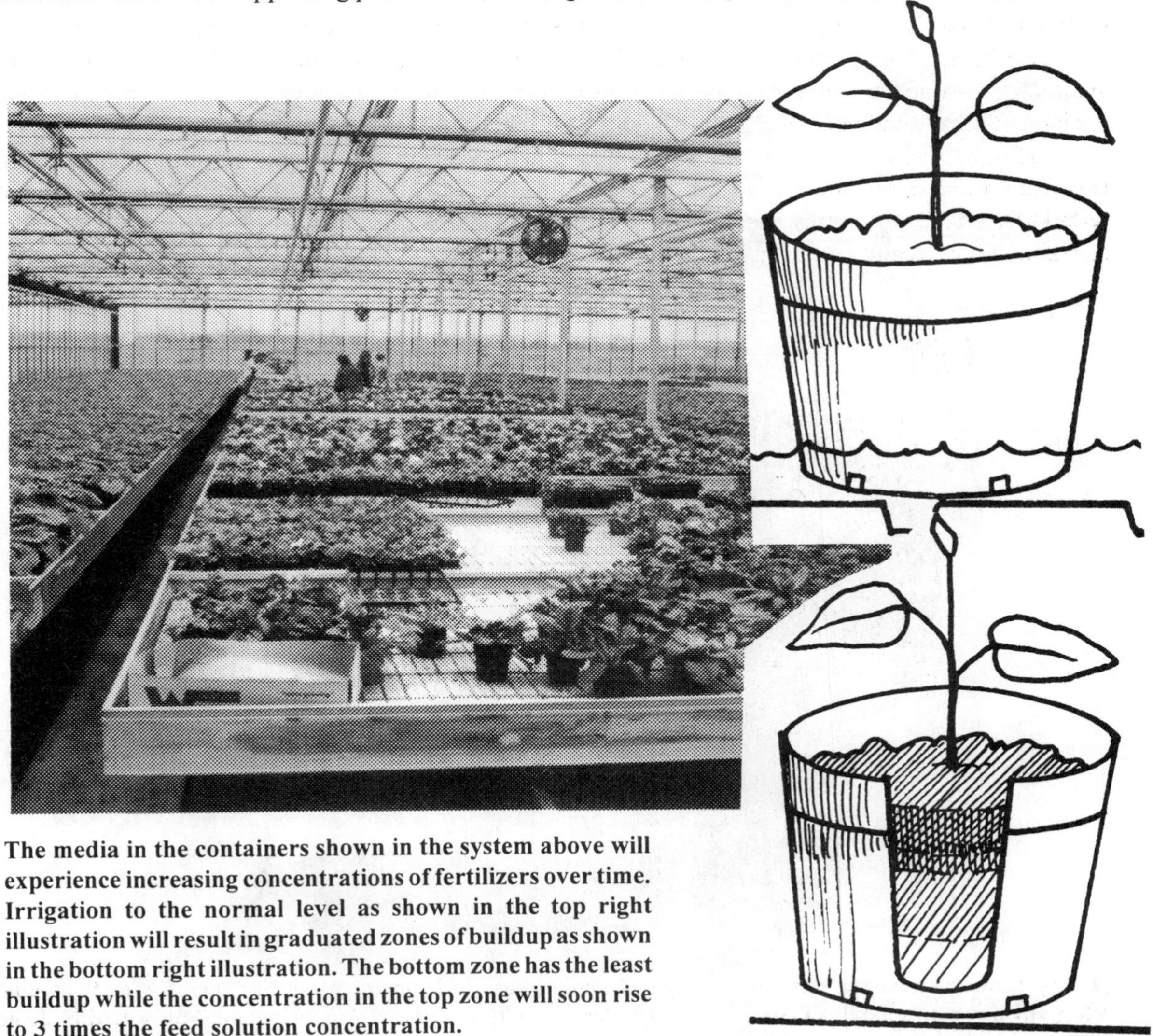

The media in the containers shown in the system above will experience increasing concentrations of fertilizers over time. Irrigation to the normal level as shown in the top right illustration will result in graduated zones of buildup as shown in the bottom right illustration. The bottom zone has the least buildup while the concentration in the top zone will soon rise to 3 times the feed solution concentration.

THE FLOATING RAFT SYSTEM

An adaptation of the Ebb and Flow system which has recently found favour with some growers. The set up is identical to an ebb and flow system. The addition is a floating raft, normally of styrofoam which floats on solution in the tray. Solution may be completely replenished on a regular basis or a constant slow flow can be used. The plants are set into small holes in the styrofoam. It has been used for production of greens when the whole floor of the greenhouse is used as the ebb and flow tray. The rafts are floated from one end to the other on a cycle the same as the growth cycle of the plants. Other growers use this system for 'cut and come again' herb production.

The Floating Raft system is very similar in setup to the Ebb and Flow system. The only difference is that there is a constantly maintained level of solution in the reservoir on which the foam slab rafts float. The modern version of the Chinampas.

NUTRIENT FILM TECHNIQUE

NFT is perhaps the best known of the water culture systems although ebb and flow is fast catching up. It was the brainchild of a group of researchers in England who developed it to study the roots of plants more closely. The success of the system was such that pressure came to make the system public. There was not total agreement among the research group so it fell to Dr. Cooper to publish an amended version of the system. Unfortunately those who read the information did not realize there was information missing. In the following years the commercial and hobby viability has been proven for the system through the intensive work of growers and researchers.

It was the first system developed for modern agriculture which was designed to completely isolate plants from media. Yes there is a small amount often used to propagate the plants. This eliminates the problem of seeds washing down the drain instead of germinating. The propagation media is seldom sufficient to provide plant support so for small plants the channels are designed to handle this task and for larger plants stem support is commonly used. The use of the ebb and flow technique has proven to be the ideal propagation method for plants to be grown in NFT systems.

Construction of NFT systems tends to be crop specific in commercial systems and this is a practice it would be wise for the hobby grower to adopt as well. There is no buffer so nutrient formulations are more important in NFT systems. For the hobby grower operating a mixed garden, the trick is to match plants with similar size, growth habit, and nutritional requirements. Compared to many other systems the root systems of plants grown in NFT tend to be smaller in volume and much different from those grown in media. There is seldom development of a tap root, all roots developed are feeding roots unless something goes very wrong in operation of the system.

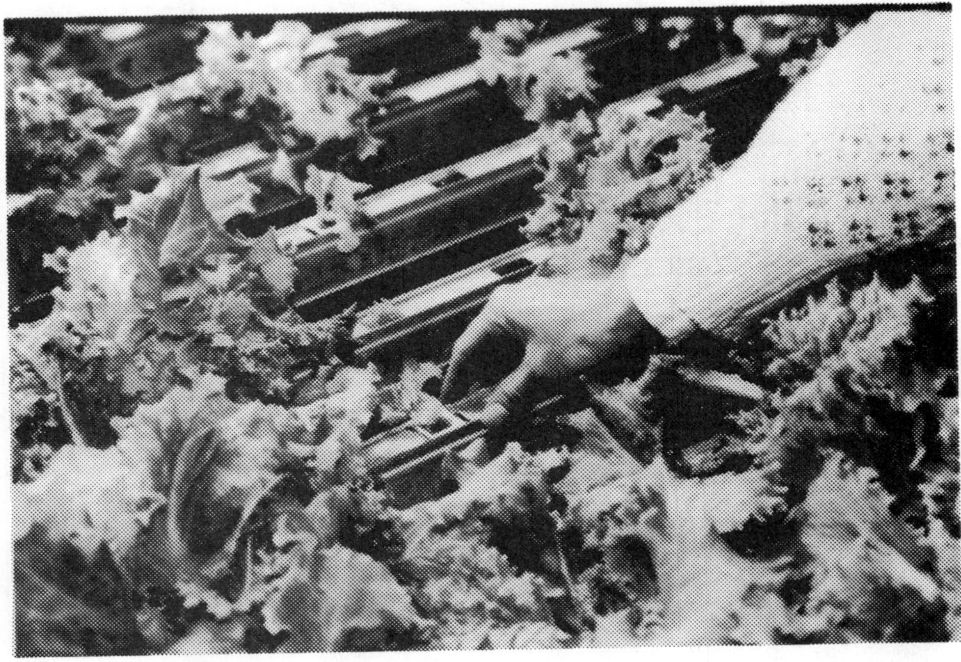

Using the wrong size of channel will not save you money. The 3/4" channel used at Phytofarms in Dekalb IL was one of the reasons lettuce crops never reached maturity. Within a matter of days the channels were completely blocked with the roots and the channels flooded over onto the floor.

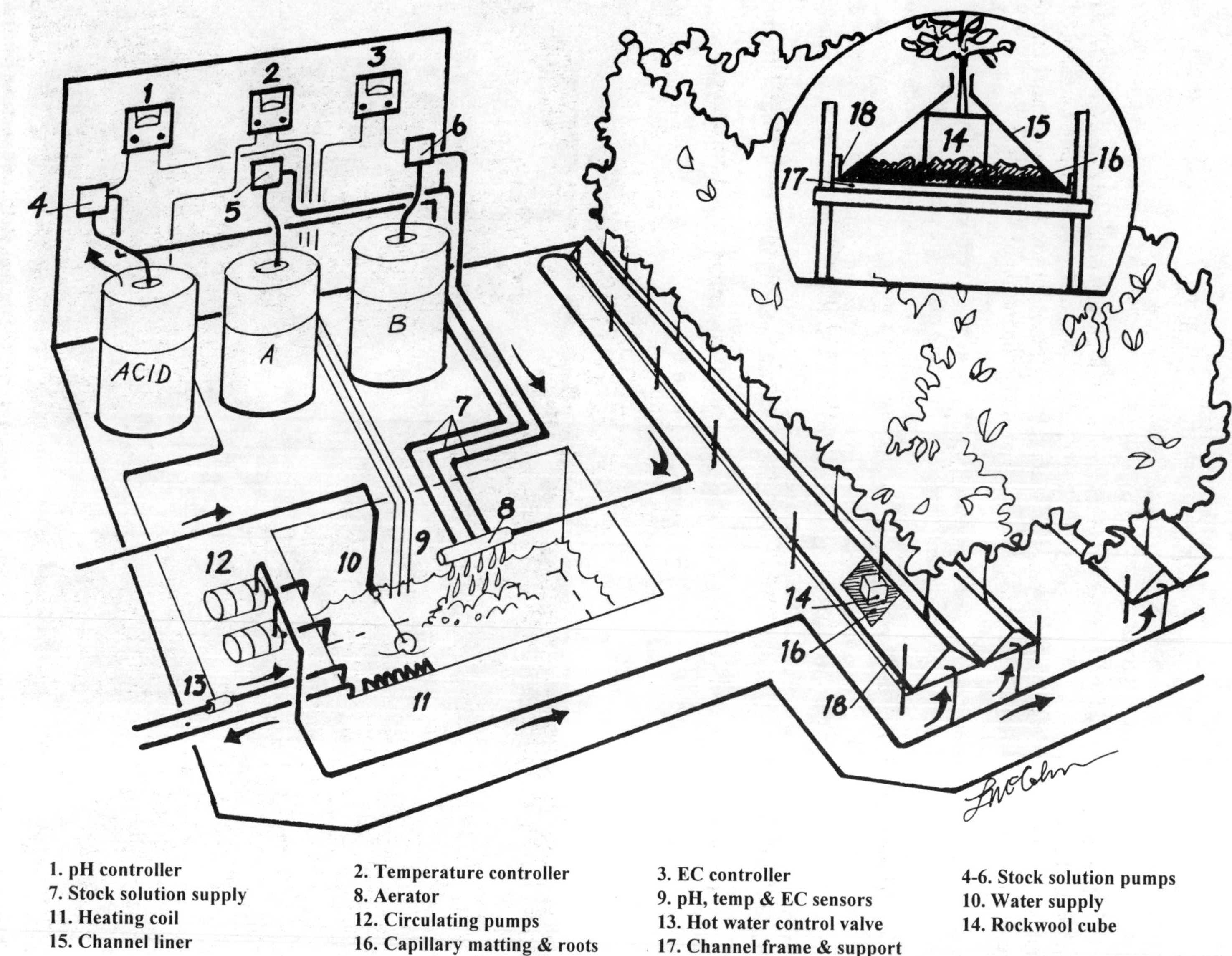

1. pH controller
2. Temperature controller
3. EC controller
4-6. Stock solution pumps
7. Stock solution supply
8. Aerator
9. pH, temp & EC sensors
10. Water supply
11. Heating coil
12. Circulating pumps
13. Hot water control valve
14. Rockwool cube
15. Channel liner
16. Capillary matting & roots
17. Channel frame & support

The growing system itself is similar to all other hydroponic systems in the components required;

reservoir,
delivery system,
container system (in this case channels) and
a recovery system for waste solution.

The essential difference is in the container system. Multiple plant channels are used instead of individual containers. These channels must be sized for the plants to be grown if optimum use of the space is to be realized. There is no problem with growing plants in too large a channel but the restrictions of a too small channel will be very detrimental to operation of the system.

The Channels

Three channel sizes commonly used for NFT construction are;

2" wide for greens such as lettuce and spinach,

5-6" wide for herbs to be grown for extended periods & crops such as strawberries,

10" wide for large, high energy crops such as tomatoes, peppers, and cucumbers.

There are several commercial producers of NFT channels in the lettuce size, (left), and some in Austrailia for the mid-size channels. However the wide channels (right) are most commonly homemade affairs from a number of materials.

There are additional restrictions on the construction of the channels.

Ideally they should be covered to eliminate the potential of algae growth in the channels. There are materials which can be added to the nutrient solution to retard algae growth but it is simpler and less of a management problem to simply eliminate light during design and construction.

The length of the channels is important. If the channels are too long there is a decreasing availability of oxygen and nutrients for plants down the line. I have seen one tomato system where the plant height decreased with beautiful symmetry down the channel from 8 feet at one end to one foot at the other. It was quite an amazing ski slope in a greenhouse. The maximum length for NFT channels seems to be 18 meters (60 feet). I prefer to work from the basis of a maximum of 30 plants per channel no matter what the spacing requirements. Plant spacing in the channels is based on the mature size of the crop. Adequate room must be left for good air movement and so plant leaves are not touching for a long time before harvest. As an example, for lettuce this spacing can be anywhere from 8-12" depending on the variety and harvest size. You may want to tailor channel length for such considerations as moving systems in a greenhouse. Shorter is OK, but longer can lead to problems and is not going to save you any significant money on installation costs.

The most common material used in channel construction is plastic. This is for the same reasons as discussed for other systems, long life, ease of cleaning, and lack of interaction with the nutrient solution. There is however a problem which must be addressed, especially with new plastic. The nutrient solution tends to run in rivulets over the surface instead of flowing in an even sheet. It is not unusual for these rivulets to miss the roots of transplants so the plants can die within hours of transplant. The simplest method of correcting the problem is to lay a narrow strip of capillary matting on the bottom of the channel and set the transplant on top. Some pre-manufactured channels have ridges running the length of the channel to direct the solution flow.

Another consideration in channel design is light. All channels should have covers to prevent the nutrient solution from being exposed to light. The algae which results is not detrimental to the plants but is does provide a breeding site for fungus gnats and other pests as well as clogging pumps and delivery tubing.

Many growers have used round PVC pipe as channeling with mixed results. The main problems which have emerged are the difficulty in having the solution reach the roots of a transplant when the propagation media sides sit a fair distance above the bottom curve of the pipe and the use of too small a pipe for the plant with the resulting clogging of the pipe. The solution to the first problem is to use a propagation media or container which is shaped to fit properly into the pipe. The solution to the second is obvious, use the proper size of pipe.

Other options for channel construction include everything from black/white plastic (black side to the interior) folded up to form a channel, to wooden frames lined with plastic, square plastic downspouts from eavestroughing or the plastic eavestroughing itself. Metal channeling can be used if it is coated or lined with plastic to isolate the plant roots from the metal. No matter what is used the channels must sit on a rigid base which provides adequate support for the combined weight of the channel, the solution, and the mature plants. To ensure proper flow of the nutrient solution the channels must have a 2% slope (1' per 50' of channel length). Long experience has shown this slope is the best for the majority of crops.

The Delivery System

The difference with the NFT channels is the requirement for control of the delivery volumes which will change over the life of the crop. This can be accomplished by valving, or multiple delivery devices per channel which can be turned off if the volume is not required. It is an added advantage if the solution is distributed over the width of the channel. The solution volumes will be adjusted so that 95% of the solution delivered at the head of the channel enters the return system. This will ensure that all plants are receiving adequate oxygen, nutrients and water. If this balance is not possible then there are too many plants in the channel, i.e., the channel is too long. The other critical monitoring at the drain end will be pH, EC and in commercial systems, oxygen.

The delivery system needs to be controlled by a cycling timer. The on/off cycle will vary from crop to crop but experience has shown that cycling the flow is an excellent way to ensure maximum disbursement of root effluents and breaking of the inherent water walls around the roots.

The Reservoir

There are several factors which need to be controlled in the reservoir; temperature, oxygen content, and degassing. Temperature control is more critical than in other systems as the solution can pick up a lot more heat than in media based systems. Additionally there is no buffer in the root zone so heating may be required to bring temperature up at night. I would note here that the concept of excessive heating of the solution in an attempt to cut heating costs in the greenhouse has been thoroughly disproven. The ideal solution temperature is still 20C (68F).

Reservoir sizing for small hobby systems and large commercial systems is quite a different proposition. The same calculation can be used for hobby reservoirs as is used for other recycling systems (lettuce 0.5 liters per plant up to tomatoes 2 liters per plant) although I would reduce the volume of original solution by 20%. For commercial growers I like to see the reservoir sized so the entire volume is used by the plants twice in a 24 hour period. This requires a control and refill system which does not need to be expensive. One of the best I have seen for the commercial grower is the Dosetron L out of New Zealand. It is compact, inexpensive, easy to operate and reliably accurate.

Tips and Tricks for NFT Systems.

1. System aeration is critical to keep beneficial organisms thriving and to suppress disease.

2. Monitor solution temperature to ensure it does not get too hot or cold over a 24 hour period. This is critical on hot summer days.

3. When using bare-root transplants do not set the root crown on the bottom of the channel. Use a packing of some sort to hold the root crown even with the top of the channel cover.

4. To achieve even solution distribution over the bottom of the channel for young transplants use a thin strip of capillary matting across the channel instead of laying a strip down the length of the channel.

5. Set the flow rate at the top of the channel so that 95% of the solution introduced at the head of the channel drains from the channel. If this is not possible then you channel is too long.

6. Cycling irrigation is best for all crops in NFT except lettuce which really doesn't care. The cycle will vary with the crop but there is an easy method of getting started and adjusting the cycle. Start and continue the irrigation until the water starts to run back into the reservoir. Shut the pump off and wait until the system stops draining. Leave the pump off for 1/2 the time of the irrigation cycle and then start the pump again to repeat the cycle.

7. Make sure the base on which you set your channels is solid and will not allow sagging.

8. Remember that NFT means Nutrient FILM Technique. The flow of water down the channel should be a thin film. If the solution depth in the channel starts to rise check your system to ensure you have used the right width of channel and that your plants are not growing excess roots because of a problem with your nutrient solution.

9. When making your channels from wood and lining them with plastic the best plastic to use is the black\white laminated plastic with the black to the inside. Carefully check the wood to ensure there is nothing that will puncture th liner.

10. You can space the channels close together for young plants and move them apart as plants grow but, you must space the plants in the channel for the mature size.

SPROUT/FODDER GRASS SYSTEMS

Periodically various companies have spent large sums of money promoting sprouting units which are ready made and expensive to buy. The average grower is a dedicated do-it-yourselfer and such units often experience slow sales with the resulting bankruptcy of the manufacturer. It is tough to justify high priced units for a low end technology. Sprout production is essentially water packaging at a very rapid rate.

Before even considering sprout production for human consumption it is essential that you investigate the market. These systems are extremely productive. Two racks (8' long x 4' wide x 5' high) containing 4 shelves will produce 800 pounds of marketable alfalfa sprouts per week. This is productivity you can calculate by the cubic foot per week instead of the normal pounds per sq. ft (kg/ sq. m) per year calculations normal for greenhouse production.

On the other hand these high production rates make sprouting systems ideal for ranchers, horsebreeders and other livestock operations. The only difference between a human sprout and an animal fodder production system is the time for the cycle from seed to harvest. The human stuff takes 3-1/2 days and the animal fodder 7 days in the same system. A word of caution regarding the animal fodder. The product is extremely rich and no animal can be fed only this product. Roughage must also be supplied. Deciding optimum rates of feeding is best done in consultation with your veterinarian.

Sprouts will provide an interesting sideline and diversification for growers but, seldom if ever, will the local market provide sufficient consumption to think of sprouts as a single profit crop. It doesn't take much space to fill local market demand. Okay, in spite of what I have just said you are still interested in building a system so lets get on with it.

World Champion jumper 'Big Ben' is fed fodder grass as a regular part of his diet. Ian Miller gives a lot of credit to this diet for Big Ben's recovery from illness and injury to continue his championsip performance at the age of 15 years.

The Propagation Process

Building the optimum system requires that we look at seed germination in its specific stages;

1. Water accumulation for seed swell.

This is preferably done before the seeds go into the germination chamber in small systems where the wet seeds can be spread by hand. Non-viable seeds can then be easily discarded. In larger systems a specific percentage of overplant will be required to compensate for non-viable seed. In a properly designed system, with non-treated seed from a reliable source, germination rates will be very high. Depending on the variety it may be desirable to use a product such as Superthrive to speed the germination after seed swell.

2. Germination.

Once the seed has swollen, the actual emergence should not be followed by any mechanical movement of individual sprouts until the point of harvest. Since germination will occur more readily at high temperatures, 80 - 90 F (26-32C) depending on variety, the irrigation system should provide for temperature control rather than attempting to use an air control system.

3. Initial growth.

The temperature of the sprout needs to be lowered during growth to reduce the onset of disease and promote the crispness of the product. This temperature can range from 65-75 deg F (18-24C)

4. Greening.

If you are going to sell a sprout it must be green, such is the demand of the consumer. This greening requires minimal light and a very short time. It can occur during the drainage time when the product is waiting to be placed in a cooler to await delivery. Greening will occur in as little as 6 hours. We do not want any appreciable root growth to occur as this will reduce shelf life.

For animal fodder systems the sprouts will be under light for the last 4 days of the cycle. This is best done within the germination chamber and will require the installation of a lighting system. High intensities of light are not required although due to the use of fog or mist caution must be used and all electrical components rated for use in such an environment.

The above 4 stages can standardly be achieved with alfalfa sprouts in 3-1/2 days. Other seed varieties can take longer which is a factor to be considered in the design of mixed seed production systems for sprout salad production. Experimentation with combinations of seeds will soon prove the wide variety of flavours which can be created by mixing seed.

This system is designed for thin layer production. It can be used for larger seeds such as mung beans but do not attempt to fill trays with larger seeds. If there are many layers of seeds the heat generated by the germinating seed can build up causing uneven germination and provide the initiation of some real disease problems. For the larger seeds where the final product is harvested before leaf formation, the depth of seed in the tray should not be any more than 1.5 times the diameter of the seed.

Design Considerations

There are several considerations in system design which will affect disease resistance and shelf life of this very delicate product.

1. Mechanical Damage

Sprouts are very susceptible to mechanical damage. Cell walls are thin and the water content is extremely high relative to dry matter content. During the entire process we are simply expanding the original seed contents with water. No plant nutrients are being used unless an alteration of taste is desirable. The production trays should not be moved during the period between seed swell and harvest.

For fodder systems it is usually less of a problem to complete the cycle in one location for smaller production systems (under 30 head). In large systems, automated conveyor systems may become economically feasible and save on energy costs.

2. Disease

Having the system contained in a minimum area with virtually no air flow from the outside goes a long way to disease prevention. The water supply should be pathogen free. This concentration of seedlings is an ideal initiation site for diseases. Cleanliness is absolutely essential. Between crops the growing chamber should be thoroughly cleaned and ideally this is accomplished with a high pressure spray on all surfaces. No plant material should ever be allowed to remain in the growing area. All trays placed into the area should be sterile.

This demonstration unit from Harvest Spring shows the 7 day cycle of fodder production. Many companies have offered ready made systems and most have failed for the same reason. Users can construct their own systems at much lower cost and achieve equal production levels. The system and technology are simple and construction materials are locally available.

3. The Production Container

My ideal container is one which is as large as the customer can display. The complete mat of sprouts should remain intact until delivery to the retailer or restaurant. Air movement helps keep the sprouts cooler and it is easier to mist them to maintain freshness. The trays should be displayed in a cooler or a misted area of the vegetable counter. If they are kept cool and well misted there will be little disease initiation even when portions are removed for use or sale.

Trays should have maximum drainage to ensure there is no water pooling in the tray. Sprouts will be kept moist through periodic timed irrigation and water pooling or accumulation will interfere with this. The structure of the tray should be sufficiently rigid that when handled it bends or warps very minimally to prevent mechanical damage of the sprouts.

In addition it is a great help if the trays can be stacked for both seed swell and the delivery process. The tray sides need to be high enough so a mature product is not touched by the tray above. It helps to have a nested pressure connection for stability.

Often you will see small clear plastic containers used to market sprouts. Wastage which occurs when these containers are used is incredible. They are very thin and mechanical damage occurs every time they are handled. This damage is a guarantee of disease which makes the product unsalable within hours. Lack of air movement in the small containers enhances the spread of disease.

The health department will require that the growing trays be food grade plastic and they may have certain cleaning requirements. In fodder production the tray can be of any size as the fodder can be cut into squares sufficient for each head of livestock being fed.

This photo shows the simplicity of the racks and the containers for fodder grass. The ones used here are propagation flats which are standard in the greenhouse propagation industry. For human sprouts, the containers must be made of food grade plastic.

4. Temperature Control

In an isolated sprout chamber this is easily handled through the irrigation system. The temperature adjustments required for different stages will be gradual even if water temperature is adjusted in stages, as the high (100%) water content in the air mitigates and tempers the rate of change. Direct, immediate contact of incoming water with the sprouts is minimized by using the smallest water droplet possible.

5. Water Control

The introduction and removal of water is critical to optimum production. Source water must be clean, as pure as possible with no particulate matter, and it is beneficial to allow for oxygen content enhancement. Moving water is a force. The droplet size must be as small as possible with fog being the optimum size of droplet. Dan "Micro-Mist" nozzles operated under 50 psi have proven to be quite effective for irrigation.

While it is the optimum particle size, fog presents design problems related to the very low volume requirements for small chambers. The expense is seldom justified in sprouting chambers unless they are of a very large size.

The better sealed the sprout chamber is the less frequently irrigation will be required. In a sprout chamber irrigation controls temperature and humidity. There should be at least 2 air changes per hour built into the design of the chamber, preferably using filtered air.

When setting water temperatures it will be necessary to make some adjustment to allow for the heat loss when a percentage of the water droplets are absorbed by the air.

6. Materials

Plastic is best, it cleans up quickly and easily and does not provide an initiation site for diseases. The problem is that more strength may be required. Steel can be coated to isolate it from the water and prevent rusting but galvanized materials must be used with extreme caution.

There are several paint coatings used in the dairy industry which are ideal for coating wooden members used in construction. Keep in mind that any coating materials may have to be approved by your local health department.

Rounded surfaces will enhance cleanup between crops and prevent the lodging of any plant material in nooks and crannies to cause problems in the next crop. If it is allowed, an ideal support material for the bench is the same plastic mesh used for fencing.

This high tech sprouting chamber is one way of approaching the production for human consumption. For the same price you can build a more conventional system with higher continuous production.

7. Rack Design

Rack design is critical to the effective removal of waste water. The water draining from one level of trays must not be allowed to fall onto the tray below. Large drops would have sufficient weight to cause mechanical damage. A solid surface collection cover under the tray level is the easiest way to accomplish this. Runoff can be easily directed by PVC pipe.

The physical measurements of the rack will be decided in part by the actual production container being used and the necessity of being able to easily place and remove the containers. The type of misting equipment used will also be a factor in the ability to effectively use floorspace to the optimum.

For most small production systems a design which creates the rack as an independent chamber is usually the least expensive to construct. It also allows expansion to occur in modules without the necessity of dedicating excess amounts of building space to the project. Moveable racks of quite considerable size can be economically constructed using commercial metal storage racking on wheels. This will allow for a system similar to the rolling benches used in greenhouses to optimize production area.

8. Harvest

A multiple number of operations are included under the general term of 'Harvest'. They can be combined for efficiency but for a quality product with an acceptable shelf life none of them can be ignored. When the sprouts in the chamber have reached the desired height (grown without light), the growing trays are removed for the final processes. For fodder grass the process is simply feeding the animals. For sprouts the process is a bit more involved.

(A). Drainage of all excess water.

Standing water presents an unwanted breeding site for disease.
It also slows down the cooling process.

(B). Greening of the sprouts.

Almost any quantity of light seems to cause this effect as the sprouts attempt to switch gear. Intensity should be high enough (1,000 f/c) to allow it to occur in the minimum amount of time so the plant does not initiate a high rate of root growth at the same time. Colour is the issue here, if the sprouts are a pleasing green for about 25% of the distance down from the tip, the consumer will be happy. The sprouts will continue to green when they are on display.

Light levels for the fodder system can be around the 200 f/c level which makes it much easier to install lighting in the germination chambers. Usually all that is required is the use of fluorescent lighting.

(C). Cooling of the sprouts to reduce metabolism and increase shelf life.

This is critical to reduce shipping damage, slow the plant metabolism to a near stall and increase shelf life at the point of sale.

All of the above can be accomplished at the same time. Trays removed from the sprout chamber can be placed in a refrigeration chamber which has the capacity to hold at least the complete contents of the sprout chamber. The lighting can be accomplished with a minimal amount of HID lighting while the trays drain. Once drained the trays can be stacked for shipping. In larger operations this would allow the next chamber to be emptied into the cooler without effecting previously treated crops.

9. Shipping

Keep it cool and avoid rough handling. These are the basics of ensuring that your crop reaches the store or restaurant in optimum condition. If you are required to produce in small containers it is best if the containers themselves are not handled individually during shipping.

10. Display Maintenance

If you want a retailer or restaurant to keep coming back for more you must ensure the product is properly handled while in their possession. If they lose a high percentage of product for any reason; because they bought too much and it stays too long, because they don't display it properly, or if no one takes time to provide the necessary temperature and humidity, you will lose sales. Take the time to ensure your product is used properly and you will sell more and build customer loyalty.

SIX DAY BARLEY GRASS
Composition Analysis

Dry Matter	125 g/kg
Crude Protein	160 g/kg DM
M.A.D. Fibre	160 g/kg DM
Ash	27 g/kg DM
In Vitro OMD	77%
Calcium	0.78 g/kg DM
Phosphorus	4.72 g/kg DM
Magnesium	1.28 g/kg DM
Sodium	0.96 g/kg DM
Potassium	4.60 g/kg DM
Chloride	18.60 g/kg DM
Iron	61 mg/kg DM
Zinc	40 mg/kg DM
Manganese	30 mg/kg DM
Copper	8 mg/kg DM
Selenium	0.07 mg/kg DM
Cobalt	0.05 mg/kg DM
Vitamin A (Measured as Beta-carotene)	43 mg/kg DM
Vitamin E (Measured as Alpha-tocopherol)	62 mg/kg DM
Biotin	1.15 mg/kg DM
Free Folic Acid	1.05 mg/kg DM

Analysis obtained from samples of sprouted Barley grown in a hydroponic chamber after six days of growth.

Chapter 14
THE SPECIALTY AND UNUSUAL SYSTEMS

Now we get to the gardens and cultures which are really impossible to classify. They borrow something from at least one standard culture but, variations are added which may be different or there may be a combination of cultural techniques. From these systems you will see that your imagination is indeed the limit when putting together a garden to suit your specific needs and crops. Just for fun and for those with more interest in the super high tech I am including several systems which were developed for the CELSS Program at NASA. Each of these systems has something to contribute to our understanding of plant production in controlled environments.

MULTIPLE PAIL SYSTEMS.

Growers are definitely an inventive bunch who can find less expensive ways of doing just about anything. One popular system uses the plastic pail, complete with lid, as the main garden component with variation on whether the pail is also the reservoir or a separate reservoir is used. The favorite growing containers are the one gallon mesh bottom nursery containers and the 6 inch mesh pots often used to propagate tomatoes and cucumbers for bag culture. The plastic pails are connected with 1" flexible tubing using thru-hull fittings installed at the bottom of the pail. A standard drip irrigation system is used for solution delivery.

Any media can be used in the net or mesh containers which will not fall out, organic, aggregate, or rockwool. The irrigation frequency is a bit higher than for systems which use more media but this is a good system for use outdoors in areas where there is too much rainfall for an open system. Pails can be placed in any pattern or spacing so there is tremendous flexibility in laying out the system. As mentioned earlier the reservoir can be a combination of all pails in the system. If you decide to do this make sure the pail with the pump in it is lower than all of the others for efficient collection of enough solution to keep the pump operating properly. A separate reservoir makes changing solutions easier to accomplish.

This system can be assembled from easily available materials, many of which assist in recycling waste products. You will find it easier to change solutions if the bucket containing the reservoir is about 6" lower than all of the other containers. A second bulkhead fitting in the container with the pump will make changing solution easier as well. Raising the other containers will allow you to put the drainage in the bottom of the bucket which will ensure complete drainage.

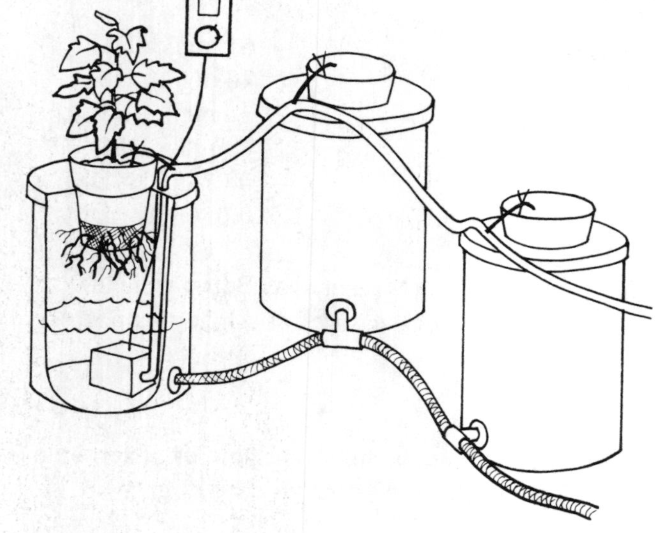

AEROPONICS

This system is one which has never been commercialized for large crop production but it is invaluable for propagation of bare-root cuttings and for successful propagation of many cuttings which just don't seem to be successful any other way. The difficulty in building an aeroponic system is getting spray nozzles which will not clog up with the salts in the solution but will also deliver fine enough droplets at an air speed slow enough to eliminate the potential of damage to the fine roots.

For small commercial systems or hobby gardens I have found plastic nozzles are the easiest to install and work with. Some 'spot spitter' nozzles and the Dan series from Gan provide economical options which work at low pressures (15 to 20 psi). To work effectively most nozzles require much higher pressures and this makes for an expensive system installation.

System construction is similar to NFT but the containers used are more like smaller high sided ebb and flow trays. The plants or cuttings are inserted into soft holders used to hold them in holes in the cover. Under the cover a series of nozzles or sprayers delivers the nutrient solution in a fine spray or mist. The waste solution is collected and recycled to the reservoir.

This system can be a very valuable tool for tree fruit growers who want to take advantage of new cultivars and the dwarfing root stocks. Dwarfing root stock and the cultivar stock can be produced for grafting completely virus free and at a fraction of the cost of purchasing the same product from commercial nurseries. This combined with the ability to get to the market with new varieties up to 2 years ahead of the competition can spell profitability with a very large $ sign.

This completely self-contained aeroponic system was used to produce bare root strawberry transplants for an NFT system. A line of nozzles on a pipe provide the spray for the roots and the excess drips down into the reservoir directly below.

Air Pump Aeroponics

There is another method of assembling an aeroponic system which I designed to overcome the problem with nozzles. It works using air pumps, aquarium type or compressor type, and long air stones or air curtains to keep the root zone at 100% humidity. Operating the system is a combination of aeroponics, hydroculture and the Gericke system. Small diameter hydrostones in 2" net containers are suspended over the solution reservoir. Long air stones are placed in the bottom of the reservoir, the more the better, the ideal would be to cover the reservoir bottom with a source of air bubbles.

The cuttings are placed in the net container so the cut end is 1/2" above the bottom of the container. Fill the reservoir so the solution level just touches the bottom of the net containers and turn on the air pumps. As the solution evaporates the level will drop. Do not replenish the lost solution. The initial contact will ensure there is moisture around the cutting to draw the roots out and the drop in solution forces the roots to seek the moisture. It is very effective.

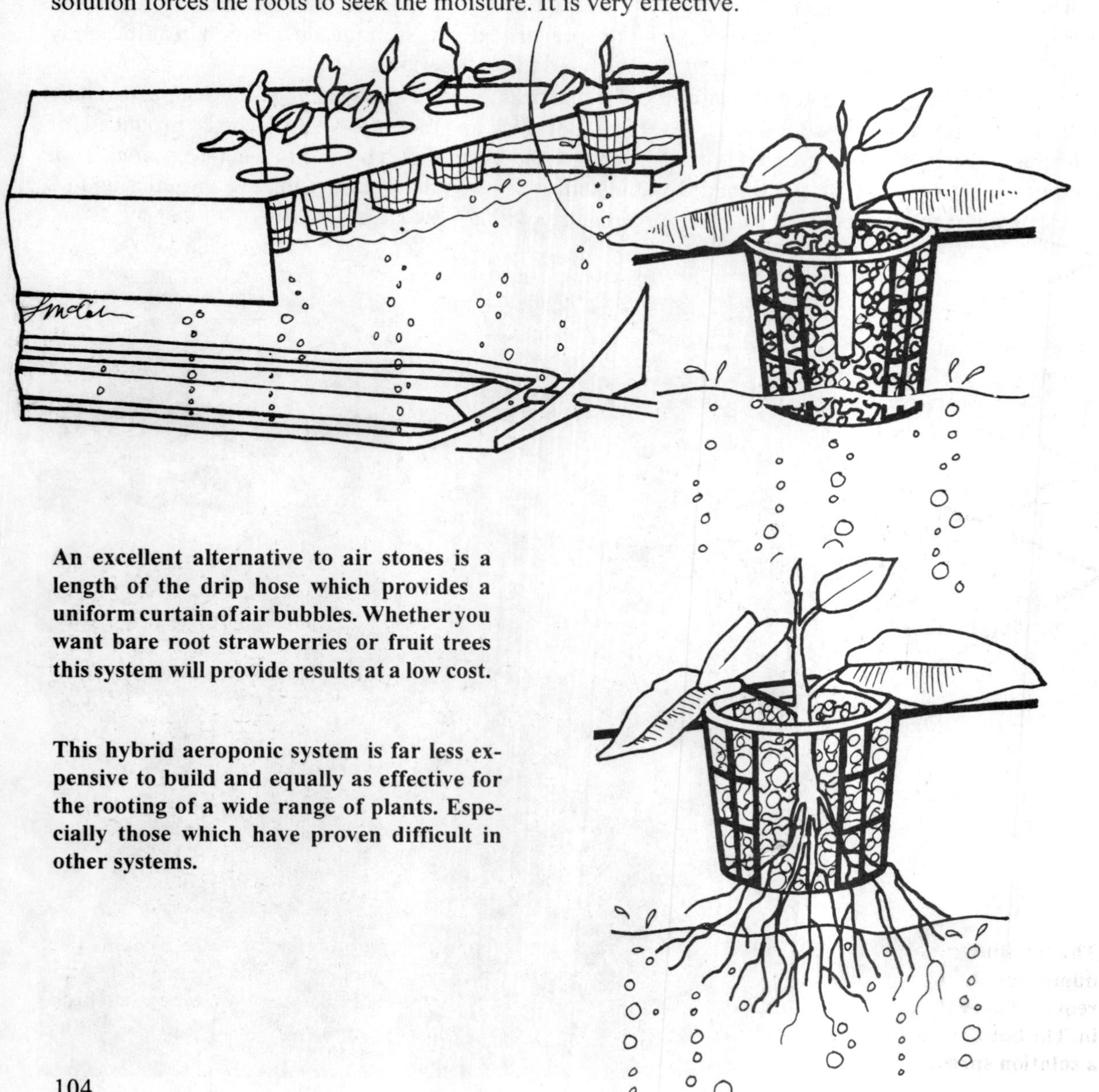

An excellent alternative to air stones is a length of the drip hose which provides a uniform curtain of air bubbles. Whether you want bare root strawberries or fruit trees this system will provide results at a low cost.

This hybrid aeroponic system is far less expensive to build and equally as effective for the rooting of a wide range of plants. Especially those which have proven difficult in other systems.

THE EIN-GEDI SYSTEM
Bomb Proof Hydroponics

This system has never reached commercial viability in North America for a simple reason. The cost of installation and operation is higher than any other system. It is a combination of Gericke, NFT and Aeroponics. In fact there is the expense of allowing for the requirements of all three systems. This redundancy is necessary if you want a system which is absolutely guaranteed to operate in spite of any interruptions to the power supply. In Israel the only available media is sand so media systems are not an option. In North America and other countries we have a wealth of options and no need for such redundant systems.

The top illustration shows the typically suggested construction for a commercial Ein-Gedi System. The pump would normally be in a separate reservoir and service multiple channels. The high pressure pumps required are expensive. The channels are really just oversized NFT channel with an aeroponic system built in. The bottom photohgraph shows a hobby system which uses a vaporizer pump as the method of creating a solution spray.

HOBBY HYDROPONIC POTATOES

Any good hydroponic nutrient solution used for tomatoes is quite adequate for the nutrition of potato crops. The main problem is finding some sort of system in which to get the maximum yield which will fit in with an existing hydroponic setup. Your best friend for this purpose is the 5-gallon pail. They are cheap, easily available and simple to modify for the purpose.

Creating an independent potato garden which can be plugged into your existing hydroponic garden is a matter of a few simple steps.

1. Assemble the necessary materials

Three 5 gal pails for each garden - 2 are sufficient in short season areas. The best pails are the ones which have a lip at the top but, have a minimum amount of ribbing.

A drill for cutting a hole in the bottom edge of one of the pails and a hole saw of proper size or equivalent for the installation of the size of thru-hull fitting you choose.

A saw or knife for cutting out the bottom of two of the pails

Some gravel or hydrostone sufficient to cover the bottom of the pail to a depth of 4 inches

A good quality soilless mix (such as ProMix C). The total required over the life of the plant will be 2.5 to 3 cu. ft.

A 1/2 or 3/4 inch thru-hull fitting with sealing O-rings.

Flexible drainage tubing which will fit onto the thru-hull you are using and of sufficient length to drain waste solution to the location where the solution is to be disposed of.

2. Prepare the pails to be a part of the garden.

A. Cut the bottom out of two of the pails leaving the bottom rim in place. (1 in short season areas)

B. Drill a hole in the side of the pail with the bottom still in it as close to the bottom as will allow the thru-hull fitting to be properly installed. Install the thru-hull fitting in the hole.

C. Set the pails with no bottom inside the pail which still has a bottom so they are in effect nested.

D. Place the gravel or hydrostone in the bottom of the pails so the drain (thru-hull fitting) is covered by 1" of material.

E. Fill the container to a depth of at least 12" with the soilless mix.

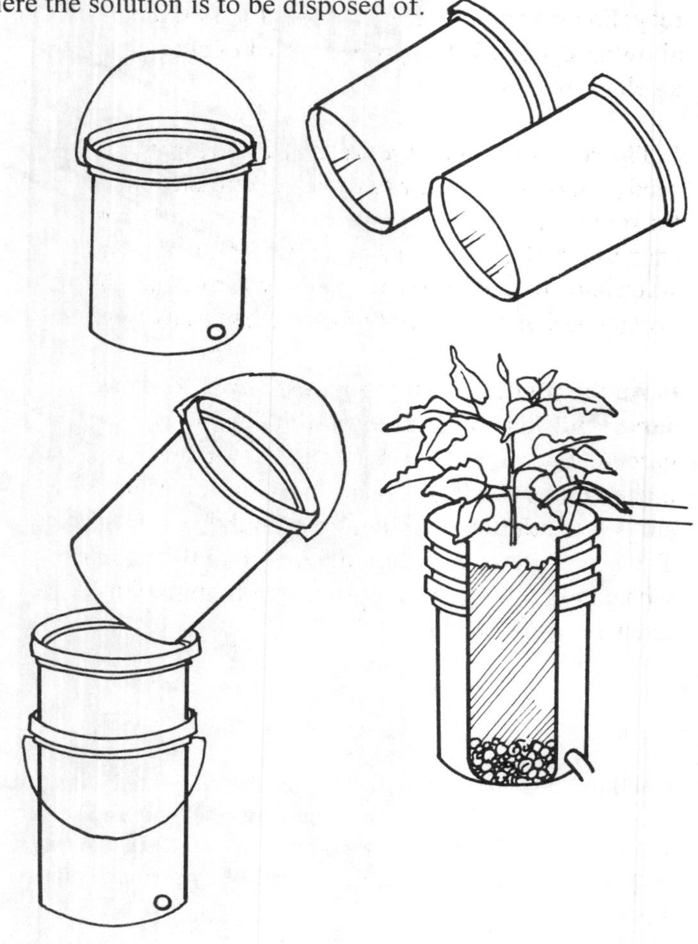

3. Place the "potato pail" in a high light location in your hydroponic garden. Keep in mind that potatoes have environmental requirements very similar to those you would provide for tomatoes. The best results will be obtained in a greenhouse under high light conditions.

4. Install irrigation drippers to feed the "potato pail." The size and volume will vary with the type of garden to which the "potato pail" is being connected. Since a large volume of media is involved compared with most hydroponic systems it is necessary to experiment a bit to match the time and dripper flow to the container size. The bottom reservoir in the "potato pail" will allow more infrequent irrigation than is usually required in your garden. Since this is essentially a drain to waste set-up it will affect the solution usage in recycling systems.

Connect the drain tubing and direct the waste to a convenient drain. This can be the reservoir in a recycling system if sufficient height is available to allow unrestricted plant growth with the container in an elevated position.

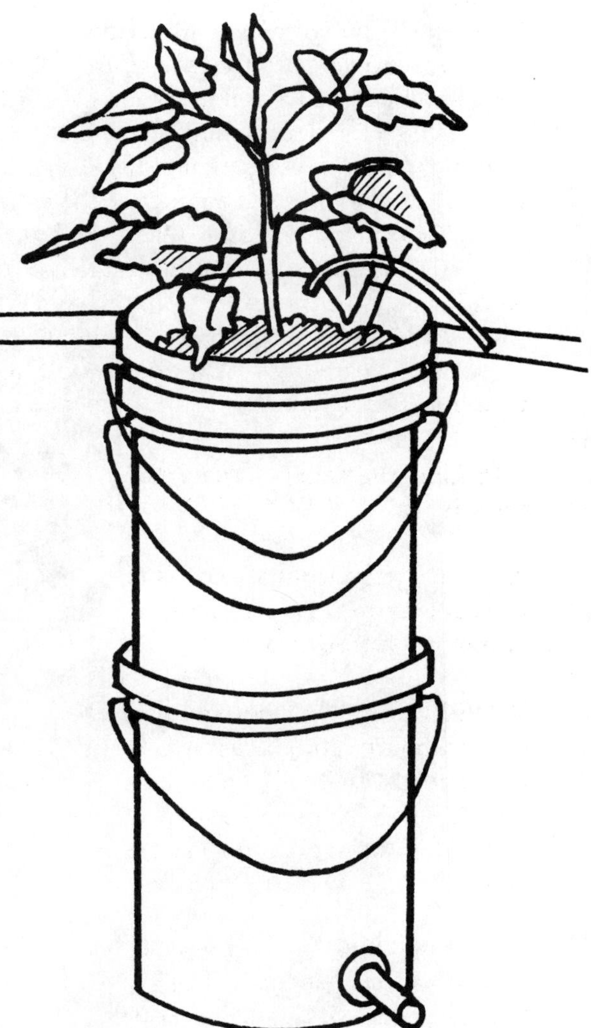

5. Thoroughly wet down the media and plant your seed potato, potato eye or in unusual circumstances the transplant. To get a jump on the season you can start the "potato pail" inside under lights by hand watering the container. It is easily moved to the greenhouse or outdoor hydroponic system any time.

6. As the plant grows it is quite simple to do the same "hilling" as you would do in the outside garden. Each time the foliar growth reaches 18 inches above the media, raise one of the inner shells and fill in additional soilless mix to the new level. The new soilless mix should be thoroughly wetted with nutrient solution immediately and tamped down to ensure the cavities are filled.

THE RAGE SYSTEM
DRAIN TO WASTE; THAT DOESN'T

The crop looks good and is quite typical of a good grower, but a look to the grow bags shows quite a different system. Drain to waste without the waste. When the solution is fed to the sawdust bags it drains into the gullies and goes nowhere, other than back into the root zone of the plants. I can hear the winces now from readers as they imagine the possible disease problems and dredge up all the nightmare stories heard in the past. Not one drop of water is wasted and the plants are healthy.

This system did not evolve overnight. When he began growing in the greenhouse Ivor couldn't keep a cucumber crop alive for more than two months before disease killed it off. After a year of this most growers would have given up in despair and gone back to the field. Not Ivor. He decided that the level of work involved was ridiculous and would probably wear him out and that he was going to keep growing cucumbers. He does have a stubborn streak. First he identified where his disease problem was coming from and then he stopped it cold without the use of chemicals.

The problem was with *Thielaviopsis*, a root fungus which was coming from the soil. Sitting the bags on the soil in a drain to waste system was an invitation to disaster. So Ivor spread the ground with a good layer of lime and covered this with plastic. He then spread another layer of lime on the plastic and covered with another layer of plastic. Instantly, no more Thielaviopsis. In addition there was the benefit of eliminating the soil as a laying area for thrips. Now his thrips problem is limited to the aerial portion of the plants where the predators (cucumeris) can handle them.

Then he took a look at the growing system which wasn't working for him and threw away the rule book. His solution was to use what I can only call a modified system modeled on the floating gardens in Mexico. The irrigation lines became the flow which refilled his miniature lake.

Proper operation of this system did not happen overnight. Ivor had experimented for 10 years before he felt he could adequately read all components of the system at a glance. In the original greenhouses the irrigation scheduling is modified by the level of water in the gullies related to the time of day and the weather conditions. In the new range this is all done by an excellent computer system designed and supplied by Argus Controls.

Ivor uses the colour and condition of the algae growing in the gullies to tell him the oxygen content of the water. He must be good at it because the plants send out roots into the gullies which are long, robust and white. Irrigation every 20 minutes is an important factor in maintaining oxygen levels. Disease simply is not happening in the gullies.

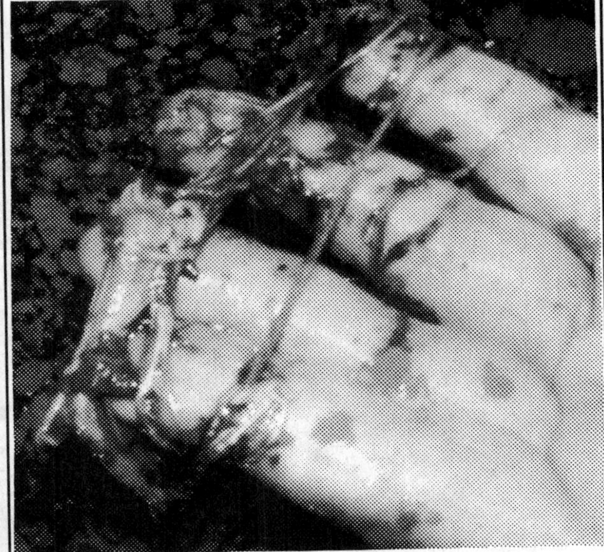

The roots are white and healthy in spite of the algae soup in which they grow.

Ivor also relates the condition of the plants to the solution in the gullies. Last year the plants were not happy and he could not find the cause. Samples were taken for analysis and the results showed excess phosphorus. Tracking back in the system led to the new injectors Ivor had just installed. They were more accurate and efficient than the ones he replaced and needed to be set properly.

The pH and EC of the solution in the gullies can alter dramatically over a 24 hour period. EC will range from 2 to 7 while there is a similar range for the pH. When taking pH readings it is important to screen algae out of the sample as it causes the sample to read more alkaline than the solution itself. Evaporation from the gullies during the day must also be factored in when allowing for the fluctuation in EC in the gully when figuring out the EC of the feed water.

By nightfall there is at least a gallon of water per plant in the gully. By sunup the solution is almost gone, suggesting a high level of metabolic activity overnight especially from sundown to around midnight, depending on the time of year. One of the safeguards of the system over recycling is that once the water is in the gully it stays there. If there is a waterborne disease it is isolated in the gully and not shared with the rest of the greenhouse.

Part V
Propagation

Chapter 15
TECHNIQUES, TIPS & TRICKS

For many outside gardeners this is a matter of tossing seeds and hoping for the best. Others make their annual trek to the local garden center and buy transplants at inflated prices from a limited selection of varieties. For the hobby hydroponic gardener propagation is an opportunity to enhance production, and incidently save a lot of money. There are many excellent books on propagation available and if you don't have one I recommend 'The Secrets of Plant Propagation' by Lewis Hill.

Typically the hydroponic garden will need fewer transplants than an outside garden at one time but for many crops such as greens, transplants will be required over the season. For this reason it is a good idea to set up a propagation area which can handle both seed germination and cutting propagation for a variety of medias. For the sake of disease and insect control it is important that you do not buy transplants from garden centers or nurseries. The potential that you will contaminate all of the plants in your garden is too high.

Healthy transplants are the key to optimum production. Many growers begin their pest management programs during propagation. The plants in the top right tray show the effects of a single error in watering which will reduce overall yield by up to 15%. The loss can never be recovered.

Size

The size of the propagation area you require will depend on the size of your garden and whether you will be starting plants for other purposes such as a soil flower garden of annuals or new landscaping. The location of the area is quite flexible but it is important to have both heating and humidity control available. The higher humidity may be detrimental to some things in your home so you might wish to use a corner of a porch or a small area in the basement.

One of the most flexible systems for propagation is an ebb and flow table with a 400 Watt clear Metal Halide for light. This may seem like big bulb for propagation but seedlings do better under high light and to achieve the same light levels would require 20 four foot fluorescent tubes (10 with Silverlux reflectors). Both installation expense and operating costs are much higher for the fluorescents. This does not mean that for the gardener who requires very few plants that the fluorescents are not useful. Using Wide Spectrum Gro-Lux in Sliverlux reflectors with 1 four foot lamp for every square foot of propagation area is a good lighting system for a few propagation flats with domes to retain the humidity.

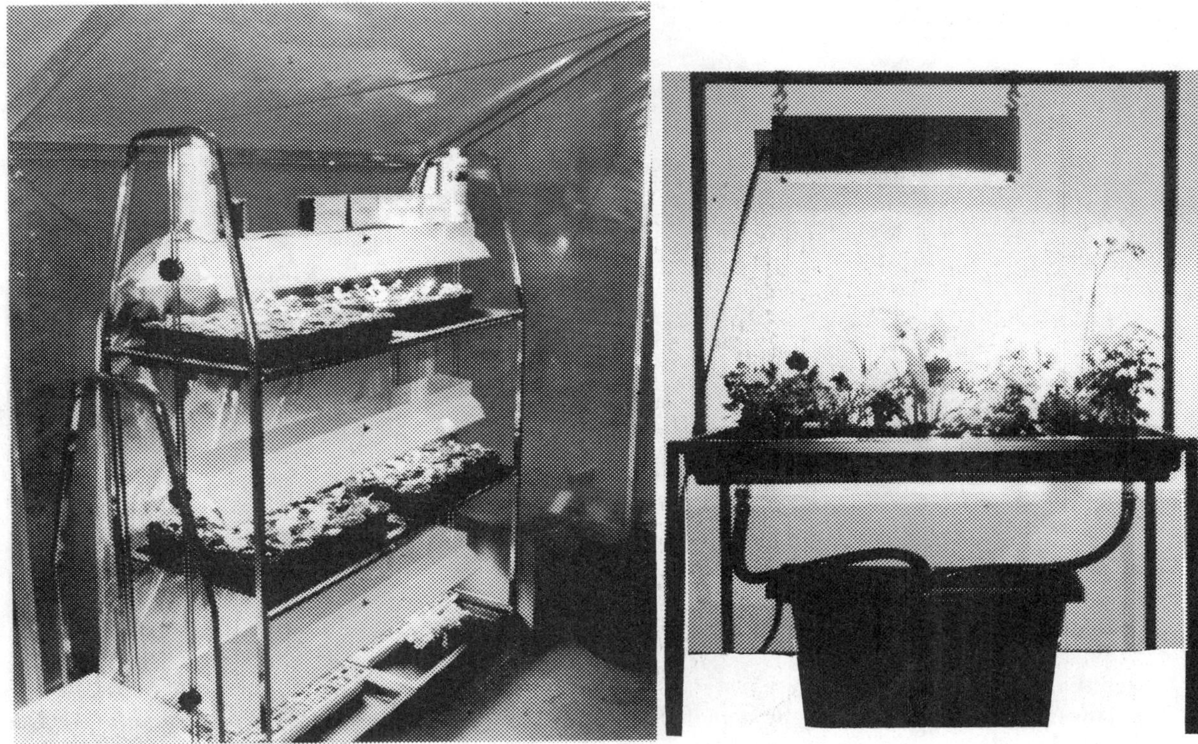

Above are two examples of systems which lend themselves to propagation for the hobby grower. Both are easily isolated to preserve light and humidity and both can be used to grow other plants such as orchids or herbs when not needed for propagation. The fluorescent unit requires hand watering while the 'Gardeners' Delite®' can provide completely automatic operation with higher light levels.

Scheduling

The first step in propagating any plant is to check out what the germination requirements are and how long it will take until it is ready to be transplanted into your garden. Some plants, such as tomatoes or peppers, will require more than one stage in propagation. The seeds will be germinated in a small bit of media (such as a rockwool cube) and then moved into a larger amount of media (such as a 4" rockwool block) for additional growth before being transplanted into the garden. Once you know the time requirements you will be able to plan your propagation scheduling and have plants ready for transplant when space is available or the weather will accomodate you. If your garden is indoors, or in a heated greenhouse, then the scheduling will be quite simple as the timing will not be weather dependent.

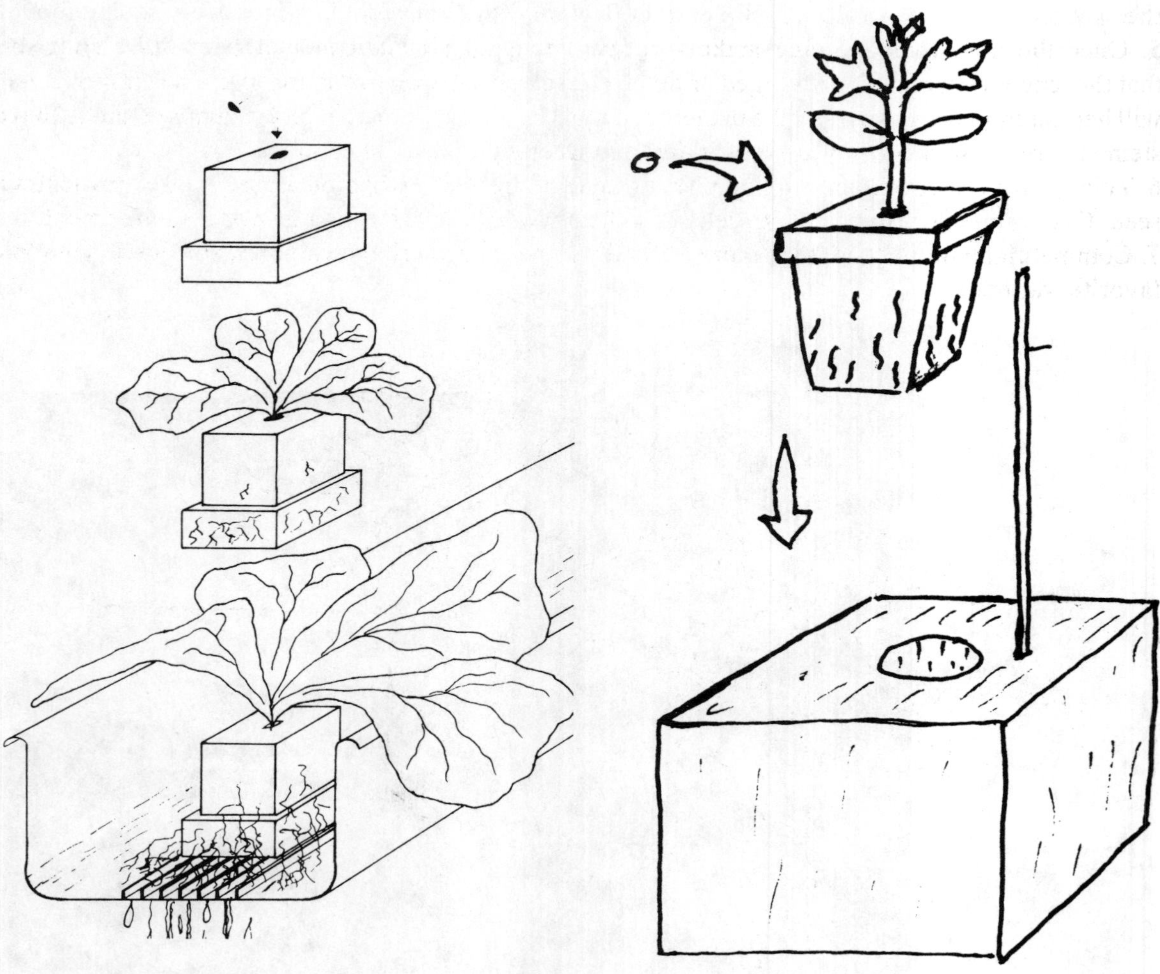

Scheduling propagation is more than just starting a seed and sticking it into a container to grow. If you want to get the maximum result during the available growing season it is often necessary to provide several stages of propagation before it enters the final growing environment. Along the way the plant may need support to reduce the potential of mechanical damage and the resulting disease. A strong transplant provides the best production, whether it is for a short term crop like lettuce in NFT or one of the 'long life crops' (tomato, pepper, cucumber, rose) in a drain to waste or recycling system. Transplanting at any stage should prevent root damage and maximize the economical use of available space, in addition to providing the plants you need when you need them.

There are some basics to keep in mind for propagation which will help you produce the best plants possible.

Seeds

1. Seeds do not do well under variable moisture regimes. Keep your irrigation regular so the media is consistently moist.
2. Do not apply any fungicides to prevent damp-off until the seeds have germinated. These materials tend to be germination retardents.
3. Start feeding the plants immediately upon germination. The food store in the seed is rapidly depleted and nutrients are essential to support the extremely rapid growth.
4. Growth promoters such as NutriBoost or Superthrive will help seedlings establish extensive root systems quickly. Soak the media with the recommended rate before planting the seeds.
5. Once the true leaves emerge make sure there is good air movement. Do not have so much that the tender tissue will be damaged or this will become a disease initiation site. The air movement will help strengthen the stems of the plants but vine crops such as tomatoes and cucumbers should have stem support as soon as they are moved into the second propagation container.
6. Your growing environment is unique. Try using varieties which will produce seed and save your own seed. Over time you will be able to select for the optimum plant for your growing environment.
7. Commercial hybrids tend to be more difficult to grow than heritage varieties, so stick to your 'old favorite' varieties.

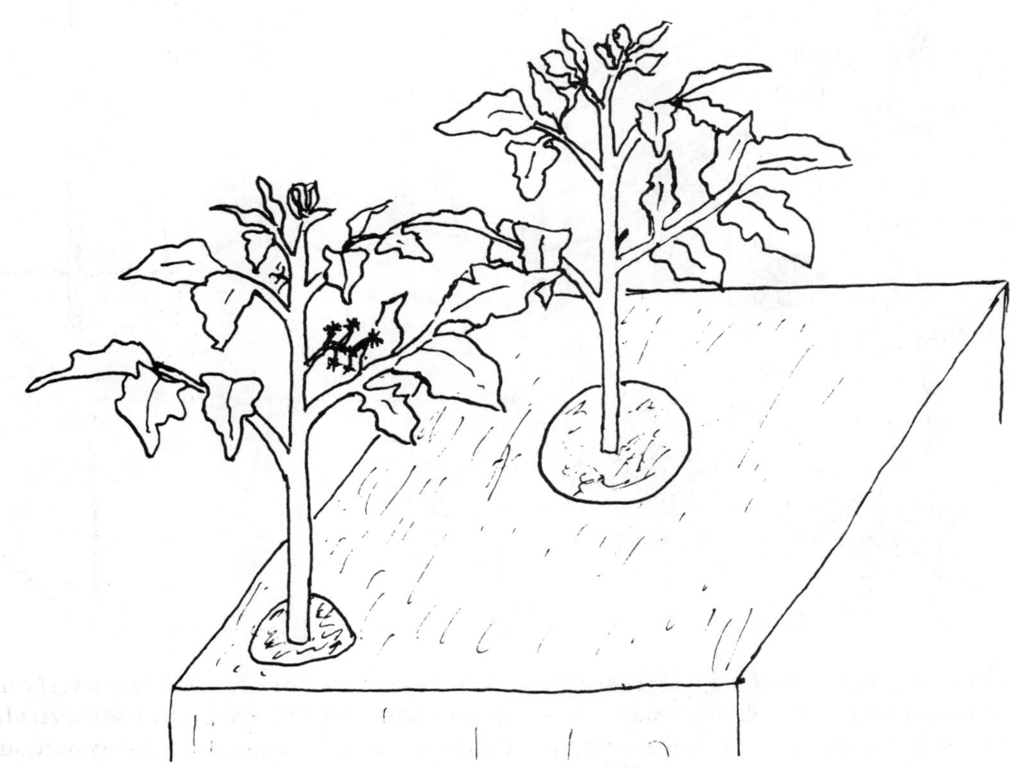

It is often necessary to graft the roots of one variety to another to obtain advantages such as disease resistance. In this situation it is best to have both seedlings in the same container or rockwool block. The seedling which is to contribute the root structure should be in the center of the media and the one which will contribute the aerial portion of the plant to the side or corner. Always do the grafting in two stages (2/3) joining of the stems, then complete separation, for best results.

Cuttings

1. Always use the 'Sip of Life' technique when taking cuttings. Take the cutting about an inch longer than required using a clean sharp knife. Place the entire cutting under water and cut again to the length required. This prevents the air bubble in the stem from being drawn further up the stem and choking the plant.
2. Cuttings are easier to root if they are placed in an area with a shorter daylength and lower light than where the parent plant is growing.
3. Root emergence will occur more quickly if promoters such as NutriBoost and Superthrive are used in addition to the rooting hormone dips.
4. Many plants respond more quickly if the temperature of the media is maintained at temperatures of 80°F, or even higher in some cases.
5. It is important to keep the upper portion of the plant at the lowest metabolic rate possible until root emergence occurs. This is achieved by keeping light levels down to about 25% of the plant growth levels and keeping humidity at 90% or higher.
6. Do not use a nutrient solution until roots have started to grow. Rooting occurs much more quickly if the plant has to 'go and look for food'.

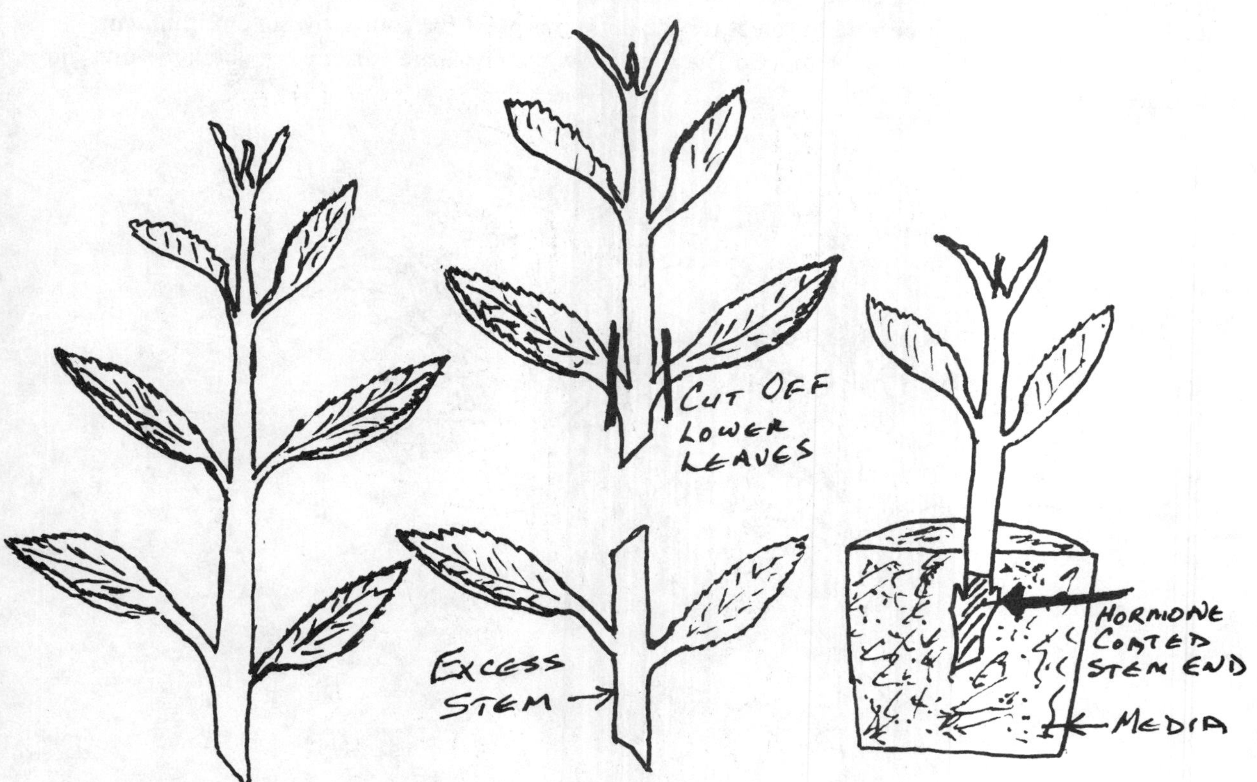

The 'Sip of Life' technique was originally developed by rose growers who also discovered that adjusting the environment had a positive effect on rooting cuttings. They place cuttings in a lower light, shorter daylength environment than the parent plant grows in. Once you have used a clean, disinfected knife to take your cutting (about an inch longer than required) place the cutting in a container of water and leave it there until you have taken all of your cuttings. Do all further cutting under water. Cut off the unwanted portion of stem and all unnecessary leaf material. Dip the cutting in rooting material and place immediately in the rooting medium or environment. This technique can be used to stabilize cuttings which are to be stored for a period before use.

Part VI
The Care & Feeding of Nutrient Solutions

Plant nutrition is an area where you have the opportunity to learn a great deal and interact very directly with the nutritional requirements of your plants. I mention this in spite of the fact that over 99% of hobby growers and over 70% of commercial growers use commercially prepared formulations of one type or another. Not a situation I agree with but, one of the facts of the industry. For those who really want to take control of their garden and tune plant nutrition to the maximum, get a copy of "Hydroponic Nutrients, Easy Ways to Make Your Own." It contains all of the latest research information and an extensive discussion of how to create nutrient formulas. It is the book to get if you really want to get the maximum from a hydroponic system.

For the average grower who uses a commercially prepared formula there is still a basis of information which will make gardening easier. There is more to running a good system than simply buying a formulated nutrient and dumping it into water. To begin with you need to know what is in your water supply.

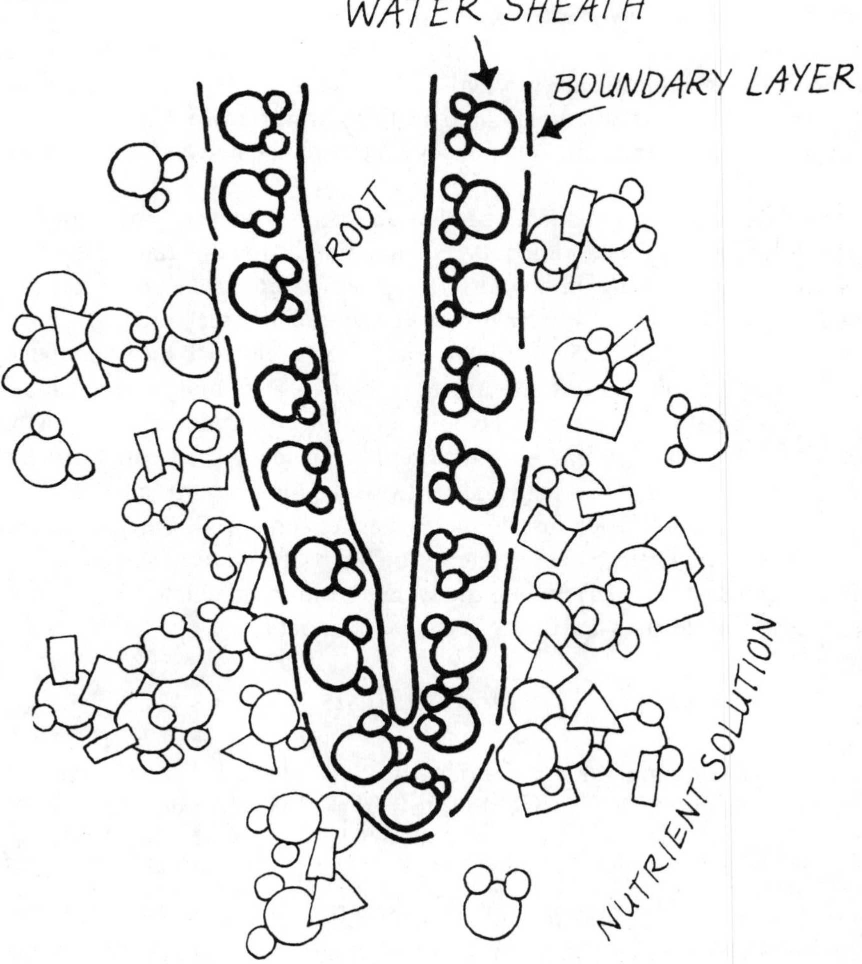

This diagram is an imaginary illustration of the environment surrounding the feeding root in a water culture system. Much more research is required before we are sure of the real picture.

Chapter 16
WATER

Water is both a nutrient and the foundation of nutrient formulation. This is a subject which is fascinating and I could, and have, written dozens of pages on it. That would be too much for the beginner but there is an aspect of water behavior that explains why hydroponic gardens require very specific irrigation control.

Water is the only substance necessary to the existence of every living organism on this planet. Yet, every living organism has evolved different ways of handling water. Plants are no exception and Bruce Bugbee at Utah State University has developed a computer model of what happens when water surrounds plant roots. Although there is currently no way of viewing the real version of the model Bruce has developed, it can help explain many confusing aspects of plant growth.

Essentially the computer model illustrates a water jacket forming around the plant roots. We are all familiar with the bonding power of water molecules. The surface tension of water allows small insects to walk on and the bonding strength of the water molecules makes possible the capillary action of many materials which enables water to run uphill.

When water bonds to different materials such as roots the bond involved is not quite the same as that involved in surface tension or capillary action. The result is the water molecules in direct contact with the root are oriented to the root rather than to the body of water which may exist in the root zone. This difference in bonding creates an invisible boundary layer between the root sheath and the surrounding water.

Although it is invisible, this boundary can have a major influence on the uptake by the root of both water and dissolved minerals. The impact was dramatically demonstrated when NFT culture was first introduced to commercial scale production. 189 growers went broke before the proper irrigation scheduling was discovered and NFT finally became commercially feasible.

Indications are very strong that the problem was directly related to the permanence of the water sheath around the feeding roots. This reduced the movement of essential minerals and oxygen below levels essential for plant growth. The sheath layer is only molecules thick, thus when the roots take in a water molecule one is drawn into the sheath to replace it, leaving essential minerals behind the invisible barrier in many cases, unless the water draw of the plant is extremely high.

This water sheath and surrounding invisible barrier have a significant impact on the way irrigation and nutrition is handled in every water or media based cultural system. Each system must create sufficient root stress that the flow into the water sheath is adequate to draw both oxygen and minerals with the water molecules across the invisible boundary.

Water Analysis

A water analysis is essential for any size of garden. I don't know what the situation is where you are but my experience has shown that the best thing to do is get an independent lab to do a basic analysis on your water supply. Even municipal water sources can have some nasty surprises. Keep in mind that commercial formulas are normally prepared on the presumption that the water to be used contains a minimum of minerals. Many of the problems with these formulas result from existing mineral content in the water. More than once new growers have found it necessary to treat their water source to make it fit for human consumption as a result of a water analysis, so there can be substantial side benefits for you.

ILLINOIS EPA — ILLINOIS ENVIRONME. .TAL PROTECTION AGENCY — .HEMICAL ANALYSIS REPORT FORM

DIVISION OF PUBLIC WATER SUPPLIES

1. Public Water Supply Name: Park Forest
2. County: Cook County
3. Facility Number: 0314740
4. Mail Report to: Name:

Post Office: Park Forest State: IL. Zip Code:

COLLECTOR: Fill in shaded area only. Type or use black ball point pen. See reverse side for explanations and instructions.

This Agency is authorized to require this information under Ill. Rev. Stat., 1979, Chapter 111-1/2, Section 1019. Disclosure of this information is required. Failure to do so may result in a civil penalty up to $10,000.00 and an additional civil penalty up to $1,000.00 for each day the failure continues, a fine up to $1,000.00 and imprisonment up to one year. This form has been approved by the forms Management Center.

Samples scheduled during: APR 1986

Received by:

Date and time in Laboratory: 1986 APR 17 AM 11: 12

5. Date and time collected: 4-16-86 11:00 am
6. Sample Collector:
7. Telephone Number:
8. Sample Type:

☒ Distribution: Sampling point address or building: Village Hall 200 Forest BLVD.

☐ Raw-Well # ____ Depth: ____ Year Drilled: ____

Pumping rate: ____ gpm Hours pumped: ____

☐ Raw-Surface: Inlet depth ____ ft.

Source: ____

Parameter	Reported As	MAC mg/l*	Concentration mg/l*
Ammonium	N		0.30

```
Parameter              As    [MAC]     Conc.
---------------------------ms/1---ms/1--
Iron                   Fe    [1.0]     0.04
Manganese              Mn    [0.15]    <0.005
Calcium                Ca    [---]     15.
Magnesium              Mg    [---]     18.0
Sodium                 Na    [---]     96.
Potassium              K     [---]     4.9
------------------------------------------
Aluminum               Al    [    ]    0.01
Barium                 Ba    [ 1. ]    <0.005
Boron                  B     [-----]   0.62
Cadmium                Cd    [0.010]   <0.003
Chromium-T             Cr    [0.05 ]   <0.005
Copper                 Cu    [ 5. ]    0.003
Nickel                 Ni    [-----]   <0.003
------------------------------------------
Silver                 Ag    [0.05 ]   <0.005
Zinc                   Zn    [ 5. ]    <0.002
Beryllium              Be    [-----]   <0.0005
Cobalt                 Co    [-----]   <0.005
Strontium              SR    [-----]   0.140
Vanadium               V     [-----]   <0.004
------------------------------------------
```

Parameter	Reported As	MAC mg/l*	Concentration mg/l*
Fluoride	F	1.8**	1.09
Chloride	Cl		16.
Nitrate + Nitrite	N	10	0.11
Sulfate	SO_4		22F.
Alkalinity (pH 4.5)	$CaCO_3$		74.
Specific Conductance @ 25°C	mmhos/cm		700.
Total Dissolved Solids/EC	TDS		420.
Filterable Residue @ 180°C	TDS		432.
pH	pH units		9.1
Hardness	$CaCO_3$		105.
Cyanide	CN	0.2	<0.005
Soluble Silicates	SiO_2		6.7
Arsenic	As	0.05	<0.001
Lead	Pb	0.05	<0.005
Mercury	Hg	2. µg/l	<0.01 µg/l
Selenium	Se	.0.01	<0.001

-Laboratory Use Only-

Laboratory Number: M6-286 CHAMPAIGN B005427

Date Forwarded: MAY 28 1986 By:

* Unless Otherwise Indicated

** For those counties of the State North of and including Henderson, McDonough, Fulton, Tazewell, McLean, Ford and Iroquois the MAC is 2.0 mg/l.

IL 532-0761
PWS-31 (Rev. 9-81)

Water analysis reports can be confusing for the uninitiated. If you do not understand the information there are many sources of help from local universities, research stations, extension agents, suppliers, and other growers. This report is one of the very important steps to successful garden operation.

Conditioning water

Once you know what your raw water contains you can find out exactly what treatment it needs. There are three types of potential problems you can encounter:

A: Suspended solids which can be filtered out.

There are inexpensive filters in a wide range of sizes and screening effects so this is usually an easy problem to solve. There are some things which will make operation easier. If there is a lot of material in the water use several filters with decreasing screen size. Wherever possible use screens which can be washed or back flushed instead of media filters which will require replacement and be an ongoing expense. If a media filter is required make sure it is the last filter in line. This will help prolong its life and increase efficiency.

B: High mineral content.

My first response to this problem is to move to having the grower mix his/her own nutrients where ever possible. This is by far the simplest solution and actually reduces costs of operating the garden.

Using higher overdrain rates in drain to waste systems and changing the reservoir more frequently can let you get away with using a marginal water supply especially if the problem is sodium which is the most expensive element to remove from water.

If the problem is severe, collect rainwater. Even if there is not enough for all requirements, it can often be stretched by mixing in some of the problem water to achieve a compromise which can be dealt with using the first response.

Some minerals can be filtered out with specialized filters, eg. iron, to bring levels down to tolerable. These are the filters which should be last in the line of filters as they do tend to be expensive.

One trick which has proven useful is to put one or more pairs of magnets on the line to increase the ability of water to carry the minerals. The new ceramic magnets are inexpensive and have very long useful lives. I have found them effective on water with both high iron and calcium. Install the magnets on the line before the filters.

To really 'clean up' a water supply there are two expensive options available, distillation and reverse osmosis. For the hobby grower they will only be feasible if required to make the water fit for human consumption.

C: Disease causing organisms.

There are four ways to treat water containing disease causing organisms; heat, UV, chlorine, and ozone.

Heat treatment is the process of raising the temperature of the water to at least 95C (203F) and holding it at that temperature for at least 30 seconds. This can cost a lot of energy and the water will take time to cool before it can be used. There are ways of reducing the energy cost but they are not feasible for the hobby grower.

UV treatment is effective but not recommended in hobby systems where control may be questionable. The UV lights are dangerous and can easily blind the unwary. Additionally you have to make sure all of the water is treated which can mean either a very low flow or an expensive installation.

Chlorine is a North American staple for treating municipal water supplies. The problem is that chlorine is a plant nutrient and the tolerance of the plants is very low. If you use chlorine you will have to make sure the treated water is very thoroughly aerated for at least 24 hours before you use it in the reservoir. A word of caution here. Some municipalities are moving to the use of 'chloramines' for water treatment. This process is deadly for plants, animals, and fish and will make your nutrient solution virtually impossible to control without some expensive pretreatment.

Ozone has long been used in Europe and is the most cost effective and efficient way of killing organisms in water. It is far more effective than chlorine. It is necessary to use a commercially designed generation system which has been properly approved. Don't worry, the ozone will not cause an environmental problem, it will exist for only a matter of seconds before the ozone reverts to a stable form. There is the added advantage that the ozone will also cause some heavy metals to precipitate out of the water. Handy if that is a problem with your water. A word of caution. If you do use ozone make sure the water is not accessible for at least 20 minutes after treatment, just for a real fail safe margin.

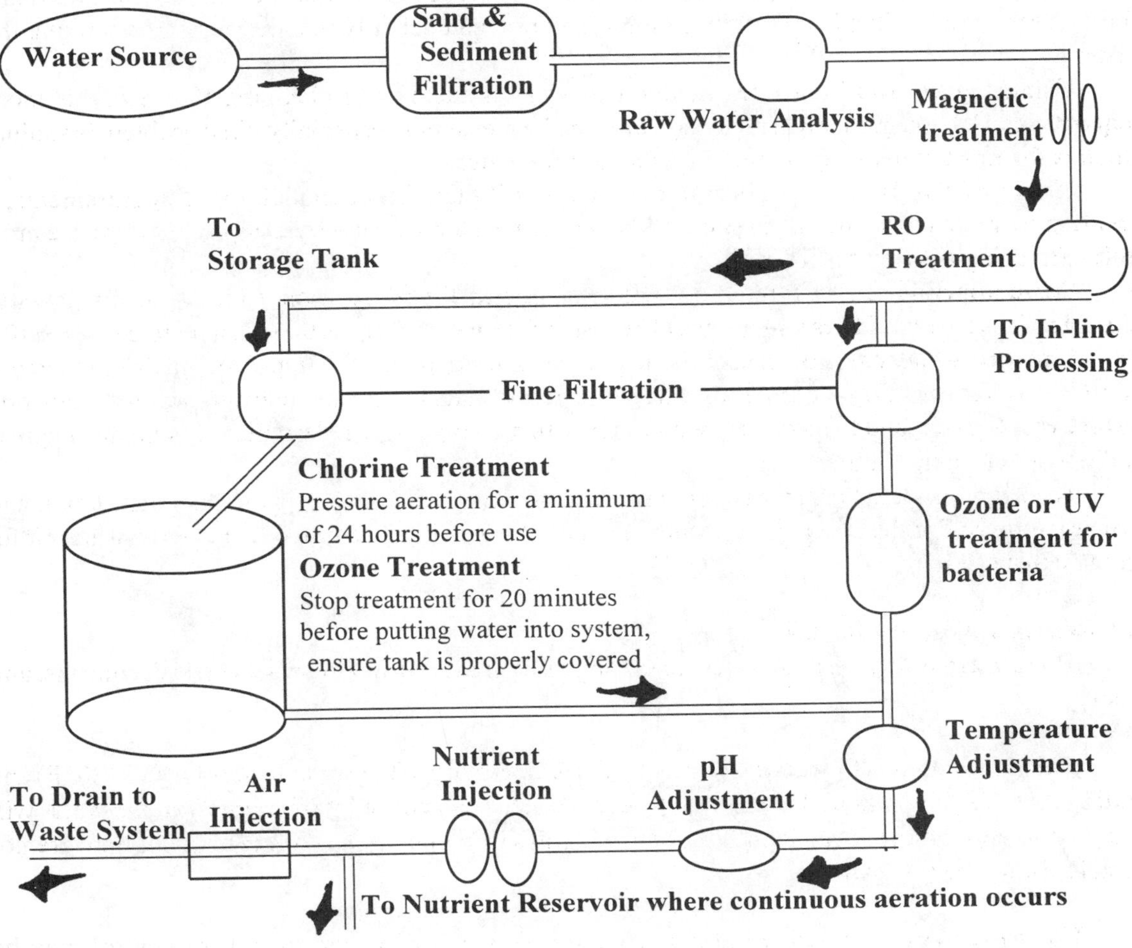

This diagram shows the logical sequence of water treatment and conditioning including all available types of treatment. For severe water problems growers are advised to have an expert design the system so that money is not wasted in treatment. Few hobby growers will have to use such an extensive type of system. Note that the only treatment after the nutrients are put into the water is aeration.

D. Pesticides and insecticides

Unfortunately these are becoming more common contaminants in water supplies. They are carried in urface runoff from farm fields, air borne sprays from surrounding property. The percolation of water carries these nasties down to the water table and aquifers where they can travel for hundreds of miles. There are simple and inexpensive tests available to check water for this problem and if it does exist you may have to find another source of water. In the event a problem is identified you will have to turn to experts to learn the proper handling procedures.

These problems will change over the year if your water is coming from a 'live water source', one which is directly affected by seasonal precipitation and fluctuations in response to environmental changes. These days that includes many municipal water supplies, so you would be wise to do an analysis three or four times during the first year.

No matter what treatment is required there is one rule to keep in mind, **'Do all of your raw water conditioning and treatment before the water goes into your reservoir'**. Growers have learned the hard way that treating a nutrient solution is the perfect recipe for creating problems. Once the solution is in the system, do not use water treatment procedures.

What your neighbours have done can affect your water supply immediately, and these sources are relatively easy to identify. Blowing pesticides from aerial applications nearby. Surface runoff from field applications. What you don't see can be even more trouble as the applications from previous years work their way down into the watertable and further down into aquifers so you may find residues from applications many miles away showing up in your water supply.

Chapter 17
HYDROPONIC NUTRIENTS

Buying hydroponic nutrients should not be a case of buyer beware but, unfortunately it is. Many small retailers see the opportunity for a fat profit and mix a bunch of salts without really knowing what they are doing. Many large companies have formulas which are fine as long as you realize that you have to add what is missing. Again these products are often repackaged by unscrupulous retailers and vital information is missing from the label. So how can you tell the good from the bad? Lets start with a few general rules;

Liquid nutrients are always costlier than powders.

Any single solution nutrient is the most expensive.

Any single powder formulation is not a complete viable formulation.

All powders should be 100% water soluble.

Avoid any nutrient which lists only NPK and doesn't tell you what all the other contents are very specifically (% or PPM).

The cheapest nutrients are the ones you make yourself.

Buying the cheapest commercial formulations can be a very big mistake. If in doubt, ask for references to other growers using the formulation.

Find out the qualifications of the person who developed the formula. Even the 'big companies' can put out some real lemons.

It is important to understand some basic information about plant nutrients to protect yourself and your plants.

First the traditional NPK numbers used on lawn fertilizer are useless as a source of information. Most gardeners are familiar with these N P K numbers on every fertilizer of any type manufactured today. Very few gardeners know what these numbers mean.

FOR EXAMPLE:
What does 20-20-20 really mean?
Is it as most gardeners think?

20% Nitrogen (N)
20% Phosphorus (P)
20% Potassium (K)

NO IT IS NOT!

WHAT IT REALLY IS,
20% Nitrogen (N)
20% Phosphorus Pentoxide (P_2O_5)
20% Di-Potassium Oxide (K_2O)

WHICH TRANSLATES IN ACTUAL % OF N P K TO:

20% Nitrogen (N)
8.8% Phosphorus (P)
16.6% Potassium (K)

You need to know what precise elements are in the fertilizer and in what proportion. Good products will also tell you what the final concentrations are at a variety of use rates.

Rather than attempt to make you an 'instant expert' on the subject of plant nutrition (after 20 years I am still learning) following is a list of the elements which need to be supplied in a complete formulation and the relative amounts. Please understand this is not a list engraved in stone nor is it 'perfect'. It is a basis of comparison which was originally developed as the best compromise to grow over 38 varieties of plant in one garden and have them all do well.

Hydroponics gives the gardener a control over the feeding of plants which is not available in any other type of garden. For the purposes of this discussion we are defining hydroponics as any system of growing in which we are feeding the plant not soil or some other substrate. In other words the nutrients are dissolved in water and as such are immediately available to the plant.

To accomplish this it is necessary to use
Nutrients which are in fact complete nutrients;
NOT soil supplement fertilizers.

There is no soil supplement fertilizer which is a complete nutritional package for a plant. In addition soil supplement fertilizers are generally made from a lower grade of ingredients than hydroponic nutrients. This means an unwanted level of contamination in soil fertilizers.

Good Hydroponic Plant Nutrients
will contain all of the elements necessary for plant growth
In The Proper Ratio To Each Other.

Many novice hydroponic gardeners are misled by reading the labels on plant foods without understanding the ratios which should be present. They assume that because all of the symbols are shown that all of the necessary elements are present in the proper quantities when nothing could be further from the truth.

The elements which must be in the nutrient formulation are divided into two groups;

The MACRO-ELEMENTS &
The TRACE ELEMENTS.

The MACRO-ELEMENTS ARE:		**% ratio**
Nitrogen	(N)	21.287345%
Phosphorus	(P)	6.244288%
Potassium	(K)	28.383127%
Calcium	(Ca)	21.287345%
Magnesium	(Mg)	5.960456%
Sulphur	(S)	11.353250%
The TRACE ELEMENTS ARE:		
Iron	(Fe)	4.825131%
Manganese	(Mn)	0.454130%
Zinc	(Z)	0.045413%
Copper	(Cu)	0.011352%
Boron	(B)	0.141915%
Molybdenum	(Mo)	0.005676%
Sodium	(Na)	0.000283%
Chlorine	(Cl)	0.000283%

You will note the ratios do not add up to exactly 100% but then I could have used a lot more decimal places too!

The ratios shown above are a general guideline only for a multi-crop hydroponic nutrient mix. The above balance of minerals will grow just about anything. There are additional elements which may have impacts on plant growth and physiology. At this time we simply do not have enough information to identify them accurately. Ensuring that you make all of the potentially unknown elements available in the naturally minute quantities is as simple as adding a teaspoon of seawater per gallon of nutrient solution.

Growth and yield of any plant species can be optimized by creating a formulation specifically designed for the variety being grown and the specific environment and cultural technique. The ability to manipulate the ratio's between the elements for various stages of growth is a precision tool available only to the hydroponic gardener.

Solution Manipulation

The second method of nutrient manipulation available to us is the concentration of nutrient solution that we use. The general guidelines that we follow are quite simple since they correspond to the different stages of growth of the plant. Common sense tells us that a small seedling is not going to require the same strength of solution, frequency of feeding, or formulation, as a ten-foot tomato plant carrying 10 trusses of fruit. The same common sense tells us a lettuce plant does not need as much food as that big tomato plant.

So how do we categorize the plants, the formulations and the concentration of nutrient solution required?

1. The age of the plant.

2. The stage of growth - seedling
- vegetative
- fruiting
- flowering.

3. The type of plant - tropical
- vegetable
  - green
  - fruiting
  - root
- flowers
- cacti & succulents
- trees & shrubs.

4. What we want the plant to do.

5. Where the plant is being grown
outdoors
in the greenhouse
indoors under lights.

Take the example of a pepper plant grown from seed then transplanted into a hydroponic recycling system with an aggregate in the pots.

For the sake of this example we will consider the strongest solution to be 100%. The specific methods of measuring concentration are covered in a later chapter. For the moment we will stick to simplicity

STAGE OF GROWTH	CONCENTRATION	TYPE OF SOLUTION
seedling	75%	rooting
transplant	100%	rooting
vegetative	100%	vegetative
flowers	100%	flowering
pepper growth	100%	flowering
ripening	75%	flowering
new flowers	100%	flowering
and so on.		

You will notice in the above example that I have combined both the solution strength and the manipulation of the element ratio at the various stages. In practice in small hydroponic systems, especially those with many different types of crops, we would simply use a single solution such as the one outlined in the above chart on the elements. The above example does however give you an idea of the type of manipulation available.

Don't let this discussion of solution manipulation scare you. A very wide variety of plants can be grown in a hobby system on a single solution. I once grew 38 different varieties of plants in the same garden with only one reservoir. Every plant did well, not up to commercial production standards but I harvested flowers, fruit and a wide range of greens plus some corn.

Garden Location Considerations

The solution strength and frequency of feeding are also affected by the type of hydroponic system you are using. No two systems are handled exactly the same in irrigation so never make the assumption that what you are going to do is the same as your friend who has a garden unless your garden is in fact identical to his in the identical environment with the same water supply.

This list is going to change depending on where you are growing the plant. Not necessarily the formulation used but there will be changes in concentration and what we consider to be 100% strength. The above list is for an indoor environment. Not all plants are grown indoors.

Outdoors we have the maximum potential light combined with a good air flow and relatively stable air (temp, humidity, CO_2) the plant will use the maximum amount of water relative to the amount of nutrients.

Move into the greenhouse and the temperature swings wildly, CO_2 depletion occurs quickly and humidity is on a roller coaster. This is potentially the most difficult environment in which to match what is going on in the aerial environment with what the concentration of the nutrient solution should be.

Indoors, life is easy, the light is constant (although generally lower than in other locations), air flow is steady as long as the fans are running, and it is simple to calculate how much fan power we need to replace the air to ensure stable humidity and CO_2.

With all of these different potentials how can we possibly make a reasonable decision on what to do with the nutrient solution? It is not as difficult as it may seem. All you have to do is keep some general relationships in mind.

The higher the humidity,
the less a plant will transpire (the less water it will take up).

The higher the air flow over the plants,
the more water they will transpire.

The higher the temperature,
the higher the transpiration rate.

The higher the light levels,
the more water the plant will transpire relative to the amount of nutrient used.

The higher the transpiration rate,
the lower the nutrient concentration we will deliver to the plants.

There will be situations where all of the environmental factors which increase transpiration will be working together and somewhere they will be conflicting. Where they all work together, the transpiration rates will be the highest or the lowest. When they conflict, the transpiration will be determined by the conflict. Balancing your control of the root environment to the aerial environment through manipulation of the nutrient concentration is a key to maximum productivity. The way to hone your skills is through experience, careful observation, and monitoring the nutrient solution concentration.

Solution Concentration

Concentration of the nutrient solution: what is it, and how do we measure it? Concentration is simply the ratio of nutrient to water in the solution. The more nutrient per unit of water the higher the concentration. How do we measure it? There are many meters, all of which work the same way, which are commonly used to measure concentration. The principle is simple, the meter measures how effectively the solution carries electricity. The result is provided in a range of scales which make for the 'different' meters.

The fact is they all tell you the same thing. It isn't the numbers on the scale that matter, but what the change in those numbers is over time. If your nutrient solution starts with a reading of 1 and 4 hours later reads 1.25 it is telling you your plants are taking up more water than nutrient so you should dilute the solution. If the reading starts at 1 and then changes to 0.75 it tells you the plants are eating a lot. What the exact numbers are doesn't really matter. How they change over time is what tells the story. If the numbers rise the plants are thirsty, if the numbers fall the plants are hungry. So much for complex scientific sophistication, even I understand this.

Where do you take the readings in different systems?
For all systems the starting point is the same.

The freshly injected solution, or the solution in the reservoir, will give you one reading.

Once the solution has drained past the roots of the plants you get a second reading.

The change in the reading tells you what the plants want,

more water
(decrease the concentration because the concentration has increased) or

more nutrient
(increase the concentration because the concentration has decreased).

The testing gets a bit more involved if you are running a media based system because the media is holding on to both nutrients and water. The aggregates hold very little while organic media will hold quite a bit. It is the concentration in the media which is critical so the drain water is not going to tell the whole story because the media may be buffering changes. In this case you add another sampling point, the media itself. For this you will need a syringe with a rigid rubber tube attached which is long enough to poke down into the media. Take your sample immediately after irrigation once the drainage has stopped.

Chapter 18
THE ELEMENTS

Let's take a look at the elements found in all plants on analysis and the concentrations in which they are present as a range. This will give us a picture of all the elements required for healthy plant growth.

ELEMENT ANALYSIS OF PLANTS SHOWN AS A RANGE
Based on Dry Weight

THE FREE ELEMENTS

Carbon (C)	=	30 - 45 %	
Hydrogen (H)	=	- 6 %	
Oxygen (O)	=	30 - 50 %	

THE MACRO ELEMENTS

Nitrogen (N)	=	0.2 - 4%	
Phosphorus (P)	=	0.3 - 3%	
Potassium (K)	=	0.3 - 3.5%	
Calcium (Ca)	=	0.1 - 10%	
Magnesium (Mg)	=	0.05 - 1.0%	
Sulphur (S)	=	0.2 - 2.0%	(high 7%)
Chlorine (Cl)	=	0.2 - 1.0%	
Sodium (Na)	=	0.1 - 1.0%	(high 15%)

THE TRACE ELEMENTS

Iron (Fe)	=	20 - 100 ppm	(high 1500 ppm)
Boron (B)	=	10 - 100 ppm	(high 600 ppm)
Zinc (Zn)	=	5 - 75 ppm	(high 600 ppm)
Copper (Cu)	=	1 - 25 ppm	
Manganese (Mn)	=	5 - 50 ppm	
Fluoride (F)	=	0 - 1.0 ppm	(high 800 ppm)
Molybdenum (Mo)	=	?	

The above chart is based on a dry weight analysis of a variety of plants. Plants are like people in that they are on the average 90% water before being dried to provide the above analysis. If we start by considering that a plant before drying is 100% weight and we then lose 90% of that weight by drying, we begin to get the relative value of the elements that we put into a nutrient solution into perspective.

THE FREE ELEMENTS

CARBON

Carbon forms up to 50% of the dry weight of a plant. It is not however an element which we include in our calculations for the creation of a nutrient solution.

HYDROGEN

Hydrogen is a major constituent of plant structure as a component of water in addition to comprising up to 6% of the dry weight of the plant matter. Supplying hydrogen to the plants is a simple enough matter since water is the base of our nutrient solution. Where hydrogen becomes a critical part of our formulation process is in the free hydrogen we introduce into the solution by our choice of the compounds used to supply the required elements.

OXYGEN

Oxygen pays a critical role in plant growth. First it is a major component of plants. More in fact than any other element. Oxygen is 88.81056% of water. Water is the solvent we use to dissolve all of the other elements used in feeding plants.

Plants obtain their oxygen from two sources EXTERNAL & INTERNAL. The external oxygen is oxygen taken in through the stomata on the leaves, oxygen taken in by the roots as a component of the water in the nutrient solution and the oxygen absorbed by the roots during the process of respiration. Internal oxygen is the oxygen liberated during the process of photosynthesis. Considerable amounts of this oxygen are released back into the air in combination with nitrogen and carbon.

THE MACRO ELEMENTS

NITROGEN

Nitrogen is a key element for controlling the oxygen levels in the plant as well as the rate of carbohydrate reduction in the respiration process. Plants can absorb nitrogen in the nitrate (NO3) form or as the ammonium ion (NH4). The oxygen from the nitrate form is used in the breakdown of the carbohydrates produced by photosynthesis. The nitrogen freed as a result is combined by the plant with hydrogen to form ammonium which is then further utilized by the plant.

Deficiency Symptoms

Plant light green; lower leaves yellow, drying to light brown colour. Stalks (stems) short and slender if element is deficient in later stages of growth. Growth is restricted and plants are generally yellow (chlorotic) from lack of chlorophyll, especially older leaves. Younger leaves remain green longer. Stems, petioles and lower leaf surfaces of corn and tomato can turn purple.

Toxicity Symptoms

Plants usually dark green in colour with abundant foliage but usually with a restricted root system. Potatoes form only small tubers and flowering and seed production can be retarded or reduced.

PHOSPHORUS

There is only one form of phosphorus available to the plant from the nutrient solution, PO_4. Once in the plant it is relatively mobile and found just about everywhere. Concentrations occur in the seeds, fruits and meristemic tissue. It is easy to understand why fruiting and flowering plants require more than green plants.

Deficiency Symptoms

This is a mobile element and symptoms appear first in older leaves.
There is commonly no necrosis of tissue.
Stunted, abnormally dark green plants usually with narrow petiole angles.
Abundant reddish or purplish pigmentation or leaves may appear bluish green or black.
Sometimes chlorosis of older leaves.
Roots may be yellow brown in colour.
Stem may be slender similar to nitrogen toxicity.
In extreme cases the growing point will be affected.

Toxicity Symptoms

Overall symptoms are:
General yellowing of older leaves, older leaf tips and margins later become yellowish or brownish, followed by coloured necrotic spots. Leaf abscission develops (similar to potassium deficiency in some plants and nitrogen excess in others).Initially mature leaves may appear 'crushed' or wrinkled.
Older leaves may 'brighten' in colour while others appear to go dark green.
In extreme cases leaf internodes will harden and bright dry spots or colour spots may appear on the leaves or fruits.

POTASSIUM

In plants, the meristemic tissues in general are particularly rich in potassium as are other metabolically active regions such as buds, young leaves and root tips. Potassium deficiency may produce both gross and microscopic changes in the structure of plants. The effects include leaf damage, high or low water content of the leaves, and decreased photosynthesis. Concentrations of this highly mobile element exist in the areas of high physiological activity.

Toxicity Symptoms

Seldom if ever occurs due to the fact plants do not generally over absorb potassium. However high levels can cause interactions with other elements such as magnesium, manganese, zinc, and iron, resulting in deficiency of these elements.

Deficiency Symptoms

As a mobile element - symptoms will occur first in the older leaves and move through the plant in reverse order to the ability of the plant parts to demand water.

Necrosis - older leaves first, initially at tips and between veins, more marked at margins
dicots - initially chlorotic
monocots - initially necrotic - tips & margins first
Newer leaves slightly darker than normal
There may be a general stunting of growth,
- small leaves
- downward cupping of leaves
- short petioles
-slender stalks (stems)
fruit - soft or puffy - poor shelf life
uneven ripening
foliar spray for correction of deficiency
- 2% potassium sulphate

CALCIUM

Although the highest concentrations of calcium are found in the leaves and seed coats, there is not a single cell which does not contain it. It is the foundation on which the cell structure is built. An absence or deficiency of calcium will stop plant growth totally.

Toxicity Symptoms

Excess calcium is seldom expressed by the plant as a direct toxicity symptom. Rather the symptoms which show are in the related elements such as iron, potassium, or magnesium.

Yellowing of whole leaves, interveinal spots in mature leaves.

Deficiency Symptoms

Pure calcium deficiencies are quite rare; even acid soils almost always have adequate calcium for normal plant growth. Because calcium is immobile within the plant, the deficiency is exhibited at the growing point and in fruit.

Because calcium is required for cell division and elongation, deficiencies first appear at root tips and other growing points. Weakened stems, premature shedding of blossoms and buds, and abnormal dark green colour of foliage are also symptoms of calcium deficiencies.

The inability of the plant to move calcium to the fruit or tubers can cause certain disorders once thought to be pathological in nature. Blossom end rot of tomatoes and bell peppers, bitter pit of apples, internal brown spot of potatoes, and tip burn in lettuce and cabbage, as well as other disorders, are attributed to localized calcium deficiencies. In many of the these disorders, it is too late to correct the problem once the symptoms are observed. Initial damage often occurs when the fruit is very small and the demand for calcium is greater than the plant can supply.

Plant Symptoms

It is important to note that plant symptoms may be a toxic response to other nutrients which are suppressing calcium uptake or an overall response to poor cultural or environmental conditions, in addition to the following symptoms.

Growing point: stunted with discoloration varying according to species.

Young leaves: marginal discoloration, upward curl, spotting depending on species, dry leaf margin, bright leaf between veins.

Fruit: cat facing, blossom end rot, mis-shapen fruit, buds abort or flowers do not set.

Older leaves: downturn, marginal chlorosis or discoloration.

MAGNESIUM

Magnesium is a key to the assimilation of CO_2 in plants. It is the final component of a chlorophyll molecule and the amount of chlorophyll present in the leaf determines the CO_2 assimilation capability of the plant. The other major role for magnesium is its function as a carrier of phosphorus in the plant. Magnesium is highly mobile and the result is that deficiency symptoms tend to occur in the older portions of the plant first. If you are monitoring chlorophyll content in the leaves then the older leaves will give a more accurate picture of the situation.

Toxicity Symptoms

These are seldom encountered. I have never seen a case or heard a report of one. If a grower were to make a mistake in formulation such as kieserite instead of epsom the result would be suppression of another cation with the resulting deficiency symptoms if the plant were to be adversely affected.

Deficiency Symptoms

This is a mobile element in the plant so the symptoms will appear in the older leaves first as an interveinal chlorosis. In cases of moderate deficiency the overall plant colour is a lighter green.

Deficiency of Mg results in loss of green colour, dead brown margins and spots in leaves, often bordered by broad yellow-orange bands. When plants are exposed to strong sunlight the Mg deficiency can result in a general withered appearance. Individual leaves suffering from Mg deficiency are stiff and brittle and the intercostal veins are twisted. Mg deficient leaves often fall prematurely.

The symptoms begin as purple brown 'rectangular' interveinal areas located close to the midrib and major veins of trifoliate leaves. These spots radiate outwards in a characteristic regular pattern. The spotted areas rapidly become necrotic and coalesce into larger scorched areas. The leaflets become generally bright pale green or yellow green then totally bleached.

SULPHUR

Sulphur is one of the base building blocks for plant proteins as well as for many other plant constituents, such as amino acids, coenzyme A (found in all living cells) plus vitamins thiamine and biotin. Adequate supplies of sulphur improve the chlorophyll supply. In legumes the number of root nodules are affected by the availability of sulphur. In other plants the size and health of the root system is affected by the adequate supply of sulphur. Because of the close relationship with nitrogen assimilation processes deficiencies of sulphur are quite often mistaken for nitrogen problems.

Toxicity Symptoms

Plants are quite tolerant of sulphur and symptoms do not usually show up until concentrations exceed 600 ppm in the solution or root zone. The salts used for formulation seldom yield concentrations this high in any formulas in common use.

There is a general hardening of the plant with a bluish-green coloration of the leaves. Leaves are smaller and stems become hard. Later leaves may curl inward and become pimpled similar to oedema.

Deficiency Symptoms

Because of the close relationship with nitrogen assimilation processes deficiencies of sulphur are quite often mistaken for nitrogen problems. Sulphur is another of the elements quite often found in water supplies so care must be taken to ensure the content is included in the formulation process.

Deficiencies should be rare in hydroponic cultures if full formulation solutions are used. They are more likely when 'supplementary formulas' are used for containers or hanging baskets. Symptoms are slow to develop and initially resemble nitrogen deficiency.

Plants are stunted and woody with slender stems. The entire plant may be light to yellowish green in colour. Chlorosis appears in older leaves and may be more pronounced in young leaves which will become yellow. Internodes are longer than normal and older leaves may be thicker than younger leaves.

CHLORINE

One of the main functions of chlorine appears to be as an enzyme actuator in the photosynthesis process releasing oxygen from water. Deficiencies appear to adversely affect the root structure and metabolism indicating a role in respiration as well. Extreme caution must be taken with chlorine in nutrient formulations. Usually sufficient exists in the source salts of other elements. If excessive quantities are present in raw water, the water must be aerated for 24 hours prior to use to eliminate the chlorine. Chlorine is also a critical factor in the drought resistance of plants because of its effect on tissue water content.

Deficiency Symptoms

Seldom encountered in hydroponic culture.

Toxicity Symptoms;

Leaves are small, dull green and the plant becomes woody. Excesses may also cause early flowering in tomatoes.

THE TRACE ELEMENTS

The Trace elements are so called because of the minute quantities required by the plants. These elements tend to be in the role of catalysts rather than fixed in any structure. They are quite mobile in the plant and the difference between optimum and toxic levels is minute indeed.

IRON

Iron acts as an oxygen carrier and as an enzyme catalyst. This makes iron critical to the processes of chlorophyll production, protein synthesis and respiration. It could be termed a photosynthesis regulator. Iron has a special relationship with manganese since it balances and prevents manganese toxicity. pH is critical to iron availability in the nutrient solution since under alkaline conditions iron combines very readily with phosphates, carbonates and the hydroxyl ions.

Toxicity Symptoms

With all of the antagonistic elements present in the solution this seldom occurs. I have never seen it. There is a possibility of occurrence after high concentration foliar application.

Deficiency Symptoms

Growing tips turn yellow to nearly pure white while the veins remain green (interveinal chlorosis). Younger leaves alone show interveinal chlorosis.

BORON

Boron influences and may even control the ratio in which anions and cations are taken in by the plant. The presence of boron enhances the uptake of cations and limits the uptake of anions. Carbohydrate and nitrogen metabolisms are influenced by boron as are the water relations of cell protoplasm and the formation of pectic substances in cell walls.

It is not unusual to find high boron content in some water supplies. Quite often where it exists in water sources the concentration is too high so the boron content of the water must be filtered and the boron removed from the nutrient formulation.

Toxicity Symptoms

Marginal and interveinal leaf scorch and chlorosis.

Deficiency Symptoms

Growing points die. Leaves later mottle slightly and flowers and stems roughen. Buds die, leaves become yellow-brown and curl inward.

MANGANESE

The function of manganese can be generally described as that of a catalyst. The highest concentrations occur in the leaves where manganese is involved in carbohydrate metabolism and chlorophyll formation. It also plays an important role in root aeration. In conjunction with nitrogen it accelerates plant growth.

Toxicity Symptoms

May show as calcium or iron deficiency symptoms. General symptoms; curling-in of leaves, death of the growing point and spotted or scorched leaf margins.

Deficiency Symptoms

Appear first in younger leaves, generally further away from the main stem, as tissue necrosis (leaf transparency) while veins retain their colour.

ZINC

Best described as a regulating catalyst zinc utilization is closely related to the quantity of light available to the plant. The higher the light levels the more zinc the plant will uptake and the result is higher metabolic activity. It is both an enzyme actuator and a component of the plant growth hormone indoleacetic acid.

Toxicity Symptoms

May manifest as Phosphorus or iron deficiency symptoms. Some plants have extremely high Zinc tolerance. Symptoms include a reduction in root growth and leaf expansion followed by leaf chlorosis.

Deficiency Symptoms

More common in summer under high light, high temperature conditions. Symptoms appear first in younger leaves which are abnormally mottled, with chlorotic spots and upward curl.

COPPER

The activity of copper in plant metabolism manifests itself in three forms: (1) synthesis of chlorophyll, (2) activity of enzymes, and (3) as an electron carrier. In leaves most of the copper occurs in close association with chlorophyll. Copper also influences the disease resistance of plants.

Toxicity Symptoms

Marked reduction in growth. Subsequent symptoms of iron chlorosis, reduced branching, thickening and darkening of rootlets. General stunting of the plant growth. Often caused by the application of copper based fungicides.

Deficiency Symptoms

Young leaf chlorosis, stunted growth, green-blue leaves and burned margins.

MOLYBDENUM

Molybdenum appears to be a factor in both nitrogen and carbohydrate processes as well as an enzyme coordinating catalyst. It acts as an electron carrier in the nitrate/ammonium reduction cycle and is involved with N_2 fixation.

Toxicity Symptoms

Not commonly noted. When observed a radical colour change in plant parts is seen.

Deficiency Symptoms

These can be mistaken for nitrogen deficiency. Interveinal chlorosis shows on the older or mid-stem leaves and moves up the plant. Leaves may also scorch or cup.

THE 'NON-ESSENTIAL' ELEMENTS

Our knowledge of plant nutrition has increased. We are becoming more aware of the interactions between plants and the root zone environment. The result is that we are discovering that there are elements which can help in creating a beneficial environment for plants. Their absence may not cause the plant to die as is required by the definition of an essential element, but when they are present the plant seems healthier.

This improved health can be a result of the plant actually metabolising the element as in the case of chlorine, an element once thought toxic. Or it can be related to the improved ability of the plant to combat fungal infection as in the case of certain forms of silicon. Another benefit observed with silicon in silicate form is the impact on the growth of certain micro-organisms in the root zone which inhibit disease organisms.

Other elements currently under intense investigation include sodium, and nickel. Where this will lead is unknown at this time but it does point out that the practise of including a teaspoonful of seawater per gallon of nutrient solution may have more basis in scientific fact than many growers think. For those with no easy access to seawater there is another alternative and that is pyrophyllite. This is a clay which contains traces of almost as many rare elements as seawater with the added benefit of providing silicon in plant useable form.

At this time it is not possible to provide accurate information on the same basis as for the 'essential' elements, but in the future I anticipate the information will improve and the list of 'beneficial' elements will increase dramatically.

Chapter 19
pH & EC

These topics do confuse growers of all types so we will look at the tools for measuring them before we get into the specifics. This way, you can follow cultural instructions without really needing to know what the underlying science is.

TESTING SOLUTION CONCENTRATION

What is - *Solution Concentration*?

In making up nutrient solutions we need a method of measuring how much nutrient is still in the solution after the plants have had a go at it. We can easily define how much fertilizer we put into the water at the beginning. For hobby growers the most common method used to discuss solution concentration is **Parts Per Million (PPM)**. How many parts of fertilizer are in every million parts of water. Understanding this is easier than it sounds as long as you use liters and grams. Metric is the measurement system which has been used by growers for many decades because it makes calculations so much easier. In metric both weight and liquid measures are related.

1 kilogram = 1000 grams
1 liter = 1,000 milliliters

For the sake of simplicity we consider that 1 gram occupies the same volume as one milliliter. So if we put one gram of fertilizer into 1000 liters of water we have one part fertilizer to one million parts of water

(1,000 x 1,000 = 1,000,000).
To convert your gallons to liters is simple math
1 Imperial gallon = 4.54 liters
1 U.S. gallon = 3.785 liters

Having the ability to talk about such small amounts of fertilizer is important because we use so little in a hydroponic nutrient solution. Where farmers talk about tons of fertilizer per acre we only need grams per liter. The instructions on the hydroponic fertilizer you use may tell you to dissolve 3 grams of fertilizer per liter of water in your reservoir, but after you turn the pump on you want to be able to track how much the plants are eating.

The only way to do this is to test the water on a regular basis using a meter. One point of confusion for many growers is the fact that they have put 3 grams of fertilizer in per liter of water. Which mathematically should be 3,000 PPM. When they then test the solution with their meter the reading may show only 2,200 PPM. The reason for this is simple. The fertilizer contains components such as water and oxygen which will not read on the meter.

For your purposes the simplest method is to mix up your solution according to instructions, then take a reading of the solution. Future readings of the solution will either be higher or lower than the first reading and it is this change which is important not the actual value of the reading.

Conductivity Meters EC & PPM

The reason for discussing only the electronic meters is simply that they are the only affordable one which works. Among the meters, which are essentially based on a very old principle, the Wheatstone bridge, there are many variations in the readouts which are offered. The meters all work on the electrical conductivity of the solution being tested.

These meters are available with readouts in micromos, millimos (EC = electrical conductivity) or parts per million (PPM). Hobby growers generally find it easier to use the PPM meters because this is the same scale most commonly used for describing hobby nutrient formulations.

It really doesn't matter which scale you use, they can be converted back and forth with ease. What is important is to know which scale you are using and to ensure that when you are getting advice or instructions you find out which scale the other party is using. By the way, none of these meters will identify the actual individual mineral content of the solution.

Choosing a Meter

There are essentials to the proper care and maintenance of a conductivity meter. These meters are available in a range of models. The features you should look for in the meter are as follows.

1. Calibration capability. Some meters feature an automatic calibration check which is very useful. Any meter you purchase should have a calibration adjustment. Standard calibration solutions are available to ensure accuracy.

2. Temperature Compensation - Manual or Automatic. Readings vary dramatically at different temperatures. It is important to be able to get an accurate reading at the temperature of the solution.

3. Properly designed probe. I still prefer the remote probe type of meter although I do use a pen type for quick checks. The inexpensive pens are quite adequate for the needs of a hobby grower. Experience with cup type probes has shown a tendency for leaks to occur around the cup in several brands. This leakage causes corrosion of the electronics and is not covered by warranty.

4. Accuracy. A good general meter should be accurate to 2% of full scale with a repeatability of within 1% for readings. A less accurate reading leaves the potential for quite inaccurate readings. Keep in mind a 2% error on a scale of 10,000 ppm is 200 ppm while the same error on a scale of 5,000 is only 100.

5. Scale. Obtain a meter which gives you readings within the range of the solution you will generally work with plus about 1,000 on either side of the high/low range you require. This will keep the meter readings as accurate as possible.

6. Power Supply. Batteries are preferred over adapters for consistent voltage supply and more accurate readings. Just remember to turn the meter off when not in use.

Care and Maintenance of Conductivity Meters.

The conductivity meter you use will look after you only as well as you look after it.

1. Calibrate the meter when you first take it out for the day.

2. Rinse the probe in distilled water after every reading and before putting the meter away. Leaving solution water on the meter will lead to salt build up and inaccurate readings.

3. Periodically rinse the probe in a solution such as 7% acetic acid vinegar to dissolve any salts which may have accumulated on the probe. Do Not use strong solutions of acid. Rinse the probe in distilled water before putting it away or using it.

4. Check your batteries regularly to ensure accurate readings.

5. Periodically examine the probe electrodes to ensure they are clean. Never use an abrasive material to clean the electrodes.

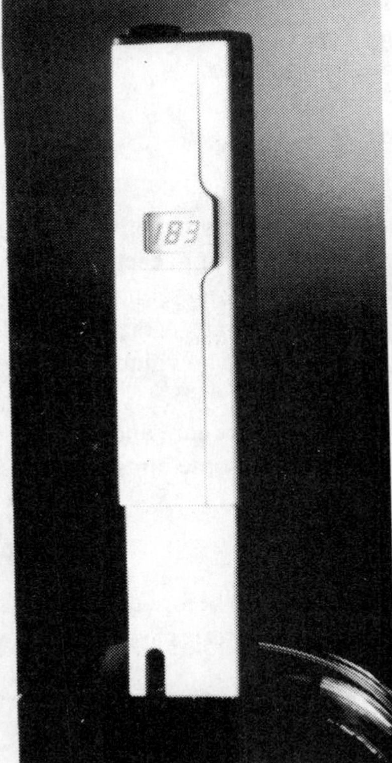

This is one of the 'EC pens' widely available to growers. Be sure to check that the meter you choose has the features and the range you require.

Keep in mind that your EC meter will not tell you what is in the water, only the total concentration of all salts you have added and the plants have not taken up. For hobby growers, the easiest way to correct problems is to dump the old solution and start over with a fresh one.

pH

Most gardeners have run across the term 'pH' at some point in time. In a hydroponic garden this term is much more important than in soil culture. pH is shorthand for 'potential hydrogen'. This is a reference to the balance of elements in solution or media as to the electrical charge carried by the elements or compounds. Luckily for the novice it is not necessary to understand all of the technical information behind pH. It is enough to understand that the scale exists, that we can easily test for it and adjust it in both solution and media to suit our needs.

The pH scale runs from 0 to 14. Many books on soil gardening publish lists of the pH preferences of plants. These lists are not accurate for hydroponic culture, but they can be used as a starting point if you are trying to figure out the right pH for your plants. The pH requirement in a hydroponic garden will be lower than for soil and the amount of reduction will vary according to the culture and the media.

Here is a quick guideline which will help you get started.

Water Culture 1.5 points lower
Non organic media Culture 1.0 points lower
Organic media Culture 0.5 point lower

Electronic pH Testers

In recent years a variety of these instruments have become available at very reasonable cost. The key component to each meter and the determiner of its accuracy is the probe. Any meter not using a proper glass bulb probe can be considered inaccurate. Metal probe "Hobby Meters" often sold in garden centers are of no value to any hydroponic gardener.

Electronic pH meters, or pens, require proper care and attention if they are to give accurate readings. Here are some hints which will extend the life of your probe.

1. **S**tore the meter away from extreme temperatures.
2. **C**alibrate the meter using a standard pH7 solution before each use.
3. **A**lways ensure the connections are tight and batteries are fresh.
4. **R**inse the probe in distilled water after each test.
5. **S**tore the probe so it is kept damp.

The word **SCARS** can be remembered so your meter is always properly maintained.

Keep in mind there are many ranges, accuracies and options available in pH meters so be sure your supplier provides a detailed care and maintenance list for your meter. If such a list is not available from the supplier, do your buying from a supplier who can provide this information.

This electonic pH pen is a good choice for the hobby grower. There are also models which commercial growers will find very useful for in-system testing.

Adjusting pH

The process of adjusting pH in both media and solution is a source of problems for many growers. There is a simple step by step process which will eliminate most of them.

1. pH adjustment should only be done on water after all filtration and other treatment of raw water.

2. pH adjustment should be done before nutrients are added to the water. The addition of nutrients to water can create buffers in the solution which will make pH adjustment more difficult.

3. Adjust the pH of the water to a value about 0.75 points above the final value required for the solution. Most full formulation hydroponic nutrients are acidic so they will cause the pH of the water to drop when they are added.

4. When adjusting pH keep in mind that the scale is logarithmic, that is, the value changes by a 10-times multiplier as you move from point to point on the scale.
For example; If the pH of your raw water is 5 and it takes 50 grams of Potassium Bicarbonate to move the value up to 6, it will require only 1/10th as much to move the value of the pH for the water up to 7.

The same applies when adjusting pH down. The amount of acid required to move the pH value from 9 down to 8 is 10 times as much as will be required to move the value of the same water down to 7.

When purchasing materials for pH adjustment keep one thing in mind, these materials are dangerous, especially in high concentrations. The dry powders sold to raise pH are just as corrosive to handle as sticking your hand in pure battery acid. Hobby growers should purchase dilute forms of these materials for safety. Always check with your supplier to find out the concentration of the material you are buying and remember, in any strong concentration they are dangerous and can burn you badly.

Maintaining pH

In recycling systems which depend on a reservoir storing sufficient solution for extended periods the solution should be tested daily for pH. One cause of pH fluctuation in solutions is the uptake of nutrient which changes over a day and in relation to the age of the plant. The other cause is the fact that plants are constantly secreting effluents from the roots into the solution. Both causes can be neutralized to a major extent by ensuring the solution in the reservoir is constantly aerated very vigorously. Ideally your reservoir should have the appearance of boiling due to the volume of air being pumped into it. This will normally keep your pH stable enough between solution changes in a hobby system if you are using a properly formulated nutrient.

The media in all systems should be checked for pH on the same regular basis as concentration of solution. The most common cause of pH change in the media is salt build up which shows a need for changes to solution concentration or the irrigation cycle.

THE EFFECT OF SOLUTION PH
On Nutrient Availability

This is most graphically demonstrated by the following charts. As the buffering capacity of the media surrounding plant roots declines, so does the optimum pH of the solution used to provide nutrients. So most of the pH preference charts published are invalid for hydroponic or soilless culture as they are based on soil culture. Optimum levels are generally a full pH point, or more, lower than those for soil culture.

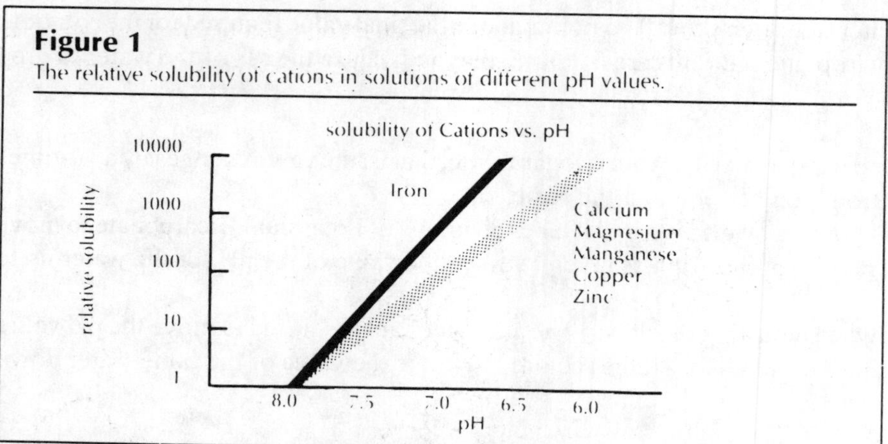

This graph shows the direct relationship between pH and the solubility of essential elements. Remember that plant roots can only absorb elements which have been dissolved in water.

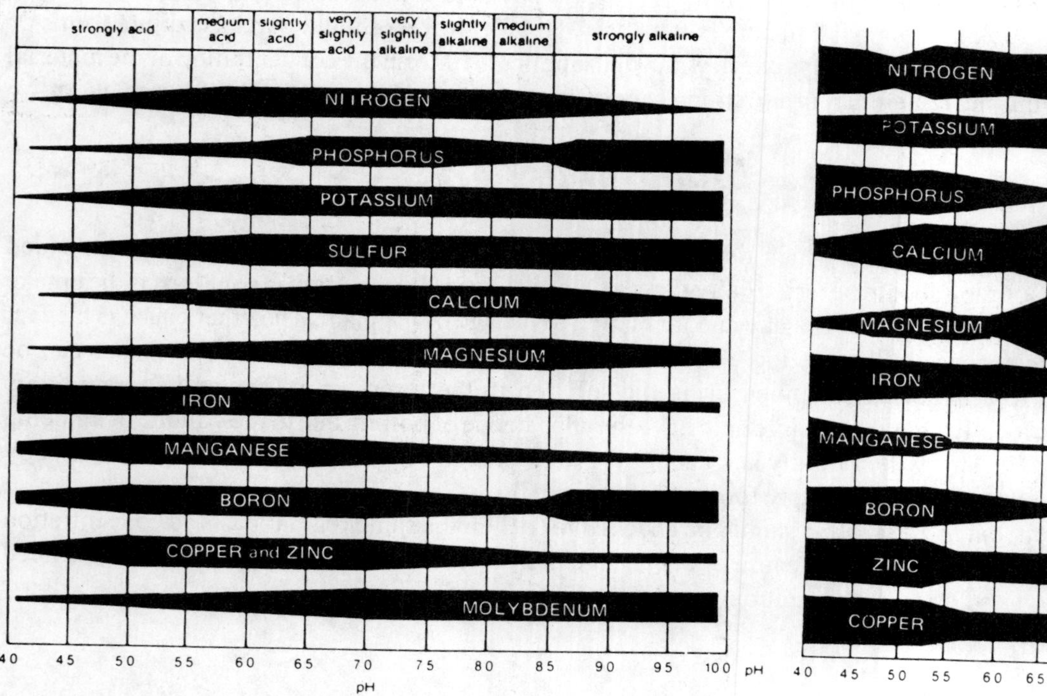

A close examination of the soil graph (left) and the soilless mix graph (right) clearly shows the effects of moving from soil to soilless culture on the 'ideal' pH for optimum nutrient availability.

Summary

pH is a very extensive topic which could be covered in a lot more detail than is presented here. Manipulation of pH is the key method growers have to ensure the optimum availability of all plant nutrients. Always ensure that you know whether any reference material you use has been written for hydroponic or soilless applications or for soil culture. For a more in-depth study of this topic see 'Hydroponic Nutrients, Easy Ways to Make Your Own.".

MEDIA ANALYSIS FOR pH & EC

To do a media analysis with either a pH or conductivity meter you need a container which is marked for volume, clear film canisters are good, and some de-ionized distilled water. The water sold in drug stores for lens care is ideal.

Put 2 parts water and 1 part media into the container.

Let it sit for at least 2 hours.

Shake the mixture vigorously and let sit for an additional hour. If the minerals haven't entered solution by now, they will not affect the root zone in the short term.

Strain the mixture through a coffee filter and take your readings.

Taking readings of soilless media can be easy as a monitoring situation. Simply take the readings in the media itself immediately after irrigation. The trend of the readings will tell you what is happening in the root zone.

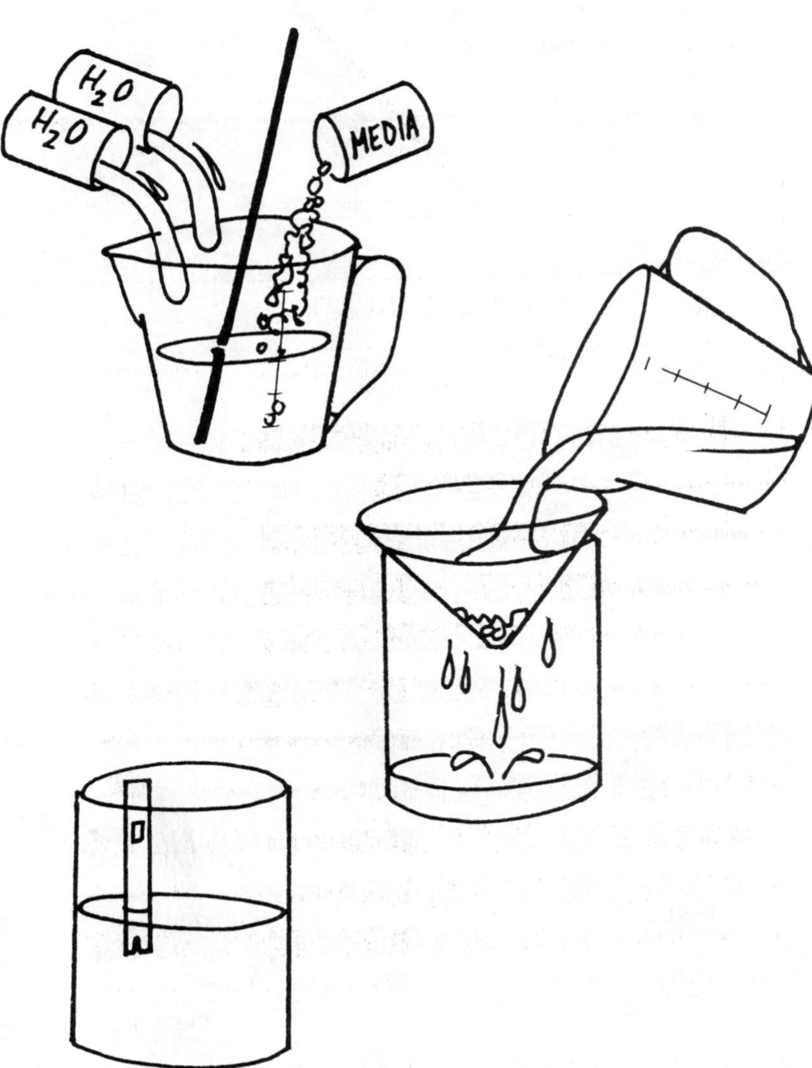

Chapter 20
CO_2
Carbon Dioxide Enrichment

When everything else is in balance, the proper application of carbon dioxide enrichment will produce worthwhile results. If you are just beginning your garden then the CO_2 will be a waste of money until you get the rest of your system operating to its best potential. Putting it in earlier will mask some problems and you won't get nearly as much benefit.

Sources of Carbon Dioxide

There are two common sources of CO_2 for horticultural applications; Bottled CO_2 and the combustion of either propane or natural gas. The following chart provides a comparison of these options.

ITEM	BOTTLED CO_2	PROPANE	NATURAL GAS
Safety	no flames, nonexplosive	burner required, CO production	burner required, CO production
Installation	simple, inexpensive	relatively simple, moderate cost	professional, expensive
Handling	easy, safe, tanks	tanks of combustible gas	easiest, no bottles
Operation Cost	most expensive	moderate	least expensive
Maintenance	minimal	regular	professional
Efficiency	100%	best conversion	poorest conversion, high water production
Gas Quality	varies by supplier	best	sulfur contamination possible
Equipment Required	tank, regulator, flowmeter, solenoid valve	tank, regulator, generator with specific nozzles	certified connection, regulator, generator with specific nozzles.
Controls	The same controls may be used for all systems		

Using Bottled CO_2

Bottled CO_2 is contained in a highly pressurized tank (839 psi) which is rated by the number of pounds of CO_2 gas which it holds. The actual tank weight is considerably higher so for the hobby grower a tank with an 80-pound rating is about the maximum you would ever want to consider. For commercial growers, suppliers send out trucks to refill the permanent installation tanks.

There are a variety of flowmeter regulators sold for CO_2 gas but not all are designed to do the job. CO_2 gas is very cold and improperly designed units commonly freeze-up. For large commercial systems it is often better to zone the operation with several regulator/flowmeters and solenoid valves than trying to do the whole range directly from the tank.

Research has shown that the optimum levels of CO_2 in the growing area (greenhouse or phytotron/growroom) can vary from 400 to 1,200 ppm depending on the species and age of the crop. One advantage of bottled gas is that control of small area systems can be left to mechanical timers by using some simple calculations.

Calculating the gas delivery time required
for any growing area is simple.

1. Calculate the cubic area of the environment.
LxWxH [e.g., 15x8x10 = 1200 cu. ft.]

2. Calculate the concentration of CO_2 wanted for your area,
then subtract the ambient level (300 ppm usually) to arrive at the enrichment required.
[Eg. 1,500 wanted - 300 ambient = 1200 required]

3. Convert the ppm required to a decimal [e.g., 1200 ppm = 0.0012] and
multiply by the cubic feet in the area to arrive at the number of cubic feet of gas required.
E.g., 1200 cu.ft. x 0.0012 = 1.44 cu.ft. of CO_2 gas.

4. Divide the result of step 3 by the flow rate set on the flow meter to arrive at the time the system must be on to achieve the desired concentration.
E.g., if the flow rate is 2 cu.ft./hr then 1.44 cu.ft.
divided by 2 cu.ft./hr = 0.072 x 60 minutes = 43 minutes on time.

This is the rate which would be required if the growing area is periodically cleared by a complete air exchange to control humidity or temperature. If no air changes are occurring and the greenhouse is tight (one air change per 4 hours) then the rate is valid only for the first cycle of the day. Subsequent cycles at 2 hour intervals would be on 1/3 of this time, or 15 minutes.

Note that commercial growers should always use a proper monitor controller to maintain desired levels economically and to integrate the system with other environment control equipment.

COMBUSTION SOURCE CALCULATIONS

CO_2 generators are rated in several ways. To help straighten things out and make conversions simple, use the above table. Once you have figured out what your combustion requirements are, it is simple to choose the proper generator. Keep in mind you should choose the smallest generator which will service your needs. I have seen greenhouses for hobby and research which had large commercial CO_2 generators installed. The pilot light alone was enough to keep CO_2 levels excessively high 24 hours a day.

To calculate your required burner operation time:

1. Convert the generator rating into cu.ft./hr of CO_2

2. Follow steps 1-3 as outlined for CO_2 gas.

Again it is important that commercial growers use a proper infrared sensor equipped monitor controller.

This information will allow you to choose the proper CO_2 source for your application. There are other integrated factors to be considered in the operation of such a system including the effects on temperature and humidity. Optimum results will only be achieved if you maintain a proper environmental balance. Carbon Dioxide is a plant nutrient and as such can be manipulated. However it will only yield results when it is part of a complete environment and nutrient control program.

When examining the potential in your system, you can keep in mind that optimum economical response to CO_2 enrichment has been shown to vary according to both environment and stages of plant growth. The order of response as related to economy and effectiveness is as follows.

1. Propagation and seedlings

2. Transplant

3. Winter growing conditions

4. Main growing area with maturing and producing plants.

Keep in mind that the plant's ability to assimilate CO_2 is increased for a considerable time after the enrichment program is ended.

Choose a CO_2 generator which is the right size for your growing environment. Using a commercial size burner in a hobby greenhouse can result in plant death since the pilot light on the commercial unit can generate more CO_2 than may be required in such a small area. The constant production results in a buildup to toxic levels due to the scarcity of oxygen.

Part VII
Lighting For Plant Growth

Chapter 21
REASONS FOR LIGHTING

Lighting for plant growth has been a topic of controversy for over 150 years. One of the problems is that the generally accepted information among growers seldom keeps up with the advances in light sources and equipment. This is compounded by manufacturers and retailers who have a product to sell, whether it is 'state of the art' or state of disaster.

Contrary to popular myth, any light source will have an impact on plant growth, regardless of whether it is the 'right colour' or economical. The number of light sources which have been used over the years is familiar to most growers, sunlight being the oldest and the only 'free' one. Although lamps available today include incandescent, and quartz halogen, these are seldom of any economic value for either the hobby or commercial grower. The two lamp types which currently best meet grower needs are fluorescent, and HID (High Intensity Discharge) which includes Metal Halide and High Pressure Sodium plus the recent variations.

Let's take a look at the various things we want to do with lighting. Identifying your real need makes choices easier.

Photoperiod alteration

This includes nightbreak lighting and daylength extension. To shorten the day length you will have to use blackout rather than lighting. What you are attempting to do here is alter the plant's perception of what is happening in its environment. It is not a question of adding light intensity for actual growth but getting the plant to believe the day is a different length than it really is.

The amount of light required for this varies with the species and variety but can be as little as 100 footcandles. In large areas it is important to use enough low output source points to provide even lighting without causing some plants to stretch.

The basic considerations for photoperiod control are;

The minimum intensity required,
Timing, and
The even distribution of the light.

Many commercial growers incorporate blackout into their shading system for automation. Hobby growers who want to use blackout should make sure the material is thick enough that no light gets through. It is surprising how much light is transmitted through ordinary black plastic.

Supplementary Lighting

Greenhouse growers often find their crops require more light energy than Mother Nature provides through sunshine. There are a variety of situations which call for supplementary lighting.

Many plants go through various cycles based on a light accumulation basis. That is, when they have received a certain amount of light energy they are ready to initiate the next stage of growth. The plant's internal counter simply operates on this restriction and there are time constraints with many plants. If enough light is not received within a specific time the plant simply aborts the next stage of growth.

All plant growth is in direct response to the actual amount of light they receive and growth is reduced if this is less than the amount of light they require. Excess light levels are of no value to a plant and can contribute to plant stress.

The bottom line on supplementary lighting is that you want to match or exceed a plant's minimum light requirement for the productivity you feel is necessary to achieve in your greenhouse. Surprisingly this level can be much higher than you may expect and some commercial growers in Northern climates have found economically profitable levels of response even in summer months when light intensity is at its highest.

Two major considerations are;

The amount of cloud cover in your area.

The quality of the greenhouse covering.

Supplementary lighting is profitable for many cut flower crops. This is a research facility in Holland where recycling is being tested for cut rose production.

If your greenhouse covering is cutting solar radiation excessively, it may be financially much more advantageous to replace the greenhouse covering or the structure itself than to invest in a lighting system.

Commercial growers who have found supplementary lighting economically useful include winter flower growers, especially roses and orchids, herb growers, and growers of salad crops such as lettuce and romaine. An increasing number of growers of vine crops (tomatoes & peppers especially) have been experimenting with supplementary lighting with mixed results. The feasibility of supplementary growing is directly related to the market value of the crop including the increases in production and quality during the lighting season and the cost of installing and operating the system.

Supplementary lighting has become quite common in hobby greenhouses. Orchid growers especially find lighting essential to good winter growth of some varieties. For those growing food crops in a hydroponic system in the greenhouse there is a way to reduce lighting requirements. Let all of the high energy requirement crops finish production. As they do, replace them with greens and herbs which have lower temperature and light requirements. You may still need lighting but it will be much less expensive to install and operate.

The basic considerations for this type of lighting are;

How much lighting is required.

The even distribution of the light.

The cost of installing the lighting system.

Some growers in overcast coastal areas have tried supplementary lighting for vine crops such as tomatoes. This is expensive and even lighting is difficult to achieve. The reflectors used in this system create an excessive amount of shade and contribute to the lighting problem.

Propagation

Virtually every grower, at one time or another, tries his or her hand at starting plants from seeds or cuttings and many of the more adventurous are experimenting with tissue culture. Propagation lighting can either be supplementary if you use a greenhouse or primary if you use an enclosed propagation area. Lighting is an almost indispensable tool for propagation as growers want to start plants several months in advance to ensure they get the best jump on the season when light is free and heating costs are minimal in the much larger greenhouse areas required for production.

When considering propagation lighting there are several things to keep in mind for optimum results.

Seedlings require only about 50% of the light intensity which is considered optimum for the growth and production stages of the plant. Overlighting seedlings can result in reduced growth, inadequate root structure, and plant stress. Also there is no need to provide more light than what plants will receive when planted out into the greenhouse or the garden.

Cuttings require only about 25% of the light intensity needed by the mature plant. Overlighting cuttings will stress them to the point that root emergence is seriously delayed or even stopped entirely.

Planting out a seedling which then experiences a drastic reduction in light levels has the effect of shutting the transplant down. There is a dramatic change in the growth pattern and the plant can be set back for as much as 3 weeks. You can often gain a significant growth advantage by delaying planting out until the solar radiation can be expected to support vigorous growth. This delay can be as little as three weeks and your first harvest date will not be any further away than if you planted had out in a time of inadequate radiation. There is the additional advantage of the energy savings through not having to heat the greenhouse during the most expensive period. Additionally you plant out a more robust seedling which will not have to acclimate to a substandard environment.

Burnaby Lake Greenhouses in B.C. use a double tier propagation system to maximize space in the greenhouse. There is a considerable difference in the rate of plant growth due to the wide variation in light levels.

The basic considerations for propagation lighting are;

The species of plant.
The type of propagation.
The transplant scheduling.
The desired size of the transplant.

Primary Production Lighting

This is mainly the realm of the hobby grower. For commercial production to be viable the outside environment must be virtually useless for growing even in a greenhouse. This is one of the situations which causes many hobby growers to move indoors.

Isolation, high transportation costs and a really lousy growing climate are the ideal combination for deciding to move your garden indoors under artificial lights. Classic examples would be the Canadian North or the State of Alaska where the sun disappears for a significant period of the year and all food is trucked in from far to the South.

The situation will vary for growers depending, not only on climate, but also the time of year a crop is required and other considerations. The options for both outdoor and greenhouse gardening are limited by the location of the dwelling as well as the environment. If you have a home with a small lot, on a north facing slope in an area with a lot of shade from neighbors trees or buildings, you may be forced to move your gardening indoors. As soon as you have to do production lighting for more than 5 months of the year plus provide heating in the face of a variable climate it is commonly more cost effective to move your garden from the greenhouse to indoors.

Specialty growers such as orchid growers who must maintain a year-round environment have been moving indoors for years. Those in town houses and apartments are joining in larger numbers as the trend moves to an aging population. The advantage the hobby grower has over the commercial is that the return is not measured in dollars and cents but in accomplishment and satisfaction.

The basic considerations for production lighting are;

The level of lighting required.
The number of days lighting is needed.
The cost of the installation.
The operational costs.
Effective distribution of the light.
The amount of heat generated by the system.

Hobby growers enjoy year-round production of food and specialty crops in indoor hydroponic systems when the local climate makes it too expensive to grow outdoors. This photo is of a garden in Northern B.C.

Design Considerations for Indoor Gardens

Designing a good indoor growing environment is a little more difficult because people commonly inhabit the same space and insist that their needs be considered. Additionally distribution of light is much more critical as the lamps are the only source of light.

What space is available for the garden?
Is it in a living space or isolated from common use?

This will have an impact on how the lighting is installed and the garden itself laid out. No one can long stand the flickering from an HID lamp in the middle of the living room while they watch TV.

What combination of plants are to be grown?

There is no sense in overlighting a garden and few hobbyists want to waste the energy dollars. Often a combination of different lighting sources can best suit the garden requirements. Keep in mind the whole plant will have to receive adequate energy, not just the top, and this will affect the plant spacing and layout.

How much power will be required for the lighting?

This is a very important consideration. New circuits may have to be installed to meet load and safety requirements. Always consult an electrician to learn what alterations will need to be made to safely install the lighting load you require. I have heard more than one report of houses burning down because a grower ignored the safety aspect of an installation. Many insurance companies can refuse claims in such circumstances. The wise grower will not purchase any fixture or equipment which has not been UL or CSA approved and will ensure the installation meets all code requirements.

Who will be going into the growing area?

HID lighting is very hot and if children or people unfamiliar with the equipment enter the growing area they can be injured. Make sure such equipment is installed so it cannot be easily touched or bumped or, that the growing area is isolated by a locked door.

This is an example of a disaster waiting to happen. This 'bare bones' installation places a MH bulb directly in the path of the grower and the bulb has a temperature of 400 degrees F. Always use properly designed and approved fixtures.

By combining hydroponic systems with proper lighting you can get an amazing selection of plants into a 10'x10' room. 1. *An underbench propagation chamber using fluorescents with reflectors.* 2. *An NFT system for greens, herbs or strawberries which can be lit by either a tracked MH or fluorescents (not shown).* 3. *A wall mounted drain to waste system for potted plants such as houseplants, cactus, or orchids lit by 400W MH on a track.* 4. *A recycling media system for tall plants such as tomatoes lit by a 400W MH on a track.* 5. *An ebb and flow table for container plants of choice lit by a fixed 400W MH.* Using area reflection ensures that the light reaches all sides of the plants.

Chapter 22

THE TOOLS & TECHNIQUES OF LIGHTING

When using lamps for plant lighting you are working with 'source point lighting' and this causes the problem of equal light distribution through a plant canopy as well as over a broad area. Light intensity decreases very rapidly with distance from the source and I am sure many readers have experienced plant stretching because of this natural phenomenon.

It is important to remember that plants 'see' light differently than people. Relying on your eye to provide a guide is one way to ensure problems. One of the best tools for gardeners, both hobby and commercial, is a spectrum adjusted Light Intensity Meter. Plants sense both the source and intensity of light. They seem very sensitive to sources. If a plant decides that light levels are too low and can identify a source it will immediately expend all available energy to get closer to that source to increase intensity to acceptable levels. It seems they learned the basics of light physics long before we did.

Providing equal light distribution using lamps is a challenge but we do have some tools to help us do a reasonably good job. They fall into four categories;

Lamps
shape, installation orientation, and size (wattage);
Installation height;
Reflectors;
Light movers.

This grower in Tsawassen B.C. spent thousands on a lighting system and 'saved' money on greenhouse construction by using heavy wooden framing. He could have increased solar source light levels by using a commercially produced frame for his poly house. Good light levels at affordable costs are the result of a properly designed operation.

Lamps

A look at the line drawings of the lamp types shows quite clearly how each emits light and shows that if the lamps are installed without a reflective fixture of some type most of the light will be lost to the plants. Referring to the diagrams (pg 156) on how light falls in intensity the further it is from the source it is obvious we cannot use one super sized lamp to get equal light distribution over a large area. In addition HID lamps give off considerable amounts of heat which can damage the plants if the lamps are too close.

The trick is to choose the combination of lamp size, and the other tools, to provide the best distribution of light at the intensity required. The area each lamp can cover will vary according to the intensity required but there are some general guidelines which may be of assistance to the novice. These guidelines are for stationary lamps at the noted installation height using minimally efficient reflectant fixtures.

FLUORESCENT
(12" above plant maximum)

Propagation & small plant growth
1- 48" tube per sq. ft of growing area

Display and maintenance
1- 48" tube per 2 sq. ft of growing area

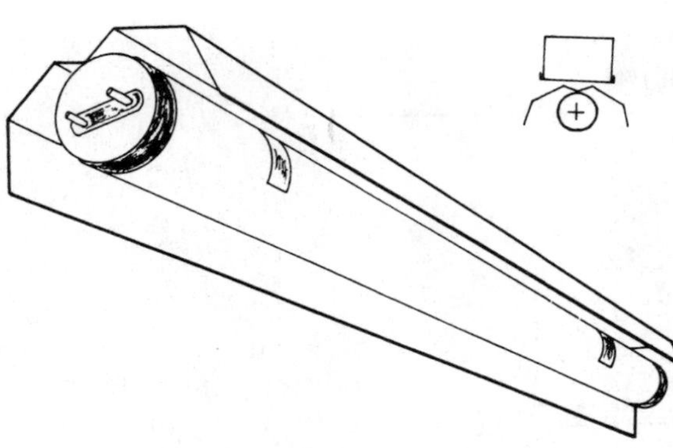

Fluorescent lamps are round, but due to the fixtures, all the light is directed downward. Without a proper reflector as much as 1/2 the light can be lost in the fixture.

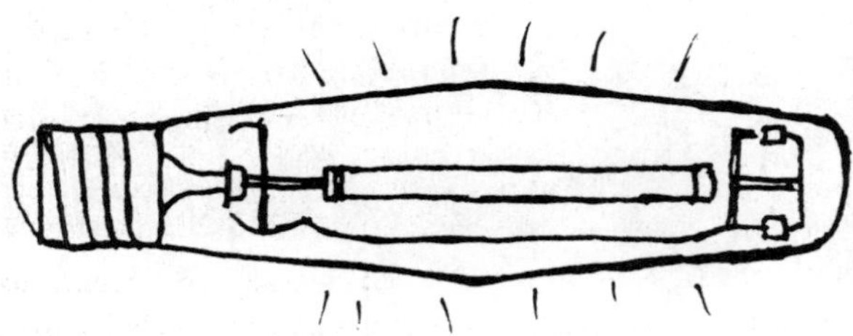

HID

Propagation - 15 watts/ ft of propagation bed
Supplementary greenhouse - 2 meters maximum - 4-6 watts/sq. ft (54-80 W/sq/m)

Sole Source Lighting
Display & maintenance - 1 meter 10 watts/sq. ft
Production growing - 1 meter maximum
Low energy plants - 10-15 watts/sq. ft
High energy plants - 20-30 watts/sq. ft

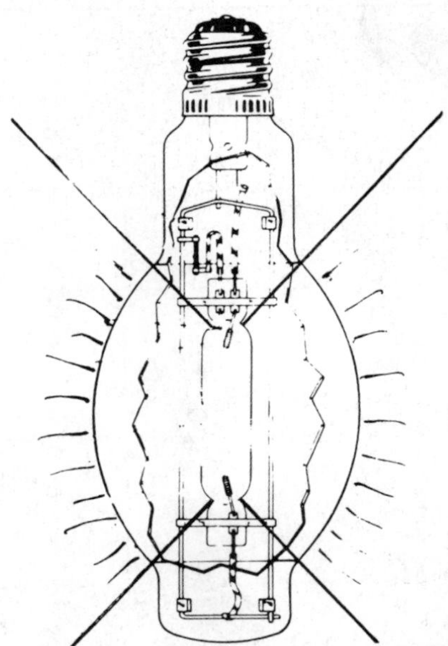

The above lamp shape is common for Metal Halide and some types of High Pressure Sodium, including those designed for use in MH fixtures. This lamp shape requires a larger fixture than the typical slim shape found in HPS (left) although the light output pattern is similar.

Installation Height

The higher above the crop lamps are installed, the larger the area they will cover but, as you are aware, intensity drops and distribution becomes uneven. The installation should allow for overlap of distribution patterns to make lighting even over the entire plant canopy.

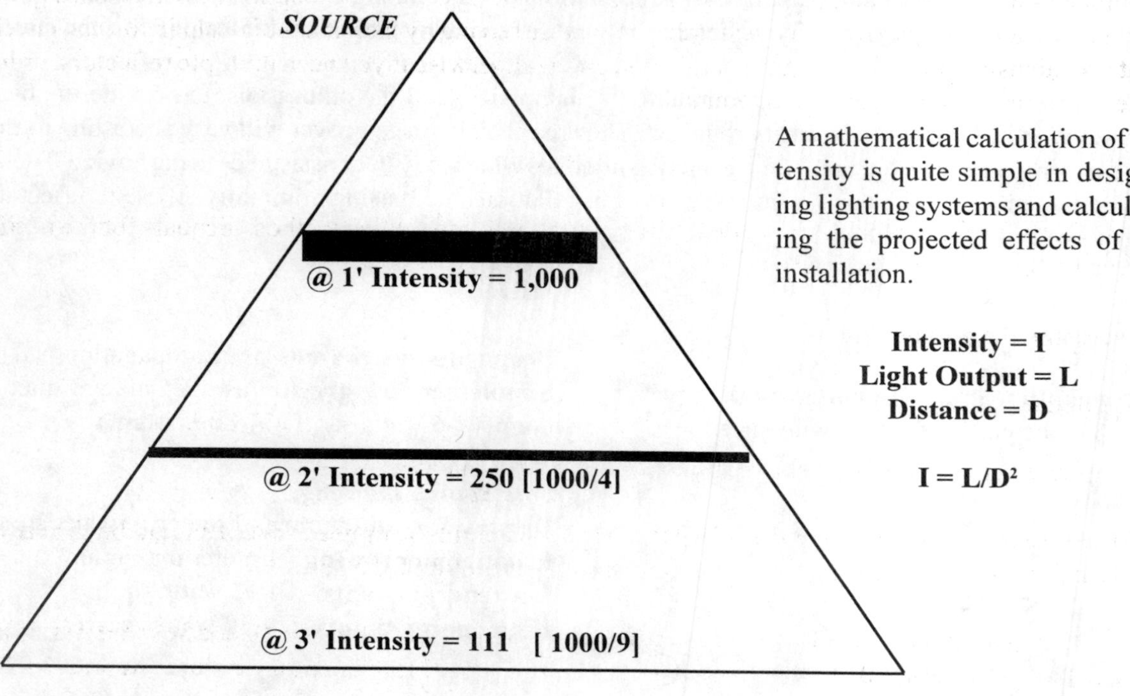

A mathematical calculation of intensity is quite simple in designing lighting systems and calculating the projected effects of an installation.

Intensity = I
Light Output = L
Distance = D

$$I = L/D^2$$

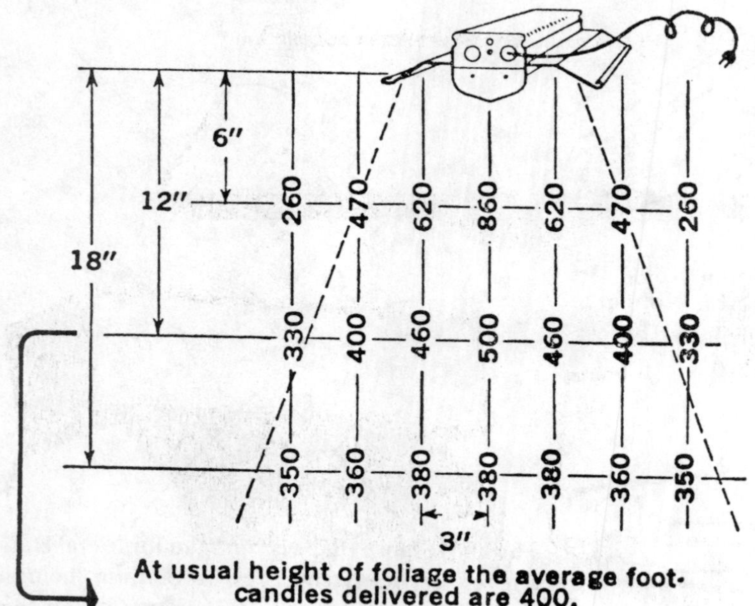

Foot-candles delivered at various distances from lights. (*Courtesy General Electric*)

As the illustration for light intensity under a fluorescent fixture show, this calculation does not take into account the effect reflectors may have and it also does not include any ambient radiation.

For lighting every grower should have a light meter to use in finalizing any installation for optimum results.

Reflectors

Reflectors are sold by many companies and they all have an assortment of claims for the effectiveness of each. Since no standards exist for horticultural reflectors and anybody can make and sell them, you must remember that 'buyer beware' is a fact of life with these products. Even the largest companies have put out less than desirable products in the past. Your best option is to invest in a good light meter and do some of your own testing. If you are buying by mail it is a big help if you can check out a local installation of the fixture before you order. Otherwise if you need multiple reflectors, order one for testing before committing yourself.

Comparison

The process for comparing reflectors is quite simple and a quick method adequate for the needs of the hobby grower is as follows.

1. Measure the ambient light.

2. Turn the fixture on and wait for 1 hour.

3. Measure the ambient light above the fixture if in a greenhouse.

4. Measure the light levels in a specific pattern (one which fits your needs and it should be the same pattern for every reflector you check) at a specific distance from the lamp.

For an accurate comparison you need to know what brand of lamp is used and how old it is. You can be fooled by the use of a new 'super output' lamp in one HID fixture and a standard one with 5,000 hours of burning in another.

There are a wide range of reflector shapes available today. For any grower the primary consideration should be safety. Reflectors which place bare lamps within reach can result in serious accidents.

Area Reflection

One aspect of light reflection which can be very effective is perimeter reflection. In greenhouses the North wall, and depending on design the North roof slope, not only lose heat they also radiate more light than they receive from the Northern sky, (Southern sky in the Southern Hemisphere). Indoor installations can lose a lot of light into construction materials which are subject to degradation due to the dampness.

The practice of covering the floor in commercial greenhouses with white plastic to reflect sunlight can be taken a lot further when lighting is being installed. Every possible piece of equipment in the growing area should be painted white with the type of paint used in dairies.

In greenhouses any non-light transmitting surface should be insulated and covered with a reflective material. In indoor installations walls, ceilings, and floors, should be insulated and made reflective. This can be accomplished in two ways, use standard construction techniques and cover all surfaces with the same 'dairy paint (which can be quite expensive) or use reflective 'yard goods'.

There are three types of these 'yard goods' being sold today. The cheapest is often misidentified as Mylar by unscrupulous retailers and is a reflective poly film designed as an insulation material for sauna construction. The poly film has no UV stabilization and will discolor and degrade very rapidly (as little as 60 days under high UV conditions). This blackened film then begins to absorb light and is often impossible to replace while the crop is in place.

There are many opportunities to improve reflection indoors. Using Foylon to cover all walls and the ceiling ensures diffuse reflection for good back lighting. Paint all wooden surfaces with a white dairy paint or porch enamel. You can also isolate propagation chambers with foylon to improve the effectiveness of fluorescents.

The mid-priced material is called Foylon and is a hybrid aluminum fabric which is also available with a very strong vinyl backing. It has the advantage of providing diffuse reflection rather than the mirror type of reflection obtained by using Mylar. Both Foylon and Mylar (usually the most expensive) are very effective reflective materials and are easy to install and have long lives. Both need to be periodically cleaned (between crops) to remove dust or other build up which would reduce reflective qualities. Price comparisons for these materials should be done on a per square foot basis to ensure you are really getting as good a deal as you think you are.

Using these materials you can install highly effective insulation and reflective surfaces on cheap wooden frames using Foylon or Mylar, and a staple gun. Angling the corners where walls meet and along the roofline will prevent the creation of light traps.

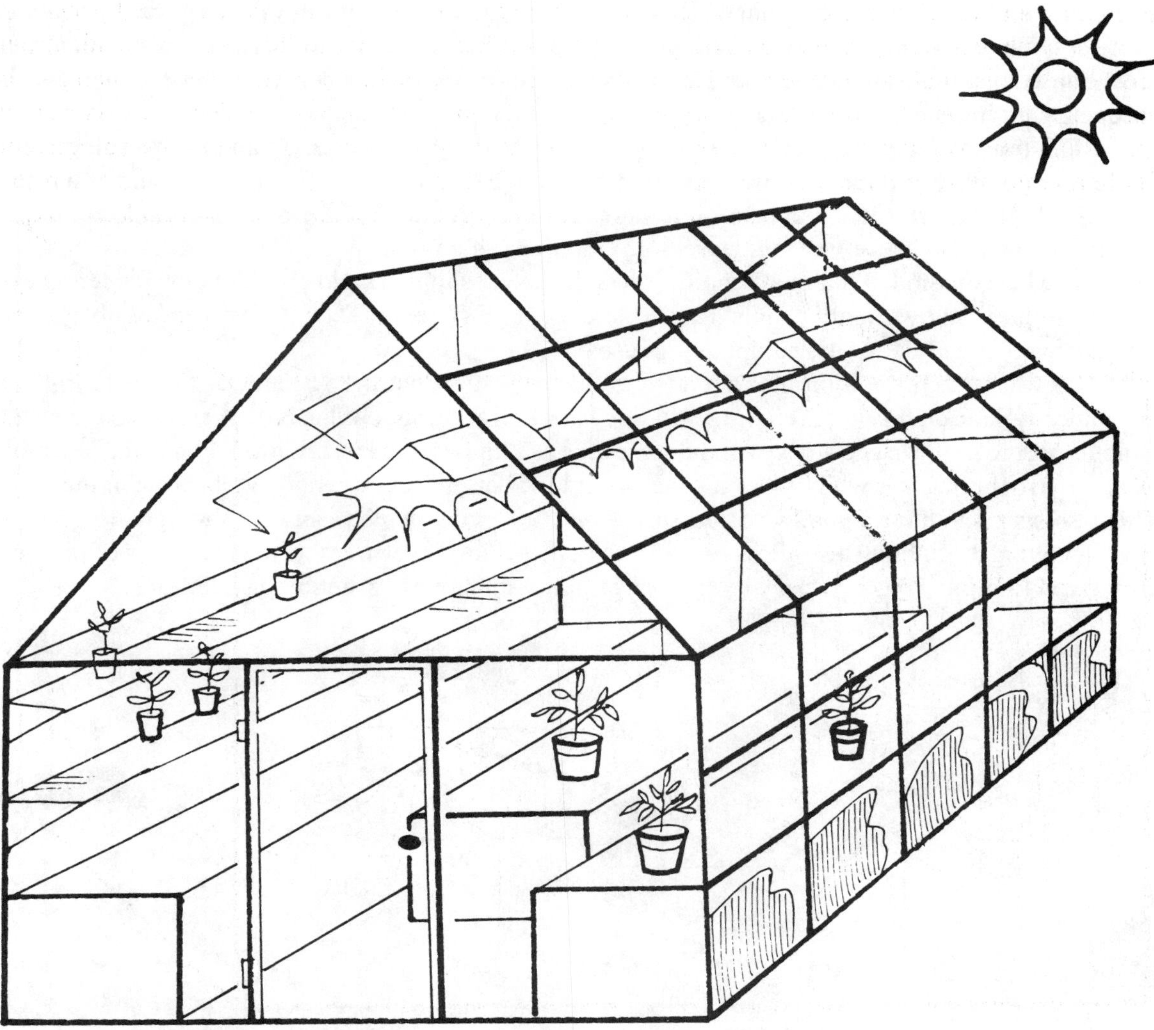

The use of area reflection in a hobby greenhouse will both improve light levels and reduce heating costs. Cover the North wall, North roof slope and all exterior underbench glazing with Foylon. Cover floor areas with white poly.

Light Movers

These are only available for HID lighting and most require your HID fixture be a remote installation setup (lamp and ballast separated by up to several hundred feet in commercial installations). A key fact to remember with these devices is the fact that HID lamps are very susceptible to vibration during operation. Vibration can reduce the life of the lamp by up to 75% in the worst cases.

One commercial grower I know got over this by using the rails and drive system designed for garage doors. He set the system up so that he covered 1/3 of his crop with supplementary lighting at 20 watts per square meter. He moved the entire lighting system each night so all of the crop got a 'light boost' every three days, and the lamps were never subject to vibration caused by motion. He was very happy with the increased production on his lettuce crop, which was superior to that of standard fixed installations at far less cost.

Commercially there are two specific designs available, those which move in a straight line (back and forth), and those which move in circles. I must emphasize that most of these devices are only of value to hobby growers, they are seldom practical for the number of lamps required in a commercial greenhouse. Some designs have found economical use in commercial propagation systems and in production lighting applications.

The tracks, drive mechanisms and drive materials vary considerably among manufacturers. Some forget just how tough a growing environment can be on mechanical equipment and as a result there are high failure rates and/or high maintenance requirements. The operation and method of installation can also cause varying degrees of vibration which will shorten lamp life.

The best method of making a choice is to call several suppliers and check out the percentage of returns, failures and warranty claims they experience for different brands. Wherever possible talk to growers who already have the equipment in use.

So what can these light moving devices do for you? What they cannot do is create light so discount any such claims in advertising. Moving lamps on a continuous basis does allow you to install lamps closer to the crop and still cover the same area as a higher fixed installation. Plants receive more light on a rhythmic basis which prevents the closer installation from causing overheating of the plant. This also seems to have a positive effect on the way the plant metabolism uses the light.

Moving the lighting also allows the light to be distributed over areas which would not be possible with fixed lighting. This is especially important in the small narrow hobby installations.

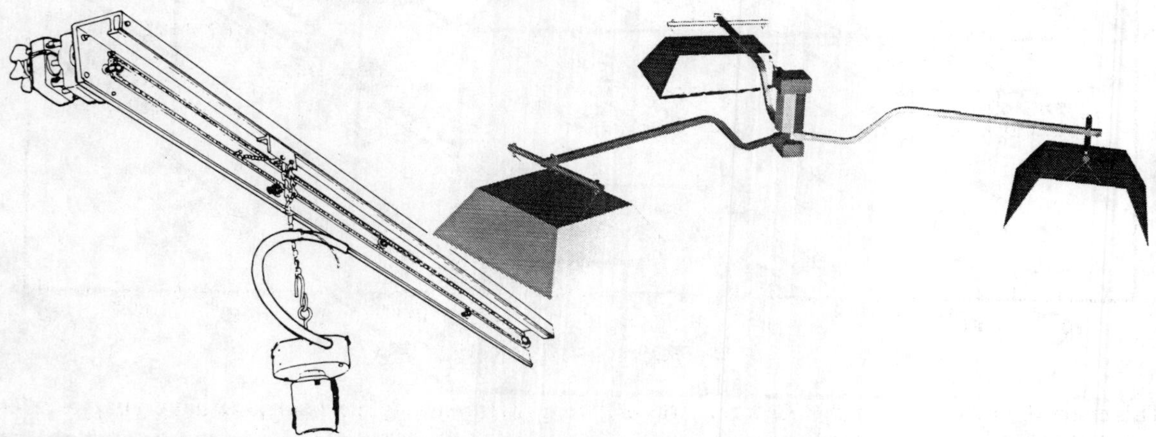

Light movers are available in a number of styles for hobby growers but they only move lights in two directions, back and forth in a straight line or rotating in a circle.

The Colour of Light

This is where most of the arguments about the 'best' light source occur. There is enough published information to make every opinion both right and wrong, so the smart gardener simply relies on the best available expertise; the manner in which the plant responds to lighting. Keep in mind what I said initially, every source of light can have a positive impact on plant growth.

Over the decades of research some of the specific light that plants respond to has been identified and this is the only guideline we have to date in choosing light sources. Look at the PAR chart for a picture of what is known. The closer you come to this spectrum (from a combination of all light sources) the more growth you will probably get for your energy and equipment dollar. Keep in mind that when doing supplementary lighting in a greenhouse or windowsill, there is sunshine or skylight providing additional intensity and colour.

Really the goal for hobby gardeners is to find out which source will provide the amount of light necessary at the most economical cost combination of installation and operation. As a rule the fluorescent lights are good for small indoor gardens growing low light crops and for propagation. High energy food crops, mixed crop gardens, and supplementary greenhouse lighting will all be most effectively handled by metal halide systems. High pressure sodium, including the new 'colour corrected' lamps, is best limited to use in greenhouses.

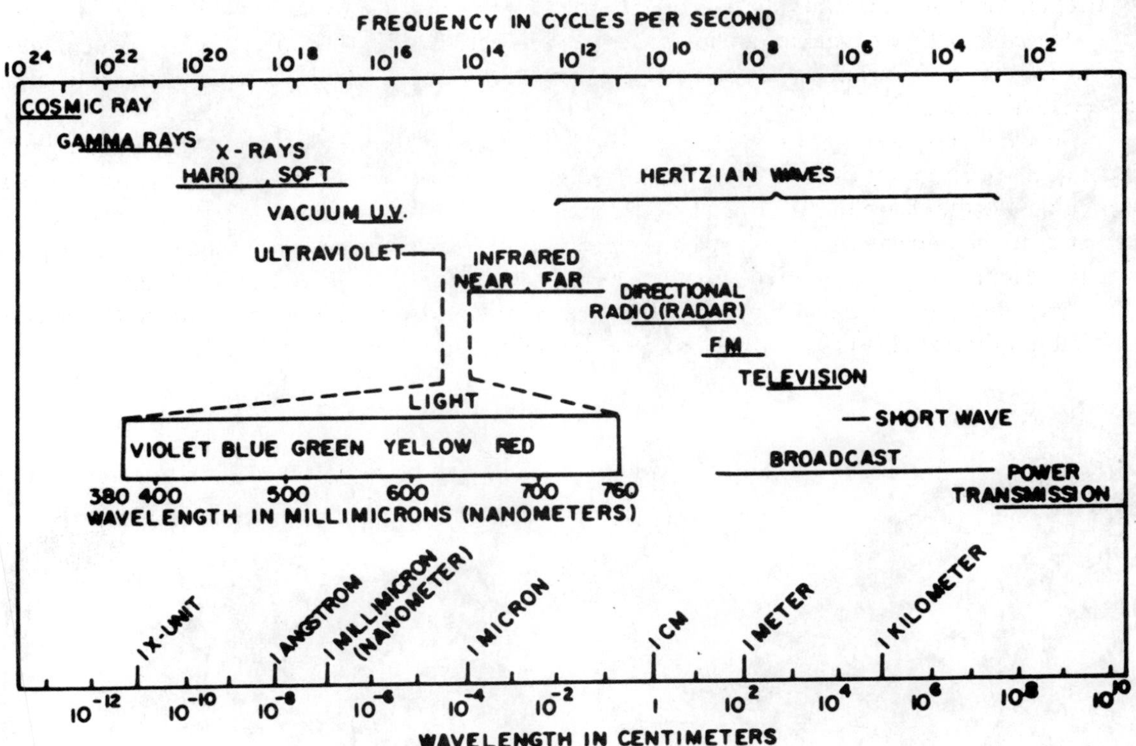

This chart shows just how small a portion of the electromagnetic energy spectrum is actually what we refer to as light. Plants can see and use a broader range of this spectrum than the human eye. For this reason a valuable tool for any grower is a light meter which can detect the same range of light energy as the plants "see."

Using Light to Mimic Seasons

The practice of changing the duration of light to cause plant response has already been discussed under photo-period control. There is another way of mimicking the seasons which can be of value to the hobby grower who wants to force flowering at 'the wrong time of the year'. It is changing the colour of the light in the same way sunlight changes over the seasons of the year.

In spring there is more blue in sunlight which is replaced as the seasons advance by an increase in the red portion of the spectrum. Many plants respond to these changes in colour by initiating flowering or going to seed. With the different types of HID lighting available this colour change can be mimicked either in the greenhouse or indoors. The simplest way is to use the Metal Halide equipment. The clear lamps are similar to the early season and the coated lamps are similar to the late summer sun. Simply swapping bulbs will 'change the season' to order.

One group of hobby growers which has benefited from the availability of HID lighting and the ability to manipulate seasons are the orchid growers. Many a prize bloom has been raised in an artificial environment in climates where the orchids would never survive outside.

Part VIII
PESTS & DISEASES

Chapter 23
PREVENTION WINS THE BUG WARS

You may have heard that there are no pests in hydroponic gardens. This is not true. To avoid insect problems you would have to leave the planet and set up your garden on the moon and even then one of the pesky little devils would probably hitchhike on the shuttle. Many field farmers have switched to hydroponic systems to escape soil borne diseases which cannot be eradicated. This in no way eliminates all of the potential diseases which can affect a crop. The real advantage of hydroponics concerning both pests and diseases is the fact we can take preventive measures. If these fail to deal with the problems which get into the garden then the confined area is much simpler to treat than the great outdoors.

PREVENTION MEASURES

Cleanliness

Your most powerful tool in dealing with both pests and diseases is cleanliness. Dead, decaying vegetation provides the perfect breeding ground for both. Keep your growing area clean and if you are outdoors or in a greenhouse this includes cutting down weeds and tall grasses both under and around your system.

The sure sign of a good grower is a clean greenhouse. No debris on the floor to breed disease or insects. Growers who have dirty greenhouses cause many of their own problems. (Photo of Crop King greenhouse in Ohio)

Culture Control

Next in effectiveness is operating your system properly. Stressed plants have a powerful voice which alerts the insect world that there are sick plants which need to be cleaned up. That is the role of many of what we call problem insects, getting rid of sick, diseased and dying plants. If you don't want the plants screaming out for Nature's recyclers then you have to keep them healthy.

The insects are always present and plants have evolved defence mechanisms to protect themselves. The presence of low numbers of insects is beneficial to plant growth as the plants are stimulated to defend themselves and are more vigorous in their growth.

Mechanical Damage

Mechanical damage is the most common site for the onset of diseases. This type of damage can come from an almost endless list of sources.

Failure to support seedlings properly causing bruising or breaking at the root crown.
Poor pruning practices.
Overcrowding plants so you are breaking leaves and branches every time you walk through the garden.
Allowing wild swings in the concentration of the nutrient solution causing root explosion.
Burning caused by the improper use of pesticides and insecticides.
Rough handling of plants in containers.

The list goes on. Every time you break, crack or bruise a plant you have set yourself up for the onset of a potential disease.

It is very common for heavy fruit loads to cause the truss to split and provide a site for disease initiation.

Oxygen Control

Adequate oxygen levels are essential for healthy plants but, oxygen is also a key to disease prevention. There is no disease free environment. Fungal diseases are the most common and the spores of literally thousands of species of fungi populate the air we breathe and the water we use. These microorganisms can be either friendly, not interfere with or enhance plant growth, or they can be very damaging. The oxygen dependent microorganisms tend to be the friendlies so maintaining high oxygen levels in the solution and root zone encourages their growth and reproduction.

Once microorganism populations are established, they tend to 'shut the door' to other organisms. It is for this reason that it is not wise to steam growing media or operate any type of sterilization system directly on a nutrient solution. Continuous or periodic killing of microorganisms simply means an increased opportunity for diseases to establish themselves and once established they are next to impossible to eradicate.

Air Movement

This is a basic prevention mechanism and the most commonly ignored by both commercial and hobby growers. Good air flow in a growing area prevents the buildup of moisture on leaves. This moisture is the ideal breeding site for many diseases. Good air movement also cuts down on plant stress in times of high humidity by encouraging transpiration. Every leaf on every plant should be moving slightly, 24 hours a day. Keep in mind that outdoors the breezes through plants are almost continuous even when the air is still, due to convection currents.

The roll up side walls used by this New Zealand grower for his NFT system are also used on larger greenhouse to provide natural air flow. The down side is that open walls allow every bug in the neighbourhood into your growing area. Solar vent openers (top right) and exhaust fans (bottom right) are common tools to provide fresh air into a growing area and cause cooling. Internal air circulation is essential in every growing area with the most common tool in a hobby system being the circulation fan.

Pest Transport

If you really want a sample of every pest and disease known to man, bring some plants from your local nursery or garden center into your garden immediately after purchase. I am constantly amazed at the selection of pests offered by retailers. In the event you do buy plants, put them into isolation and stress them for a week to see if anything develops on them. If nothing shows in a week, you should be relatively safe. If a problem shows up, you can decide whether the plant is worth saving or should be disposed of.

Also, take the time to apply common sense in your own movements. Don't go out visiting garden centers, wandering through other gardens, or playing in the outside garden and go directly into your growing area or greenhouse. Growers themselves are more responsible for the introduction of insects into the growing area than any other single source. You wander into your growing area with an insect on you. It takes one look at your succulent plants and screams "Lunch!"

Maintenance

Prevention involves making sure that all components to your growing environment are operating properly. You have to get to know your system and constantly check to make sure that what should be happening, is. The enhanced growth rates in your garden mean that the plants themselves will cause changes in such things as temperature, humidity, air flow patterns and CO_2 levels. You have to adjust your system to compensate for these changes on an ongoing basis. Even Mother Nature makes 'mistakes' and plants grown outside still survive, so don't expect that you will be perfect. The plants will survive your learning process.

Chapter 24
DEALING WITH PESTS & DISEASES

Disease

There is only one answer for the hobby grower when disease strikes. Get rid of the diseased plants immediately. DO NOT WAIT. You will not cure the disease and even if the plant is your most prized, it is doomed and has the potential to take the rest of your plants with it. Always remove it in a way that minimizes the potential of contact with other plants. An easy way is to cover the plant with a plastic bag before removing it. Get it away from the growing area and preferably it should be burned.

Insects

The first step is to recognize when insects move into your growing area. To ensure you can do this there is an essential tool kit every grower should have;

A copy of 'Rodales Colour Handbook of Garden Insects'.
Sticky strips in the growing area.
A magnifying glass (at least 10 power).
A hand held light scope (30 power).

It is no good calling anyone and asking what to do or what is approved for use on your plants if you have no idea what the problem is.

Observation & Inspection

Set up a regular program of observation and prevention to keep pest problems to a minimum.

1. Never go from any other garden or area of plant concentration into your hydroponic garden.

2. Release predators for common pests at the same time you put plants into the garden.

3. Set out sticky traps throughout the garden.

4. Check the traps daily using a magnifying glass.

5. Have the phone number of a local specialist who can advise on what solution will be best for insect problems.

Integrated Pest Management (IPM) is a powerful tool for all growers. Success with IPM is based on knowledge which includes the life cycle of both pests and predators and how their reproduction is affected by environmental conditions. Here are two sample life cycle charts for common pests. Companies which sell predators can provide similar information for all pests and predators. The best book available on IPM at this time is 'Common Sense Pest Control' and every gardener hobby or commercial should have a copy.

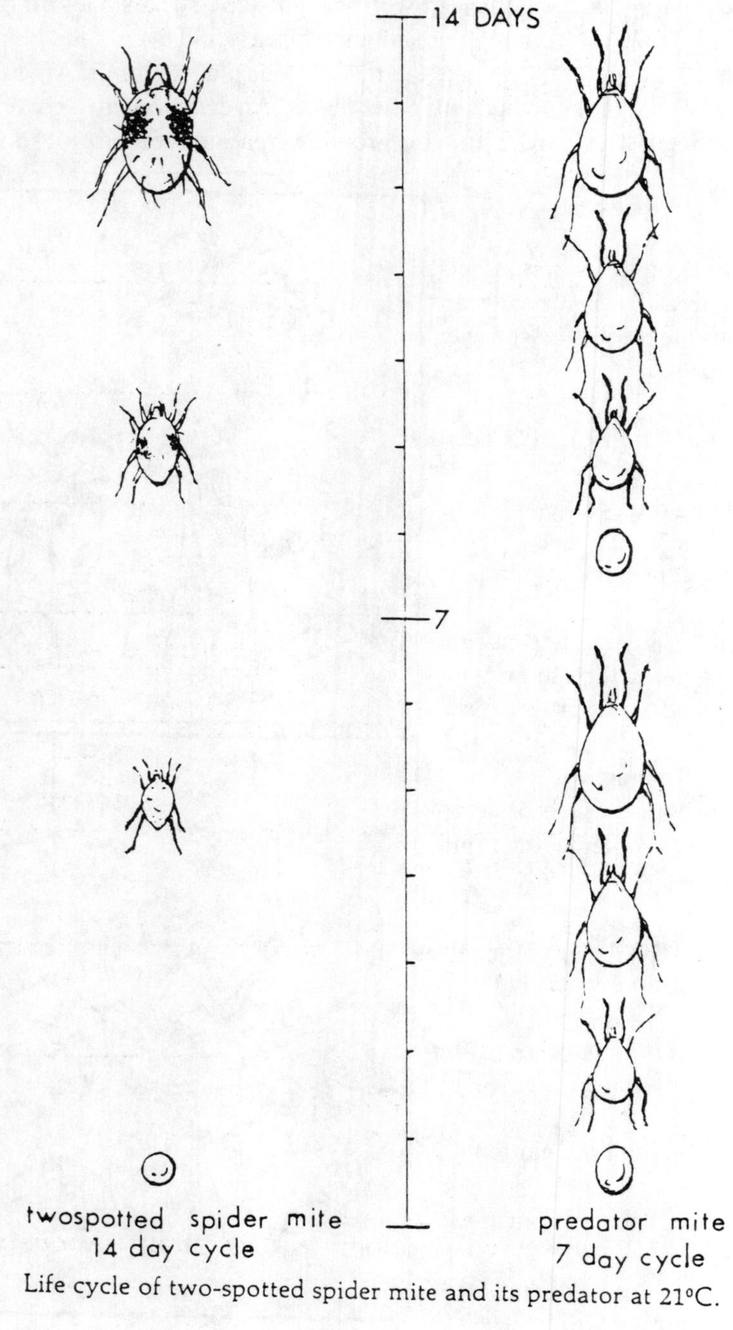

Life cycle of two-spotted spider mite and its predator at 21°C.

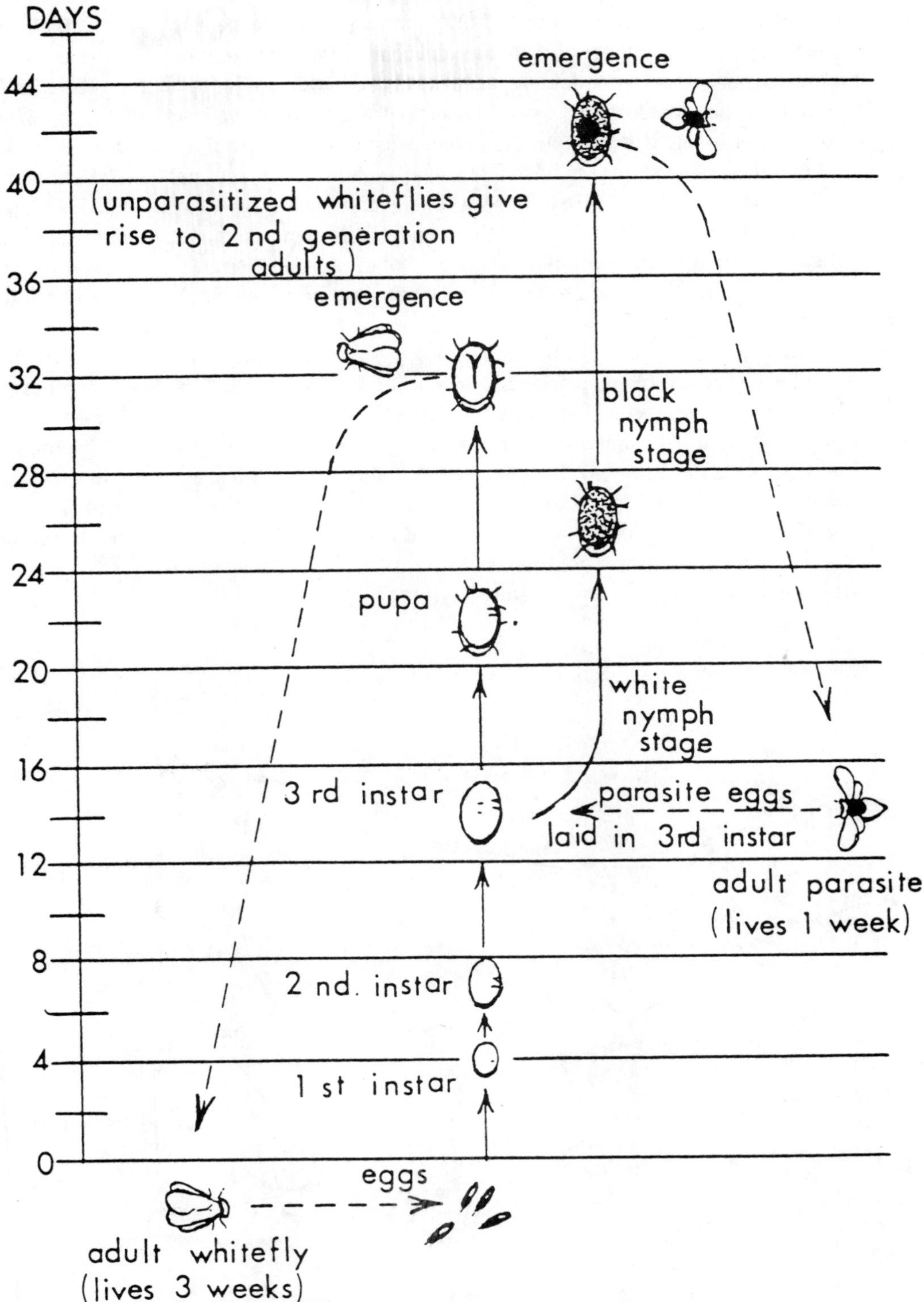

Life cycles of the greenhouse whitefly and its parasite *Encarsia formosa*.

When you identify a problem, **TAKE ACTION IMMEDIATELY**. You will not believe how fast these little critters can multiply. For every one you can see there may be up to 1,000 you don't. Go away for the weekend without attending to the problem and when you return you may not see your plants for the feeding insects. If you intend to use natural predators, do the same thing the commercial growers do, introduce the predators at the same time you transplant your plants into the growing area.

If you do find yourself with a population of insects; aphids, whitefly, spider mite, or thrips to name the most common, sprays are the best first step. There are both 'organic' and 'chemical' sprays and the brand names, availability, and use approvals will vary depending on where you live. These are 'knock-back' sprays which you will use to kill the population down to a manageable level for natural predators and environment manipulation. Your choice of spray will also be decided by whether you already have natural predators in the growing area. Choosing the wrong spray will kill both the pest and the predator.

When using these sprays either buy them in a fogger or use a pressure sprayer. You must get the material on every speck of plant surface and sprinkling will not do the job. Applying these sprays (organic or chemical) incorrectly can damage your plants and cause disease problems. For the hobbyist the best procedure is to apply the material in the evening, just before sundown or in a growroom before lights out. Early the next morning, go in and rinse the plants using a pressure sprayer.

One spray session will not get rid of the infestation. Once the insects get out of control it will take many sessions to get the population to the point where the natural predators can get the upper hand. The egg stage of insects is impervious to everything including a nuclear blast, so a weekly spray program will be needed to get the new ones as they hatch.

Most of the natural pesticides are 'contact killers'. That means they must contact the pest if they are to be effective. For the hobby grower this means using a pressure sprayer to ensure every nook and cranny in the plant is coated with the spray.

Chapter 25
TROUBLE SHOOTING

It seems that no matter how hard you try, at one time or another, your plants will show a symptom of something which is not 'normal'.

A change in colour,
slowed growth,
deformed leaves or fruit,
spotting,
leaf drop.

These are all common ways for your plant to tell you something is, or was, not right. Finding the cause of the problem can be easy or difficult depending on you. If you maintain good records and check your garden faithfully, isolating a cause will be easier. If you don't keep records and tend to take things very easy on the garden checking, isolating a cause can be very frustrating.

Every time a plant changes its appearance or growth habit it is telling you that something in its life has changed, either as recently as an hour ago or, as long ago as 90 days. The fact that the information is related to a past event means there is no instant fix right now for what caused the change. The cause may still exist and can be fixed now or it may only have been temporary two months ago with the results not being noticed until today. There is nothing to be done about a cold humid morning two months ago which caused blossom end rot on the fruit developing today.

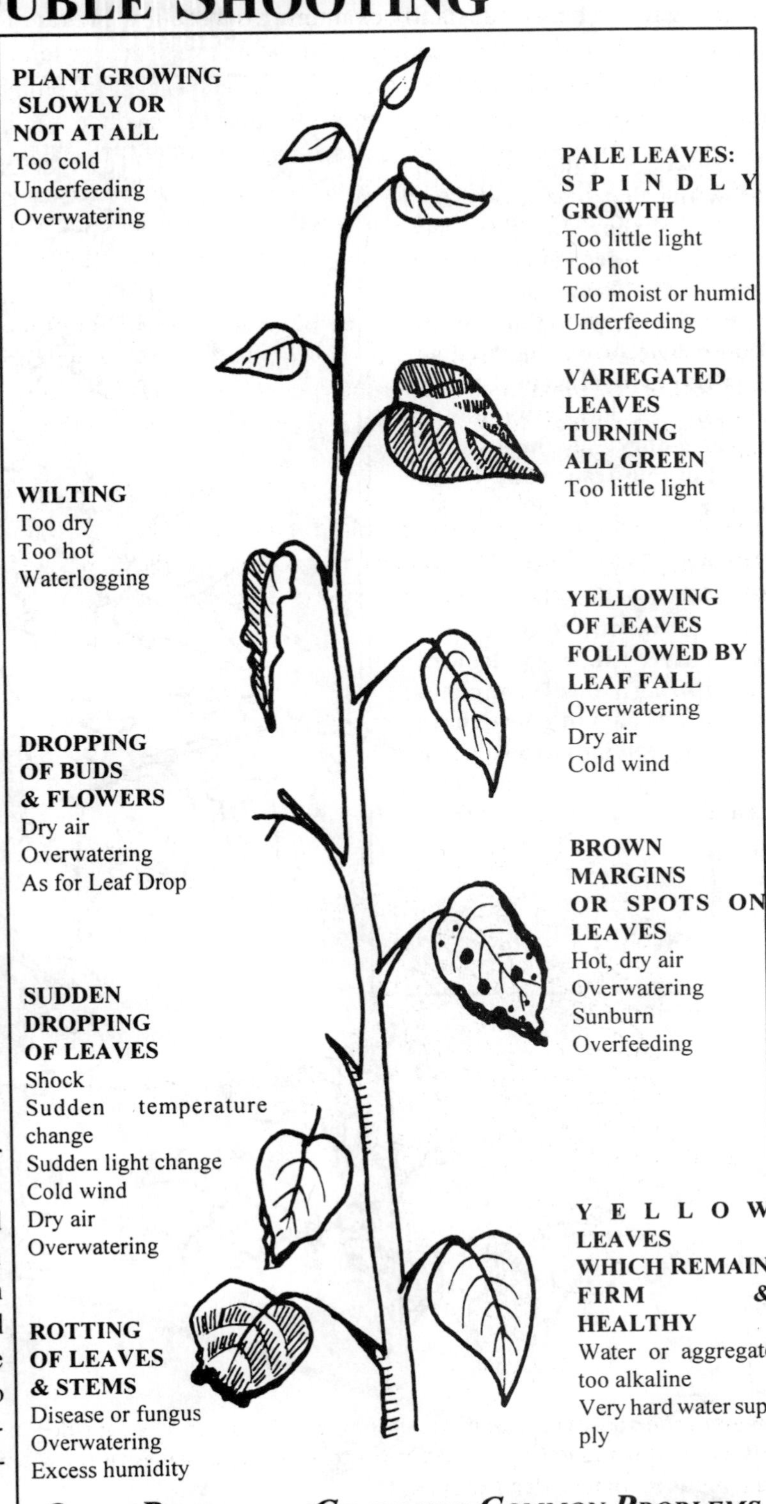

QUICK REFERENCE CHART FOR COMMON PROBLEMS

What happens in the growing point of your plant today can affect plant growth for the next three months. The embryos of leaves, branches and flowers which will appear for up to the next three months already exist in the growing point. This is why good growers always judge the health of the plant by 'looking to the head', constantly examining the top few inches of the plant.

When your seedling begins to grow the first true leaves, the quality of your transplant has already been determined. When you set that transplant out in your growing system, all growth that will occur during the time it takes the first tuss to be ready for harvest, has been initiated in the embryo of the growing point of that transplant. If you understand this it is much easier to understand why what you do or fail to do today will affect the life and productivity of your plant for months to come.

Every time you look at the growing point of your plant, the next 90 days of growth have already been initiated so when many symptoms show up there is nothing you can do to correct it.

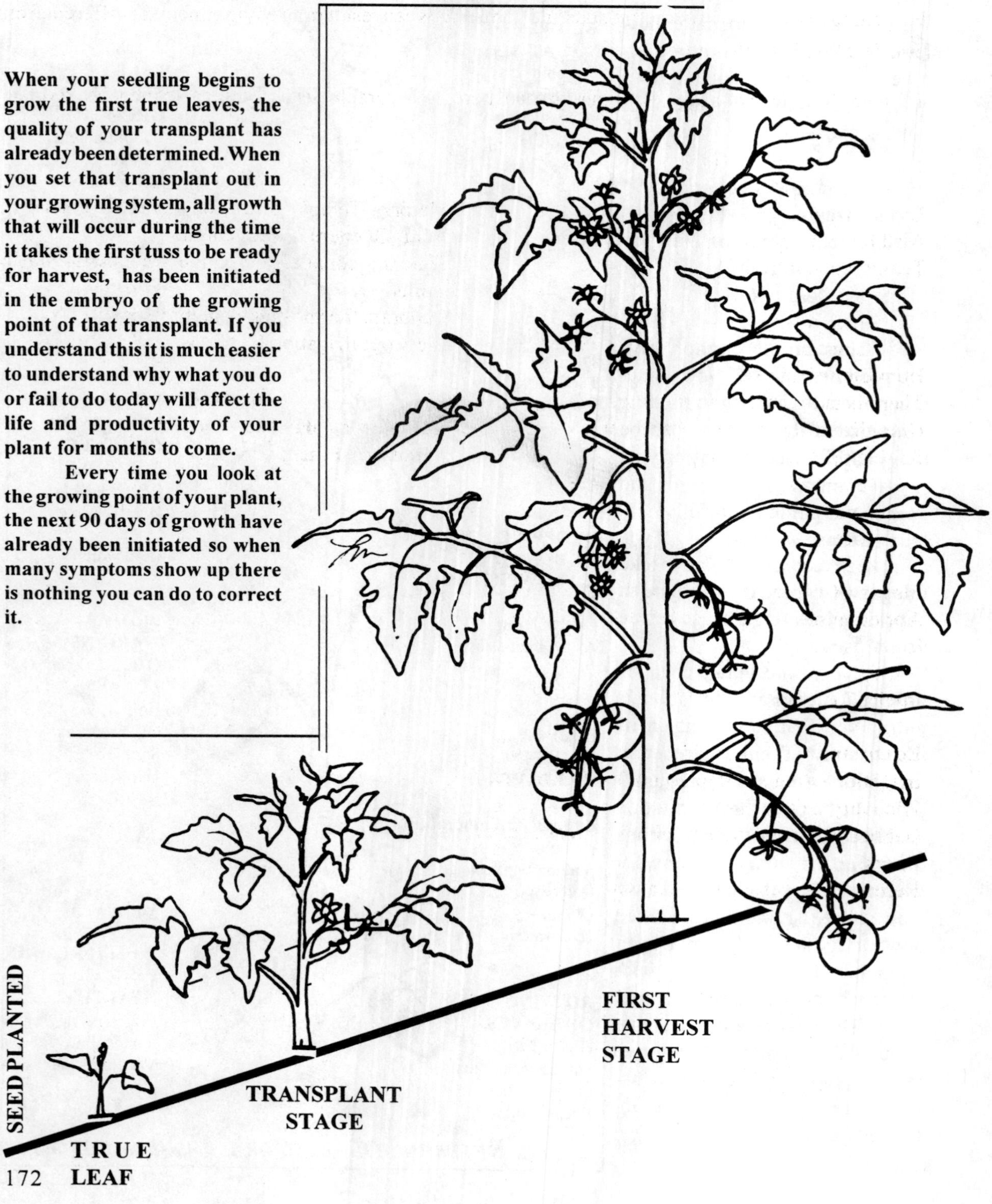

SEED PLANTED

TRUE LEAF

TRANSPLANT STAGE

FIRST HARVEST STAGE

If you want to be able to do your own trouble shooting you will have to maintain a log for your growing area. Commercial growers use computers for this purpose and so can you if you can afford it but, I prefer you to use a hand written log for the first couple of years at least. This is so you establish the habit of regularly examining the plants and every aspect of the garden including all equipment. Automation is nice, but a broken wire, or broken timer, can kill off your crop while you are away. Forgetting to calibrate your thermostats and humidistats can result in an environment far different from the one you planned.

To help you design a log for your garden here is a sample list of things to be checked.

Daily

Environment
Air Flow through plants
Temperature - High Low
air
media
solution
Humidity - High Low
Thermostat - check with thermometer
Humidistat - check with hygrometer
Solution pH - EC - Temp
reservoir
media
drain

Plants - Colour - Size - Head Condition - Leaf Appearance - Flower development - fruit load

Sticky Traps

Equipment
Irrigation - Pump - Timer - injectors (air/nutrient) - delivery device flow
Garden - drainage system - check for leaks - drain filters
Reservoir - level - leaks - contamination

Weekly

Motors - Temperature - connections - leaks
Vent Openers - movement
Timers - connections - time - condensation in works
Calibrate thermostats & humidistats
Blow out irrigation lines

Monthly

Raw Water - pH - EC - temperature
Filtration - Filters

FINDING THE CAUSE

Once you discover a change in the plants you have to figure out what the cause is. A common mistake for new growers is to blame the nutrient they are using for every problem that shows up. If you have a fully formulated nutrient, and are monitoring properly, this is the least likely cause. If you are not monitoring then you will have to do some EC, pH and temperature testing now for the solution and the media if one is being used.

The sequence of steps I go through when trouble shooting is as follows.

1. Take a very close look at the symptom using a 30 power light scope.

2. Figure out where on the plant the problem started.

3. Check the environmental history of the growing area and the actual environmental conditions in the growing area.

4. Check the irrigation scheduling and the output of the delivery device for the plant.

5. Check the EC, pH, O_2 level, and temperature of the nutrient solution.

6. Find out what has changed in the past several weeks. Including equipment breakdowns, power outages, raw water analysis, unusual weather, new equipment installation, new brands of supplies or old brands from new suppliers, and the introduction of new plants, plus anything else I can think of.

You can see that with good record keeping it will be very easy to review the situation and figure out the probable cause. I say probable cause because not always is the most obvious cause the real one. It can be the result of a chain reaction of events so if correcting the first most obvious cause doesn't change things for the better then you will need to look further.

Another advantage of good records for the beginner is that when you take the information to someone who is experienced they can very likely find the problem without ever seeing the garden, as long as you have complete information on steps one to six above.

Sample Troubleshooting

There are a number of very common plant symptoms and problems which seem to be encountered by every gardener at some time. Here are two, followed by some of the usual trouble shooting questions to help you get used to the process.

TROUBLE: Young plants wilting or completely dying off.
QUESTIONS TO ANSWER: Growing medium too wet or waterlogged? Is the drainage system funtioning? Is the media too dry? Are there excess salts on the media? Have there been wild swings in the environment recently? Have the plants suffered mechanical damage recently? Is there discoloration at the root crown? Do the roots show evidence of discoloration or have an odour? Is the nutrient concentration what it should be? Is the irrigation scheduling properly set?

TROUBLE: Yellowing
QUESTIONS TO ANSWER: Has anything changed in the environment recently? Have you changed the nutrient solution formulation or source salts? Did you forget to change your nutrient solution? Are you using a new water supply? Is the irrigation system working properly? Is condensation dripping from a galvanized surface onto the plants?

Use the information in the tables to assist in determing the cause of your problems. Please keep in mind that if you call someone for assistance they will need very specific descriptions of the problem. The location of the problem on the plant, where and when it started, anything that changed from 'normal' just prior to the appearance of the problem are all essential bits of information.

If you ignore plants until they show a multitude of symptoms, finding the cause can be very difficult as the symptoms spread and multiply. The key to good trouble shooting is detecting problems early and acting quickly. This plant is showing so many symptoms that the grower was unable to determine the cause on his own. A common problem amongst growers who do not inspect plants closely on a regular basis.

Table 1: Plant Response Symptoms

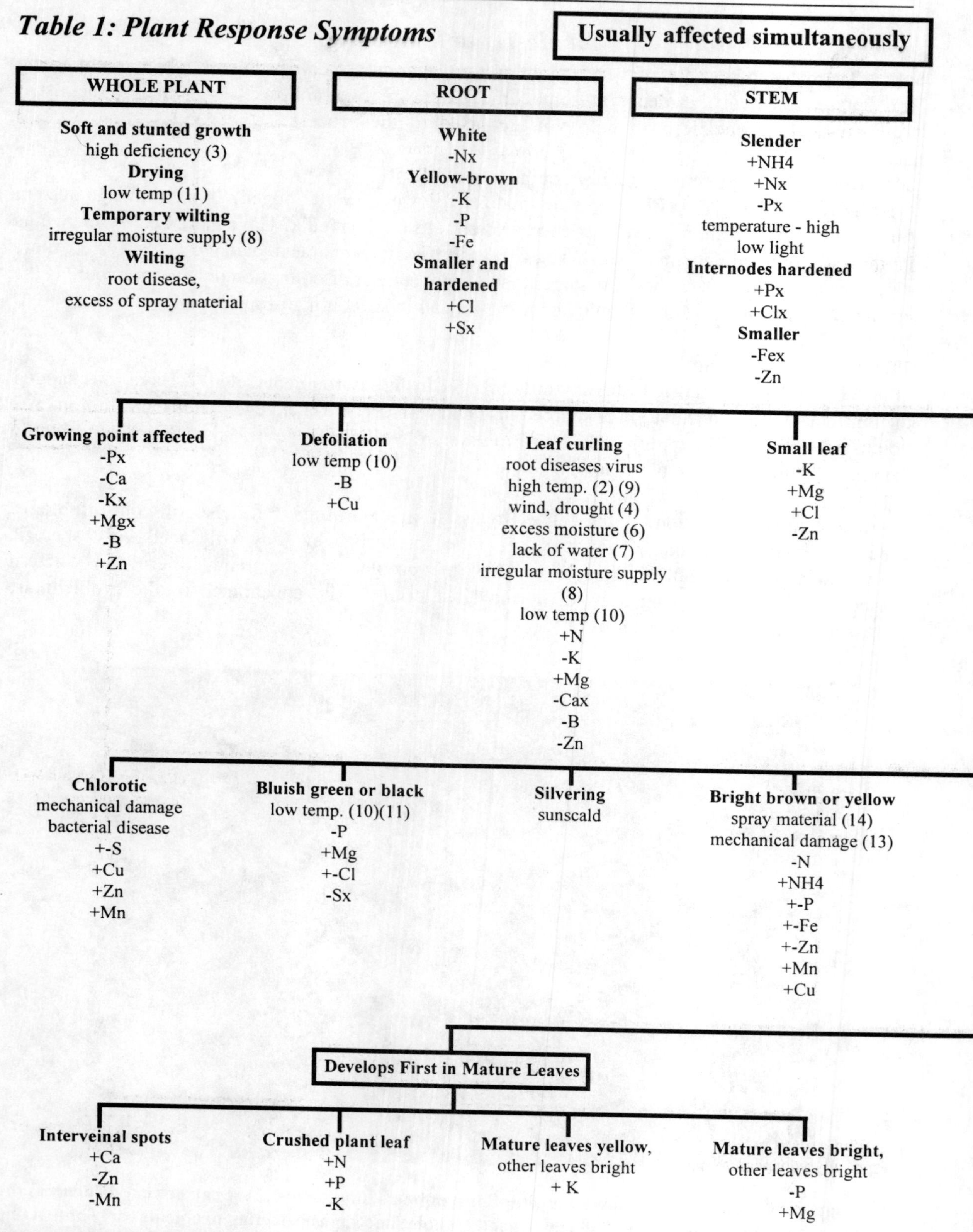

NOTE: The bracketed numbers refer to types of disorder described in Table 2.

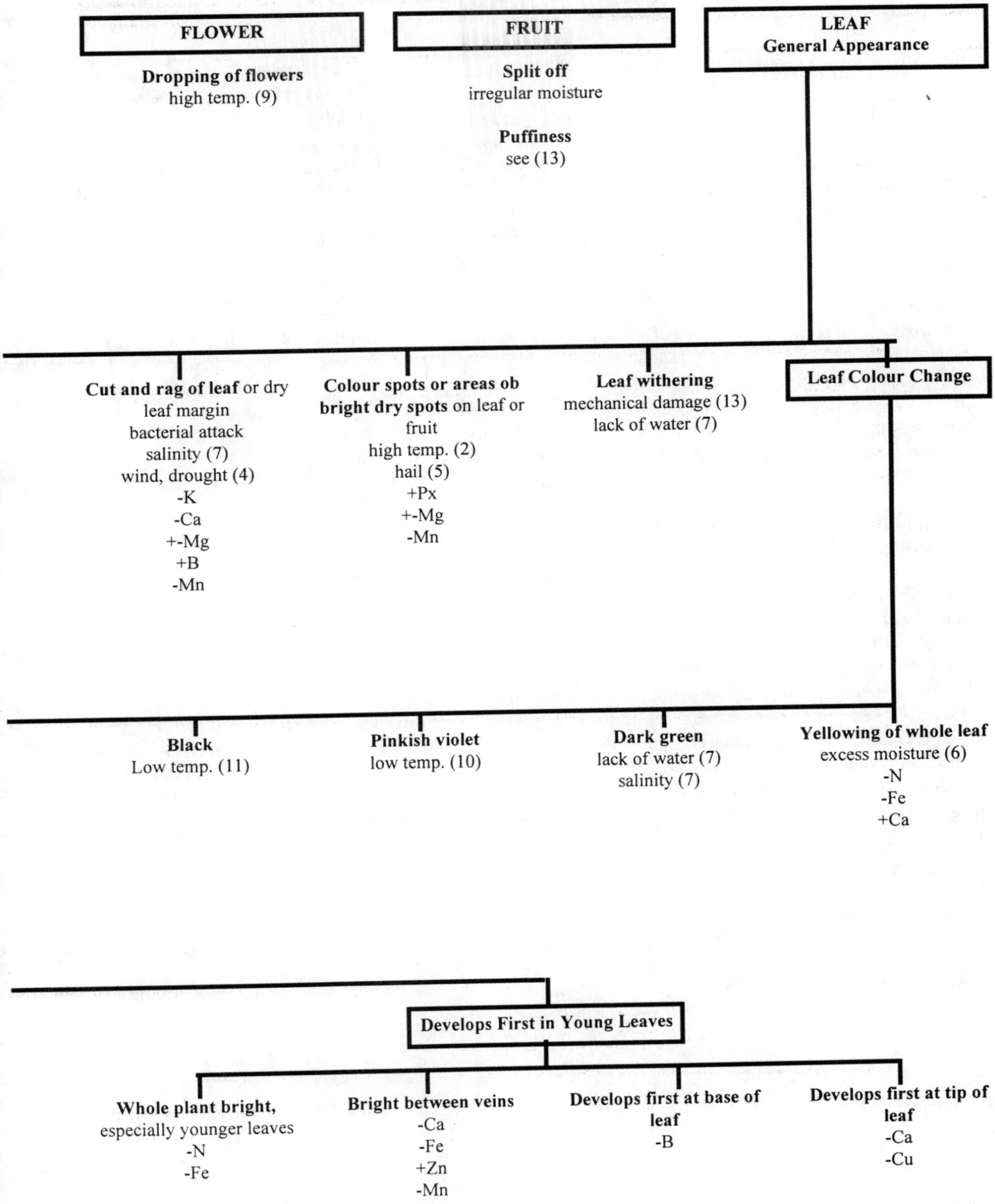

FLOWER
Dropping of flowers
high temp. (9)
FRUIT
Split off
irregular moisture
Puffiness
see (13)
LEAF
General Appearance
Cut and rag of leaf or dry leaf margin
bacterial attack
salinity (7)
wind, drought (4)
-K
-Ca
+-Mg
+B
-Mn
Colour spots or areas ob bright dry spots on leaf or fruit
high temp. (2)
hail (5)
+Px
+-Mg
-Mn
Leaf withering
mechanical damage (13)
lack of water (7)
Leaf Colour Change
Black
Low temp. (11)
Pinkish violet
low temp. (10)
Dark green
lack of water (7)
salinity (7)
Yellowing of whole leaf
excess moisture (6)
-N
-Fe
+Ca
Develops First in Young Leaves
Whole plant bright,
especially younger leaves
-N
-Fe
Bright between veins
-Ca
-Fe
+Zn
-Mn
Develops first at base of leaf
-B
Develops first at tip of leaf
-Ca
-Cu

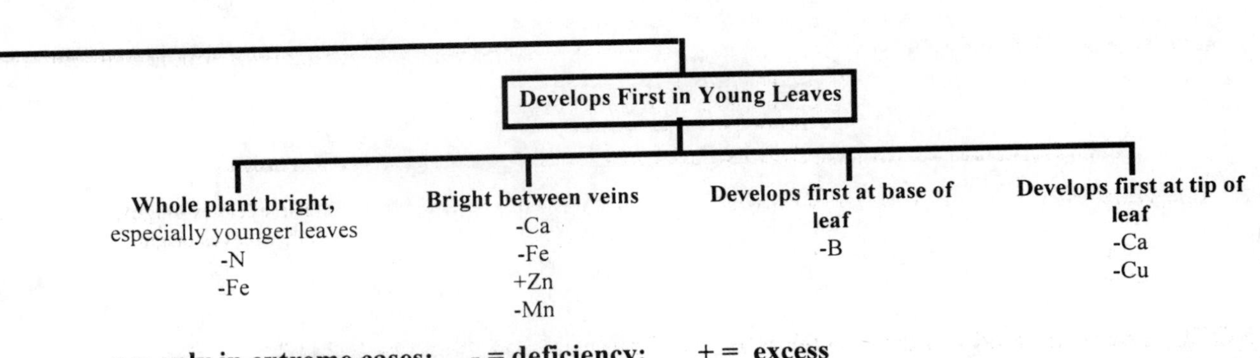

x = only in extreme cases; - = deficiency; + = excess

Table 2: General Key to Foliar Symptoms of Mineral Deficiencies in Plants
(Originally prepared by T.M. Eastwood and C.H. Hobbs for a Plant Physiology Seminar at Purdue University, Lafayette, Indiana, 1912)

I. Initial Injury on Mature Foliage

Mineral Deficiency

A. Generalized Injury
1. Necrosis of tissue
a. Stunted, light green plants; older leaves yellow in colour, followed by drying and browning in advanced stages .... Nitrogen
2. No Necrosis of tissue
a. Stunted abnormally dark green plants usually with narrow petiole angles; abundant reddish or purplish pigmentation; sometimes chlorosis of older leaves .... Phosphorus

B. Localized Injury
1. Chlorosis starts at tips and margins of older leaves, progressing between veins, followed by brown necrotic spots which usually fall out giving a ragged appearance; leaves crinkled and curlled, most noticeable in early stages .... Potassium
2. Irregular chlorotic spots between veins of older leaves, followed by rapid necrosis and defoliation; die-back of twigs and small leaved rosettes common in fruit trees .... Zinc
3. Chlorosis starts between veins in older leaves, leaves become yellow or almost white with veins usually remaining green; necrosis not usual .... Magnesium

II. Initial Injury on Immature Foliage
A. Generalized Injury
1. Entire plant light green to yellowish green in clour. chlorosis most pronounced in young leaves which become yellow .... Sulphur
B. Localized Injury
1. Necrosis of tissue
a. Interveinal chlorosis of young leaves; leaves become yellow or white in colour, all veins remaining green; small brown necrotic spots follow chlorosis .... Manganese
b. Chlorosis generally begins at bases and margins of young leaves, followed by necrosis; leaves become distorted or in more severe deficiencies, terminal buds die and turn brown or black in colour; gummy or corky deposits occur in fleshy organs .... Boron
c. Chlorosis generally begins at tips and margins of young leaves, progressing between veins, followed by necrosis; leaves become distorted or in more severe deficiencies, terminal buds die and turn brown or black in colour; roots characteristically short, bulbous, with necrotic apical meristems .... Calcium
2. No Necrosis of tissue
a. Interveinal chlorosis of young leaves, veins remaining green; entire leaf including veins becomes yellow or white in colour .... Iron
b. Plants exhibit lack of turgor; wilting most pronounced in tops; sometimes chlorosis of young leaves .... Copper

Table 3; Tentative General Key to Foliar Symptoms of Mineral Toxicities in Plants
(Compiled for available litersature and practical observation)

I Initial Injury on Mature Foliage **Toxicity due to**

A. Site of Injury General

1. Necrosis of tissue

a. Leaves become slightly darker green, sightly smaller; sometimes abnormal rolling and curling of young leaves occurs; in advanced stages growing tips wilt and dies, especially in bright weather .... Magnesium

b. General yellowing of leaves, older leaf tips and margins later become yellowish or brownish, followed by coloured necrotic spots; leaf abscission develops (similar to potassium deficiency in some plants and nitrogen excess in others) .... Phosphorus

2. No Necrosis of tissue

a. General hardening of plant, dull green, small leaf, hard stems; some plants have purplish-brown spots on older leaves, followed by leaf drop .... Chloride

b. General hardening of plant, blusi-green in colour of leaf, small leaf, hard stems; later leaves may become curled inward and pimpled, leaf margins brown and terminal growth becomes pale yellow .... Sulphate

c. Early Stages; slender growth, longer internodes,, light green leaves; Later Stages; stunted growth in general, leaves develop mosaic-like mottling, followed by dull coloured spots, leaf wilting and abscission occurs .... Potassium

B. Localized Injury

1. Necrosis of tissue

a. Marginal chlorosis of leaves develop, which extends inward between veins followed by brown necrosis and curling of leaf edge; leaf abscission (injury similar to potassium deficiency in some plants and iron deficiency in others; a terminal chlorosis) .... Nitrogen

b. Interveinal chlorosis develops, spots becoming whitish and necrotic, may become coloured or possess water soaked concentric rings, some plants have rosette-leaf growth and twig die-back with defoliation (injury similar to magnesium deficiency in some plants and iron deficiency in others) .... Calcium

c. Chlorosis of leaf margins and tips, chlorosis extends inward, particularly between veins until whole leaf becomes pale yellow or whitish; marginal burning and necrosis with crinkling of lead edges; leaf abscission ... Boron

d. Water-soaked areas develop along main veins which remain green in leaf of some plants; areas become transparent; interveinal chlorosis develops as well, later turning brown and when the entire leaf is brown defoliation occurs (also see zinc in immature) .... Zinc

e. Chlorosis of lower leaves followed by brown spots, then defoliation (also see zinc in immature) .... Copper

II. Initial Injury on Immature Foliage

A. Generalized Injury

1. Necrosis of tissue

a. Chorosis of leaves, young leaves become quite yellow; terminal buds die; also older leaves may droop without wilting, veins become coloured red or black; leaf abscission (injury in early stages simialr to iron deficiency) ..... Zinc

B. Localized Injury

1. Necrosis of tissue

a. Interveinal chlorosis of young leaves, become yellow or whitish with dark brown or nearly white necrotic spots; leaf becomes distorted and crinkled-the main difference from deficiency; plants like corn have whitish streaks in older leaves .... Manganese

2. No Necrosis of tissue

a. Interveinal chlorosis of young leaves, veins remain green, later entire leaf becomes yellow or whitish - similar to a deficiency .... Iron

b. Chlorosis of young leaves, veins remain green .... Copper

Table 4. Physiological disorders of vegetable plants caused by mechanical or climatic factors.

Main cause	Secondary Cause	Part Affected	Disorder Symptom	Similar Symptom Nutrient Problem
1. Sunscald	leaves laid bare by wind, after pruning	leaf, underside only	silvering	P-
2. Temporary high temperature	low wind; fall of leaves due to leaf or root diseases which may be the result of dry media.	leaves fruit	rolled-up leaves during hot hours bright dry spots, sometimes depressed	
3. Light deficiency	too much shade in the area	whole plant	soft and stunted plant, long internode	
4. Wind, drought		leaf	a. dry leaf margin, leaf curl b. cut and rag of plant leaf c. general appearance of damaged plant	P-, K-, N+
5. Hail		leaf, stem, fruit	bright, depressed spots in the tissue	
6. Excess moisture	inadequate root aeration	leaf	yellowing, first in younger leaves, leaf often curled	
7. Lack of water	wind, saline water, infrequent irrigation	leaf	dark green colour, withering, leaf curling	
8. Irregular moisture supply	irregular irrigation, rainfall, high media EC	plant, fruit	temporary wilting, splitting of fruit	
9. High temperature	fan or, vent failure	leaf, flower	leaf curl, flower drop	
10. Low temperature above freezing	heating, vent or, thermostat failure	leaf, flower	leaf curl, leaf colour pinkish violet especially on veins	N-, P-, K-
11. Low temperature below freezing		leaf, whole plant	drying of plant, withering black leaves and fruit	
12. Excessively high or low temperature		fruit	puffiness, fruit inadequately fleshed	
13. Mechanical damage	leaf-rubbing, wind, over planting	leaf	leaves withering, bright brown colour	
14. Spray material, excessive leaf fertilizing	ammonium, sulfur spray, sulphate	leaf	leaf burned, bright brown colour	

Appendix 1.

CONVERSION TABLES FOR BRITISH AND METRIC UNITS

Weight Conversions

1 ounce	= 0.063 pound	= 0.028 kilogram
1 kilogram	= 2.2 pounds	= 35.28 ounces
1 pound	= 0.454 kilogram	= 16 ounces
1 kilogram	= 1,000 grams	= 1,000,000 milligrams

Volume Conversions

1 litre
= 1,000 millitres
= 1,000 cm^3
= 1,000,000 ul
= 0.028 m^3
= 0.035 ft^3
= 1.06 qt
= 0.263 gal US
= 0.219976 gal imp.
= 33.80 oz
= 200 tsp

1 foot^3
= 28.3161 litres
= 0.037 yd^3
= 29.95 qt
= 7.447 gal US
= 6.229 gal Imperial
= 957.3 ounces

1 yard^3
= 764.534 liters
= 27 foot^3
= 21.71 bushels

1 bushel
= 0.035 meter^3
= 35.24 liters
= 1.24 foot^3
= 0.046 yard^3
= 32.0 quarts
= 9.3 gallons imp

1 quart US
= 0.947 liters
= 0.033 foot^3
= 32 ounces
= 192 teaspoons

1 gallon US = 3.785 liters
= 0.8327 gallons Imperial
= 0.134 foot^3
= 4 quarts
= 128 ounces
= 768 teaspoons

1 gallon Imperial = 4.5454 liters
= 1.2009 gallons US

1 ounce (Av.)= 0.029 liters
= 0.00104 foot^3
= 0.031 quart
= 0.0078 gallons US
= 6 teaspoons
= 28.3495 grams

GLOSSARY

acid;
Any substance having a pH of less than 7.

acidic;
Pertaining to an acid or its properties; Forming an acid during a chemical process; A nutrient which will drop the pH of a solution or media when it is added.

adsorption;
The surface retention of any solid, liquid, or gas on a host solid or liquid without penetration of the host.

aeration;
The process of introducing air into a media or solution through any means such as but not limited to stirring, spraying, injection or bubbling.

aerobic;
Dependent on the presence of oxygen for a life process or metabolism

aggregate;
Any mineral mass which is in a crushed or particle state; Sand and gravel being the ones most commonly used in hydroponic culture. Also refers to mineral based materials such as expanded clay or oil fired shale which are used as grow media.

air drainage;
The natural flow of cold air from high to lower levels.

air cap;
Also called bubble pack. A double layer of polyethylene sealed into small bubbles. Often used for insulation in greenhouses.

alkaline;
Any substance having a pH of greater than 7.

alkaloid;
One of a group of nitrogenous bases of plant origin, eg., caffeine.

alleopathy;
The harmful influence on a plant by another living plant that secretes a toxic substance.

ambient;
The existing, surrounding environment which is uncontrolled and uninfluenced. Also referred to in relation to all environmental characteristics.

anaerobic;
A process or organism which exists in an environment which has no available oxygen. An oxygen deprived environment.

angstrom unit;
The unit of measure commonly used to describe radiant energy wavelenth. Equal to 10^{-10} of a meter.

asexual;
Having no sexual organs. Capable of reproduction without sex.

antibiotic;
A chemical substance, produced by microorganisms , that has the capacity in dilute solutions to inhibit the growth of, and even destroy, bacteria and other microorganisms.

atrium;
A central court, surrounded by four walls and open to the sky.

automatic damper;
A device for regulating the flow of air which is controlled by a thermostat.

auxiliary bud;
A side shoot growing out of the stem at the joining of a leaf stem and the main stem.

back-flow preventer;
A device which permits the flow of water in one direction only. Required by law in many areas any time fertilizers or other chemicals are introduced into the flow of water originating from a municipal or other source which supplies water for human consumption.

bacteria;
Extremely small, relatively simple microorganism. Traditionally classified with fungi.

base;
Any element or chemical capable of accepting a proton. The hydroxyl ion is a base OH^-.

basic;
Pertaining to a base or its properties; Forming an base during a chemical process; A nutrient which will raise the pH of a solution or media when it is added.

bed;
Any specifically designated or constructed location which contains a media for the purpose of growing plants.

biodegradable;
Any compound capable of being broken down by microorganisms or their enzymes.

bitumenized;
Painted with bitumen.

blackbody;
Any body which will absorb all incident radiation and reflect none. Used to describe the sky on a clear dark night which draws heat radiation from a greenhouse.

bolster bag;
A plastic tube, generally under 1 meter in length, which contains growing media for use in a drain to waste system.

bolting;
The very rapid evolution of a green plant, eg., lettuce, from vegetative growth to seed in response to environmental conditions. The stimuli are usually high temperature and long days.

botany;
The branch of the biological sciences which specifically studies plants and plant life.

boundary-layer;
The specific layer of a surrounding liquid or gas which conforms precisely to a plant part. The division between layers of air or water generally caused by temperature gradients.

brittle tissue;
Plant tissue which lacks flexibility and breaks easily when touched.

BTU
British Thermal Unit; The amount of thermal energy required to raise the temperature of one pound of water one degree Fahrenheit.

calcareous;
Resembling, containing, or composed of calcium carbonate.

cambium;
A layer of cells between the phloem and xylem tubes of most vascular plants that is responsible for secondary growth and generating new cells. The rapidly dividing tissue between the bark and the wood in woody plants.

capillary action;
The movement of a liquid in response to capillary attraction to a solid or solid matrix.

capillary attraction;
The attraction of a liquid to a solid when the liquid bonding is weaker than the bonding attraction between the solid and the liquid.

carbohydrate;
Any of a group of chemical compounds, including sugars, starches, and cellulose, made up of carbon, hydrogen and oxygen.

catalyst;
Any agent or compound which causes a change or initiates a process without being changed itself.

cation;
An atom or group of atoms with a positive charge.

cation exchange;
The process whereby cations of a solid, which have water molecules are associated, are exchanged for cations of like charge in solid on the basis of equal charge exchange.

CEC cation exchange capacity;
The measurable potential for cation exchange inherent in any specific material or compound.

cellulose;
The natural glucose polymer which forms the skeletal structure of the plant cell.

chelate(s);
Generally trace elements which have been temporarily bonded to a molecular structure which keeps the trace elements available to the plant roots for uptake.

chloroplasts;
The cells in the green portions of plants which produce the chlorophyll. They function in photosynthesis and protein production.

chlorophyll;
The green pigments in plant cells which act as photoreceptors of light energy for photosynthesis.

chlorosis;
Yellowing of plant parts as an indication of nutrient deficiency or other damage.

clone;
A plant produced through asexual reproduction including, but not limited to, cuttings, layering, and tissue culture.

companion planting;
The practice of combining plants in a garden in such a way as to provide a protective benefit to the overall planting.

compost;
The result of the controlled decomposition of organic matter, also an old term for media specially mixed for containers.

conductivity;
The ability of a solution to carry electrical energy as a result of the elements and compounds in the solution.

conductivity meter;
An electronic meter designed to measure the ability of solution to carry current and provide a readout related to the concentration of elements and compounds in the solution.

controlled release fertilizer;
A fertilizer which has been combined with a material which slows the rate at which the fertilizer will dissolve in water. The material may degrade over time or respond to changes in temperature or other stimuli. Commonly used in commercial potted plant production.

controller;
Any device which regulates the operation of one or more pieces of equipment. The device may operate on the basis of time or a combination of time and the measurement of any number of environmental conditions.

copolymer;
A mixed polymer, the result of mixing two or more substances at the time the polymer chains are formed.

cultivar;
A cultivated species of plant for which there is no known wild ancestor.

cupping;
The curling of leaves up or down in response to environmental or nutrient problems. Can be so severe the plant leaf will curl into a tube.

cutting;
A portion of a plant, usually ending in a growing point, removed for the purpose of asexual reproduction.

cycling timer;
A timer which repeats a sequence of on/off events and has a clock with a duration of less than 24 hours.

damping off;
The process of blackening of the base of the stem of a seedling which causes it to die. Caused by several fungi and most severe on weak or damaged seedlings.

degree days (DD);
A unit of measure used in calculations to quantify the amount of energy required during a heating season. One degree day is one day when the temperature is one degree below 65°F. For it to be a full degree day the reduction must occur for 24 hours. Multiple degree decreases result in multiple degree days within the same 24 hour period.

diffusion;
The movement of a concentrated element, compound or gas, through a liquid or gas from areas of high concentration to areas of lower concentration in a natural tendency to reach a state of equal concentration.

dormancy;
The resting state of a plant during adverse environmental conditions. Also necessary for the reproductive cycle of some species of plant.

drawdown;
The process of removing a commodity from a storage facility.

dry weight;
The weight of organic material after all water has been removed from the tissue.

dry-feed;
The application of dry fertilizer to a garden.

EC; see conductivity

ecosystem;
A specifically defined environment including all living organisms contained in it and the processes they initiate and effect.

effluent;
Waste material from an organic process. In plants, the root effluent is both gaseous and solid in the form of protein.

element;
A substance made up of atoms having the same atomic number. eg., hydrogen, gold etc.

embryo;
The early stage of development of a multi-celled plant.

emulsion;
The stable dispersion of one liquid in another with which it will not mix. eg., milk, which is oil dispersed in water.

enzyme;
Any of a group of catalytic proteins that are produced by living cells and that mediate and promote the chemical processes of life without themselves being altered or destroyed.

etiolation;
The yellowing or whitening of green plant parts grown in darkness or under inadequate light.

exotic;
Any plant introduced to an area which is not native to the area.

flat;
Shallow tray used in propagation, generally 10"x20" in North America and often containing a set of smaller containers designed for the tray.

flume;
A narrow open channel designed to conduct liquid flow.

foliar feeding;
The application of dissolved fertilizers to the leaves of plants.

footcandle;
A unit of measurement for illumination. Originally defined as the light received by a surface one foot away from a candle. abbreviations; ftc., f/c.

forced air;
Air which is drawn or pushed through a defined area by electric fans.

formula;
The recipe which gives the proportion of ingredients required to yield a specific nutrient solution.

frond;
The leaf of a fern.

fungicide;
Any naturally occurring or man-made material which kills fungi.

fungus;
A nucleated, usually filamentous, sporebearing organisms devoid of chlorophyll. Many species are the cause of plant damage and death in horticulture.

galvanised;
Zinc coated.

generalized;
Symptoms not limited to one area, generally spread over the plant or leaf.

genus;
The principle subdivision of a plant family comprised of groups of closely related species.

germinate;
The process of causing the initiation and development of a plant from seed.

gravel;
Crushed rock varying in size. May be freshly machine crushed or the result of natural erosion.

growth chamber;
Any chamber designed for plant growth which provides all of the essential environmental and energy inputs including food and disposal of wastes.

growth regulators;
Naturally occurring plant hormones which control the speed and type of growth which occurs at all stages of plant growth.

habitat;
The part of a physical environment in which a plant lives.

harden off;
The process of acclimatizing a plant to live in a new environment which is generally harsher than the environment it is leaving.

hardy;
A word used to describe plants which will tolerate adverse environmental conditions. There are degrees of tolerance which are defined by environmental zones with specific ranges of conditions.

heat capacity;
The amount of heat energy required to raise the temperature of a defined system 1°F.

heel cutting;
Any cutting which has a piece of older stem wood at the base.

herbagere;
A fancy name for a sprout production system.

hormone;
An organic compound which is synthesized in one portion of a plant, and translocated to another part of the plant, where it influences a specific physiological process.

horticulturist;
An individual trained and experienced in the application of the art and science of growing plants.

host;
The plant on or in which a parasite lives or the dominant member of a symbiotic relationship.

humidistat;
An instrument which controls equipment designed to affect the humidity in an environment.

humidity;
The presence of water vapour in the air. The higher the vapour content the higher the humidity.

hygrometer;
A device which measures the amount of moisture in the air relative to the maximum amount of moisture the air could hold at a specific temperature.

hygroscopic;
Any structure or material which is sensitive to the amount of moisture in the air and can cause the moisture to condense from the air or is itself changed by the presence of the moisture.

hydroponicist;
An individual trained and experienced in the application of the art and science of growing plants in fully controlled, rootzone ecosystem, environments.

hydroponics;
Growing plants by feeding the plants directly without an intermediary process involving live organisms.

hypertonic;
A nutrient solution with a higher EC than a solution taken as a standard.

hyphae;
The filaments composing the mycelium of a fungus.

incident radiation;
The radiation from the sun which falls directly upon the plants.

inert;
Having no activity, reactivity or effect.

inert growing medium;
Any material used in the root zone of plants which remains stable over time and does not interact with the nutrient solution or plant roots.

injector;
A device which will add a liquid concentrate at a specific rate to another fluid.

inorganic;
Matter other than plant or animal. Matter not composed of carbon as the principle element.

insolation;
Solar energy received, commonly expressed as a rate of energy per unit of horizontal surface area; mW/m.

interveinal;
Occuring between the veins on the leaf of a plant without affecting the vein.

ion;
Any electron, positron, element or compound which has a net electrical charge.

ion exchange;
The movement of an ion in replacement of another ion.

kinetic;
Pertaining to or producing motion.

kinetic energy;
The energy contained in a body due to its motion. Equal to one-half the bodies mass times the square of its speed.

larva;
Growth stage of many insects. The stage after the egg hatches.

leaching;
The dissolving of a mineral by a liquid solvent from its mixture with an insoluble solid. In horticulture the solution is then carried away from the roots of the plants by the percolation of the solution down through the soil.

lime;
The powdery product of crushing limestone. Commonly used to raise pH in medias and soils.

limiting factors;
Any factor which by its absence, or availability in less than optimum value, reduces or limits the growth of a plant.

localized;
Symptoms limited to one area of a plant or leaf, Environmental conditions within a defined area

macro-elements;
Those elements taken up by the roots of plants which are used in large quantity and tend to become fixed in internal plant structures.

marginal;
Occuring first on the margins of leaves and often spreading inward.

media;
The material in which plant roots grow.

medium;
The special combination of agar, nutrients and hormones used in tissue culture. Also, used as another name for media.

metabolic;
Pertaining to metabolism.

metabolism;
The combination of all physical and chemical processes by which a plant grows.

mica;
A sheet silicate. A specialized form of mica is the source of vermiculite.

mineral;
A naturally occurring substance with a characteristic chemical composition. In Hydroponics, a generic name for an element taken up by the roots of plants.

micro-elements;
Also called trace elements. These are the elements used in very small amounts by plants. They tend to be very mobile in the plant and large accumulations in the plant are very toxic.

mottling;
The irregular light and dark pattern of colouration on a leaf. Blotchy in appearance.

necrosis;
A scorched, dry, papery appearance on a plant, generally leaves

oedema;
The appearance of 'blisters' on the leaves of plants caused by poor environmental control which results in low transpiration and excess water levels in the plant.

osmosis;
The process which enables plant roots to take up water and minerals. It is the movement of water and minerals from an area of low concentration (the nutrient solution) to an area of high concentration (the plant cell) through a semi-permeable membrane (the cell wall).

parasite;
An organism that lives in or on another organism of different species from which it derives nutrients and shelter.

pathogen;
A disease producing agent, usually referring to a living organism.

petiole;
The stem that supports the blade of a leaf.

pH;
A term used to describe the hydrogen ion activity in a solution or system. The concentration of hydrogen ions determines how other elements interact and their availability to plant roots.

phloem;
The complex, food-conducting vascular tissue in the stems of higher plants.

photoperiodism;
The physiological response of plants to day length, and to the length of the dark period or a combination of both.

photosynthesis;
The process occurring in plants where light energy is used to synthesis plant foods from carbon dioxide in the air and water plus other minerals.

physiologist;
One who study the activities in cells and tissues using physical and chemical methods.

phytotoxicity;
The measure of the strength of a phytotoxin. Also, the sensitivity rating of a plant to a toxin.

phytotoxin;
Plant products which have toxic effects on herbivores and other invasive organisms.

phytotron;
Another name for a larger growth chamber.

pistil;
The female part of a flower.

plumule;
The primary bud of a plant embryo.

polarity;
The property of a physical system which has two points with different (usually opposite) characteristics.

pollen;
The small male reproductive bodies produced in pollen sacs of the seed plants.

pollination;
The transfer of pollen from a stamen to a pistil. Often enhanced by environmental manipulation, plant movement through shaking or vibrating or the introduction of bees into the growing area.

protoplasm;
The colloidal complex of protein that composes the living material of a cell.

psi.
Pounds per square inch. The unit of measure for pressure in atmospheric and water systems.

pupa;
The intermediate stage of an insect life cycle between the larva and adult stages. This stage is enclosed in a hardened cuticle or cocoon which makes it almost impossible to kill insects in this stage.

pyranometer;
An instrument used to measure the combined intensity of incoming direct solar radiation and diffuse sky radiation.

radiant energy;
The heat energy emitted by a pre-heated body whether plant material or a portion of a structure or heating system.

reflectance;
The ratio of the amount of incident energy on a surface to the amount of energy reflected from the surface.

reservoir;
Any container of a variety of constructions which holds water in reserve for use.

respiration;
The processes by which plants exchange gasses with their environment and also the process of liberation of energy due to the chemical breakdown of food in plant cells.

respirator;
Protective breathing equipment used to filter air when toxic pesticides or other chemicals are being applied in a growing environment.

salts;
Chemical compounds which contain metallic elements.

sand;
A loose material consisting of small mineral particles, or rock and mineral particles. Coarse silica sand is the sand most commonly used for hydroponics.

scarify;
Break the outer shell of a seed through abrasion or cutting to promote germination by making water absorption for seed swell easier.

scorch;
The browning of plant tissue in response to heat or parasites. It can also be symptomatic of disease.

selective black paint;
Specially formulated black paint which absorbs more infrared than usual black paint.

semipermeable;
A membrane which allows certain solvents to pass it, but not certain dissolved or colloidal substances.

simples;
Fertilizers which contain only one element such as Urea or unformulated fertilizer salts such as calcium nitrate.

siphon;
The movement of a fluid from a higher to a lower level using a tube and the combination of gravity induced suction and atmospheric pressure.

soft tissue;
Plant tissue which is very soft and succulent. It is very susceptible to mechanical damage.

solar altitude;
The angle of the sun above the horizon.

solar furnace;
A furnace which uses solar radiation as the energy source.

spaghetti system;
The name given to an irrigation system where the final delivery to the plants is through thin tubes with no delivery device controlling the flow.

spindly;
The thin and soft growth of plant stems and leaf petioles due to environmental or nutrient problems.

spots;
Clearly defined areas of discoloration as compared to surrounding healthy or 'normal' plant tissue.

stomata (stoma singular);
The minute openings in the epidermis of leaves of higher plants which are regulated by guard cells and through which air and water vapour are exchanged.

stopping;
The practice of removing the growing point of a plant in order to direct all energy into the reproductive process or cause the initiation of new growing points.

stress;
An excess or scarcity of an environmental or nutrient requirement of a plant to the degree that the normal growth of the plant is interrupted or adversely effected.

stunting;
Abnormally small plants for the age as related to normal plant size.

sub-irrigation;
The practice of providing irrigation water, or solution, to the bottom of the growing container and relying on the growing media to distribute the solution throughout the container.

sump;
A small reservoir used to collect drain water in a gravity system before it is pumped back to the main reservoir.

sun pit;
A greenhouse with the eave at ground level and roof glazing oriented to collect winter sun.

synergism;
An ecological association in which the physiological processes or behaviour of an individual are enhanced by the nearby presence of another organism.

systemic;
Used in reference to a disease within the plant tissue, not initiated from the external cells. Also refers to materials and compounds which are taken up or absorbed by the plant and designed to fight disease.

temperature;
The property of an object or environment which determines the direction of energy flow in the form of heat to surrounding objects or environments. Objects or environments possessing excess energy, radiate to objects or environments possessing less energy.

thru-hull fitting;
A fitting designed for the marine industry which provides a leakless connection point in plastic, and other, containers.

trace elements; See microelements

transpiration;
The process whereby the plant eliminates water and cools itself. The passage of a gas or liquid (in vapour form) through the external tissue of the plant.

turgor pressure;
The actual pressure developed by the fluid content of a plant cell. This is the pressure which swells the cells and keeps the plant erect and allows orientation of the leaves.

ultraviolet radiation;
Electromagnetic radiation in the wavelength range of 4-400 nanometres. This is at the beginning of the range of the visible spectrum and radiation in the smaller values is very harmful to plant and animal life.

vapour barrier;
A barrier, usually plastic, installed to keep moisture within a specific environment.

vapour pressure deficit;
The difference between the vapour pressure in plant tissue and the vapour pressure in the surrounding atmosphere.

vapour pressure;
The partial pressure of water vapour in the atmosphere.

venturi;
A device designed to cause a restriction in the flow of fluid through a reduction in the diameter of the passage which can be used to draw an additional fluid into the flow.

virus;
A group of infectious agents which cannot exist without a living cell. They are generally composed of a protein sheath surrounding a nucleic acid core which utilizes the living cell as a resource for existence and reproduction.

wetting agent;
A compound which renders a surface nonrepellent to a wetting agent.

wilt;
The 'drooping' of a plant or its leaves caused by a loss of turgor in the plant cells. This can be the result of stress or disease.

xylem;
The chief water-conducting tissue and the major supporting tissue of higher plants.

INDEX

Nutrients are the cornerstone of any garden. They are the building blocks plants use to turn sunshine into growth. This is the first book published anywhere which provides gardeners at all levels of expertise, from beginner to commercial grower, with the ability to take control of plant nutrition. It is not always necessary to make your own plant foods but it is essential to know what is in the plant nutrients you use and why your plants respond as they do.

'Hydroponic Nutrients' provides even the brown thumb beginner with the two critical items necessary for success in hydroponics and optimum plant growth in all types of gardens; the ability to translate the mysterious label numbers into something which makes sense and the understanding of the role each nutrient plays in plant growth.

This is the expanded 2nd edition of the book relied on by growers and educators around the world. Like the first edition, this edition has drawn high praise from hobbyists, educators and commercial growers in many countries. The reason is simple. It is easy to read. The information is clear, up to date and easy to understand. There are many sample formulas included which make getting started easy indeed.

The Essence of Hydroponics is Plant Nutrition

Why Let Someone Else Control Your Potential Yields And Growing Success?

When You can Take Control Save Money and Get Better Results in Any Garden

Get Your Copy Today

156 printed pages, charts, tables, appendix, softcover

All the latest information on Plant Nutrition

To Order Write:

Growers Press Inc, P.O. Box 189,
Princeton, B.C. Canada V0X 1W0
Or Phone/Fax your order to [604] 295-7755

This Book is
Readable, Accurate, Up-to-Date, and Easy to Use
And it Contains Information on Every Plant You Grow !
No Matter How You Grow It !

Registration Card

If you did not purchase this copy of
Basic HYDROPONICS ***for the do-it-yourselfer***
directly from Growers Press Inc.

It is to your benefit to register your purchase now

1. We will send you a complimentary copy of The 21st Century Gardener

2. We will advise you of new publications covering all aspects of greenhouse and hydroponic gardening and controlled environment plant culture.

3. We also distribute 100's of gardening books of all types from around the world. Upon registration we will send you a free copy of our current catalogue.

NOTE:

All information provided is held confidential and is not made available to any other company for marketing or any other purpose.

Name ____

Address ____________________________________ City ______________

State/Prov. ______________ Country ____________ Postal/Zip Code ____________

General Survey Information
To help us create the right books for your needs
Level of Gardening

HOBBY - Beginner ____ Advanced ____ **Commercial**: Under 2 acres ___ Over 2 ____
Greenhouse ____ Outdoor ____ Indoor _____
Cultural Systems Used ____________________________________
Main Crops Grown ______________________________________
Are your planning a future in commercial growing? ____________________

Areas of Special Interest

Greenhouse: Operation ___ Management ___ Construction ____ Other ____________
Environment: Control _____ Lighting _____ Plant Nutrition ______ Other ____________
Culture: Year-round Growing _____ Propagation _____ Special Crop ______________
Notes ____
____

Mail Completed Form to; Growers Press Inc., P.O. Box 189, Princeton B.C. Canada V0X 1W0
or Fax Form to [604] 295-7755